Jesus in Solidarity with His People

A Theologian Looks at Mark

William Reiser, S.J.

A Liturgical Press Book

 THE LITURGICAL PRESS
Collegeville, Minnesota

www.litpress.org

Cover design by Greg Becker. Photo by James Schaefer.

1   2   3   4   5   6   7   8

Library of Congress Cataloging-in-Publication Data

Reiser, William E.
    Jesus in solidarity with his people : a theologian looks at Mark / William Reiser.
        p. cm.
    Includes bibliographical references (p.) and index.
    ISBN 0-8146-2717-X (alk. paper)
        1. Bible. N.T. Mark—Theology.   I. Title.

BS2585.2 .R39 2000
226.3'06—dc21   00-035666

But if, like the apostles, we never move away from him but remain with him in all his trials, he will then privately explain and interpret for us what he had said to the multitudes, and illuminate us much more brightly. But if there is someone who is able to climb the mountain with him like Peter, James and John, that person will be illuminated not only by the light of Christ but also by the voice of the Father himself.

Origen, *First Homily on Genesis*

So now, having already suffered through that humility, already died, already been buried, already risen and ascended into heaven, he is both there, seated at the right hand of the Father, and here, suffering want in his poor. . . . Fear Christ up above, recognize him down below. Have Christ up above lavishing bounty, recognize him here needing charity. Here he's poor, there he's rich. . . . But still, as a poor man here, he's hungry, thirsty, in rags.

St. Augustine, *Sermon* 123

Contents

Preface

Two theological premises have guided my reading of Mark's Gospel. The first is that God and the people of God must be understood together, for such is the nature of biblical revelation. Israel is God's firstborn child; the people of Israel are God's beloved spouse. Draw close to God and one adopts God's people; marry the Lord and one weds the people of God, imagery that naturally enough caught the attention of the author of the letter to the Ephesians (Eph 5:22-32). The story of God thus entails the story of God's people, especially the poor and defenseless ones among them, and the history of God's people becomes the story of Israel's God.[1]

The consequence this relatedness holds for our thinking about the person of Jesus is that one cannot adequately understand the interior life of Jesus without taking into account the life of the people of God in its social, cultural, political, and religious dimensions. Jesus lived and died in solidarity with his people: he died for them because he had lived for them. And with good reason. Jesus would have discovered the presence of God among the poor, an experience repeatedly confirmed by his followers over the centuries. Immersion in the lives of men and women forced into poverty and other dehumanizing conditions becomes paradoxically life-giving and affirming for those who are led by the Spirit.

When Jesus stood before God in prayer, the people of God silently stood alongside him. His perfection—his own growth in the Spirit—was shaped, tested, and nurtured by a thoroughgoing immersion in the lives of the men and women of Galilee and Judea. By the time the writings that make up our New Testament were gathered together, the Church had reached the conclusion that in Jesus' walking among us the very mystery of God had embraced both the human world and the human condition in a manner so intimate and so profound that the way human beings viewed themselves and their history would be forever changed. As a

---

[1] I have developed this point at greater length in "The Interior Life of Jesus as the Life of the People of God," which appears in Robert J. Wicks, ed., *Handbook of Spirituality for Ministry*, vol. 2 (New York: Paulist Press, 2000).

Christian, Mark certainly believed this. Realized solidarity provides, I would suggest, a contemporary key to interpreting Mark's story of Jesus theologically. Indeed, many men and women have already made the prayerful discovery that the experience of solidarity and their search for God are mysteriously linked. What is of utmost importance in reading and understanding Mark's Gospel, therefore, is not the reader's constant mindfulness of how much God (or Jesus) loves the people but *the reader's mindfulness of how deeply he or she loves the people of God.* It is the reader's love for the world, not God's, that brings the Gospel text to life.

The second premise that has guided my reading is that the whole Gospel is an Easter story. Mark is sometimes described as "a passion narrative with an extended introduction,"[2] but I prefer to think of it as an Easter story with an extended afterword. There would hardly have been any good news to share if Jesus had not been raised from the dead, and the Christian conviction about Jesus' victory over death can be heard in the Gospel's opening verse. The title "Son of God" presupposes his being raised and glorified by the Father, while the title "Christ" presupposes that Jesus has successfully completed his mission as God's anointed. Easter is woven into the story from the start, affecting everything Mark writes afterwards. Once we appreciate that the raising of Jesus from the dead is truly "the beginning," the scene of the empty tomb does not seem like such an abrupt ending.

Talking About Jesus Today

The ideas behind this book have taken shape in the course of teaching, preaching, and thinking extensively about Mark's Gospel. Several years ago I published *Talking About Jesus Today: An Introduction to the Story Behind Our Faith,* a book that more or less followed Mark's framework for looking at Jesus. At the time I was particularly drawn to a liberationist reading of the Gospel (I still am) and to a wonderful retelling of the Jesus story, initially prepared as a radio dramatization entitled *Un tal Jesús,* which has since appeared in English.[3] I was also fascinated by sociopolitical ap-

---

[2] "To state the matter somewhat provocatively, one could call the Gospels passion narratives with extended introductions." See Martin Kähler, *The So-Called Historical Jesus and the Historic Biblical Christ* (Philadelphia: Fortress Press, 1964; German edition 1892) 80.

[3] José Ignacio and María López Vigil, *Un tal Jesús: La Buena Noticia contada al pueblo de América Latina,* 2 vols. (Salamanca: Loguez Ediciones, 2nd ed. 1984). ET: *A Certain Jesus,* 3 vols., trans. Trinidad Ongtangco-Regala (Quezon City, Philippines: Claretian Publications, 1996). Available in North America under the title *Just Jesus* (New York: Crossroad Publishing Co., 2000).

proaches to the New Testament writings as exemplified, say, by Ched Myers' *Binding the Strong Man,* and Richard Horsley's *Jesus and the Spiral of Violence.* Since then I have had the satisfaction of working my way through N. T. Wright's splendid book *Jesus and the Victory of God,* a work that, if it were not for its christological astigmatism, would be just about flawless. Wright's picture of Jesus purports to be "from below," a reading of the Gospels starting with the human, historical facts about him. In the end, however, it turns out to be a picture "from above," and the importance of history as a theological datum, particularly the historical experience of suffering, is left underdeveloped. Nevertheless, the book is an enviable achievement, and I depend upon it here, especially its exposition of the apocalyptic aspects of Jesus' teaching.

I wish I had waited a little longer before finalizing some of the reflections in *Talking About Jesus Today;* the basic intuitions about Jesus needed to mature. What does one do *after* one has recovered the human, historical Jesus? What *else* does one say about Jesus after that recovery? Here three things need to be noted. The first is that the saving power that believers have discovered in Jesus' humanness and his rootedness in a particular history of suffering do not come into focus apart from the resurrection. That much I knew, but the full implications of this fact are still coming home to me. The second is that there is no christology apart from ecclesiology, no story of Jesus that is not also a story of the Church. That is a point Luke Timothy Johnson and others have been emphasizing in their critiques of the work of the Jesus Seminar. And the third thing is that christology and ecclesiology carried on apart from the historical experience of communities of suffering will be woefully inadequate, as the German theologian Johann Baptist Metz and others have explained so well.

In the summer of 1996 the Sisters of Saint Martha in Calgary, Alberta, invited me to give their community an eight-day retreat devoted completely to the resurrection, a retreat I repeated the following summer for their community in Antigonish, Nova Scotia. Devoting an entire retreat to the resurrection struck me as an excellent idea for several reasons. It would force me to re-hear all the scenes in the Gospel from the perspective of Easter, and not only the resurrection appearances recounted in Luke, Matthew, and John. Many Ignatian retreats typically tended to follow the pattern of the *Spiritual Exercises,* a sort of short course in Christian faith, an annual review of the essentials of Christian spirituality. But instead of starting with a meditation on sin or creation, why could a retreat not begin with whatever mystery of the faith or with whatever Gospel moment the individual retreatant was drawn to pray over?

Furthermore, the Jesus to whom Ignatius wanted those making the Exercises to direct their prayer was obviously the risen Lord. One could claim, therefore, that resurrection faith was just as legitimately the presupposition of the *Spiritual Exercises* as was, for example, the First Principle and Foundation or Ignatius' wise conviction that God would deal directly with men and women in their prayer.[4] For Ignatius, the director was never to get in the way of God's action by second-guessing or pushing the retreatant in the matter of electing how best to serve God. I mention this point because the evangelist never intended to get in the way of our coming face-to-face with the risen Jesus, either. Mark recounts his story and then leaves it to us, and to the Spirit that guides each one of us, to undergo the dynamics of discipleship, to identify (or not) with the men and women who so clumsily attempted to stay with Jesus and who in the end reacted with fear when it turned out that the whole story, from start to finish, was actually about what God was doing in and through Jesus. Fear and terror are odd notes on which to conclude a Gospel, unless perhaps Mark is confiding to us something about the challenge he himself had faced in following Jesus risen.

I have often wondered whether I possess the courage to stand on a street corner and talk about my faith in Jesus. I have no idea whether Mark ever did so or was even inclined to attempt it. The young man who fled naked rather than fall with Jesus into the hands of the arresting party says a lot about how terrified Jesus' followers suddenly were, but that stray detail could hardly have been a tip-off as to the evangelist's identity. There is nothing timid about the character of the first evangelist. For myself, I feel perfectly comfortable in a pulpit or a classroom, because these places grant me permission to speak publicly as a believer. Street corners, town squares, and shopping plazas yield that permission less easily. Besides, one cannot use the same discourse in civic space that one does in church. I do know, at any rate, that talking about Jesus today necessarily is going to be somewhat different from the way Mark spoke in his day, as every preacher realizes. Even street preaching would require a fresh idiom. Mark's cultural horizon is not ours, Jesus' even less so. Still, if we suddenly found ourselves faced with the prospect of terrible suffering, whether the suffering born of intolerance pure and simple (as in the case of Christians facing Muslim fundamentalists in the Sudan or Angola or Hindu extremists

---

[4] For the Principle and Foundation, see Saint Ignatius Loyola, *The Spiritual Exercises*, no. 23. Ignatius' advice to the one giving the *Exercises* appears in no. 15. The texts can be easily located in any standard edition of the *Exercises*.

in northern India) or the suffering created by catastrophic political and social upheavals like civil wars or genocidal aggression, then our way of reading Mark's story would be profoundly affected. The world disclosed by Mark's text would start to feel remarkably close. There is a certain surrealism to studying Mark's Gospel, with its unswerving attention upon the cross, in the secure quiet of a seminar room. Yet talk about Jesus is something we must do. I have found that we talk about Jesus most effectively when each of us is also carrying on a conversation with the world and when our imaginations have been engaged by what Thomas Merton referred to as the world of broken bones.[5]

I began writing these pages while giving a short course on Mark's Gospel to university students in La Paz. Bolivia proved to be a rich location for hearing this Gospel afresh. The rural world of Andean *campesinos* comes awfully close to many Markan scenes, while the recent history of Bolivia and its neighbors brought the political dimension of the Gospel into a very sharp focus. I have written this book for people who regularly draw on Mark in their ministry—catechists, spiritual directors, preachers, college teachers like myself, and our students. Those who draw on this Gospel in their work will want to be as sensitive as possible to the spiritual and theological currents in Mark's narrative. I am assuming that the reader is already familiar with the text. If not, it will be important to sit down at once and slowly read the sixteen chapters of this short Gospel, perhaps even out loud.

Mark may have been underappreciated by early church writers, but that neglect has certainly been compensated for today. Nevertheless, while there are numerous resources one might consult for historical, textual, political, cultural, and social background, and while there are many books and articles that draw out the spiritual and ethical significance of Mark, readers should also learn to trust and relish their own insight into the Gospel, discovering for themselves Mark's literary devices, his allusions to the Old Testament, the richness of his picture of Jesus and his disciples, and so on. The consolation of making our own discoveries helps us to own the story. Even in the face of the extensive historical information and marvelous insights of contemporary biblical scholarship, Ignatius' directive maintains its relevance:

---

[5] Thomas Merton, *New Seeds of Contemplation* (New York: New Directions, 1972) 70. See also William Reiser, "Solidarity and the Reshaping of Spirituality," *The Merton Annual,* vol. 11 (Sheffield Academic Press Limited, 1998) 97–109.

The person who gives to another a method and order for meditation or contemplation must faithfully narrate the story to be meditated on or contemplated by merely passing through the principal points and adding only brief
clarifications; so that the one who is going to meditate, after having first accepted the basis of the historical truth, will then go over it and consider it
by himself. Thus it would happen that when he finds something that would
offer a greater elucidation or apprehension of the story (whether it happens
through his own reflection or a divine inspiration in his mind), he will harvest a more delightful taste and more abundant fruit than if the same thing
had been more extensively narrated and explained by someone else. It is not,
indeed, the abundance of knowledge, but the interior sense and taste of
things, that usually satisfies the desire of the soul.[6]

Contemporary readers will probably not be satisfied with the methods of scriptural interpretation developed by Christian preachers and
commentators of the first five or six centuries.[7] We can surely learn to appreciate their efforts at relating Scripture to daily life and growth in the
Spirit, and the inventive way they made God's word speak to their time.
But a historically conscious, ecumenically sensitive age approaches those
ancient texts from its own distinctive suppositions, expectations, and remembrances of suffering.

Needless to say, books like the present one will come and go, but the
evangelist's text remains. The reason why people keep writing about sacred texts, however, like preaching itself, is ultimately to help the Christian community be more deeply engaged by the central narratives of its
faith. The pages that follow are not an exegetical treatment of Mark's
Gospel. For that I highly recommend Morna Hooker's commentary, *The
Gospel According to Saint Mark*.[8] What follows is simply the result of one
person's theological engagement with Mark's Gospel. Given the sheer vol-

---

[6] *Exercises,* no. 2. See *The Spiritual Exercises of Saint Ignatius,* trans. Pierre Wolff
(Liguori, Mo.: Triumph, 1997) 3–4.

[7] The volume entitled *Mark,* in the series *The Ancient Christian Commentary on
Scripture,* ed. Thomas C. Oden and Christopher A. Hall (Downers Grove, Ill.: InterVarsity Press, 1998), contains a splendid selection of comments and reflections about scenes
that can be found in Mark's Gospel—and also in the other three. The contributions assembled for this volume were not specifically commenting on Mark. On the patristic inattentiveness to the First Gospel, see Brenda Deen Schildgen, *Power and Prejudice: The
Reception of the Gospel of Mark* (Detroit: Wayne State Univ. Press, 1999) 35–62.

[8] I would also recommend consulting Bruce Malina and Richard L. Rohrbaugh, *Social-Science Commentary on the Synoptic Gospels* (Minneapolis: Augsburg Fortress Press,
1992). Unfortunately, I finished writing these pages before the publication of Joel Marcus,
Mark 1–8: A New Translation with Introduction and Commentary (New York: Bantam Doubleday Dell, 2000).

ume of literature on Mark both of a technical and popular nature, I am virtually certain that whatever insight I have into this Gospel has already been reached by others. No matter. The fact that many people have sung about love will not deter others from composing new songs.

I have tried to stay focused on Mark's text and not to allow my familiarity with Matthew and Luke to influence the way I read Mark, although these two evangelists would amplify our picture of Jesus considerably. This bracketing does no disservice to Mark if one accepts the widely held view that Matthew and Luke had the advantage of reading Mark but not vice versa. Mark, we must remember, was a storyteller, not a trained theologian (unless in the broad sense where every believer who thinks about faith can be said to be a theologian). Yet the story he wrote is for us a work of theology, a segment of the biblical God's long conversation with the human race. Roberta Bondi's description of theology's service would surely apply in Mark's case:

> Theology, I would now say, is about saving lives, and the work of theology . . . is saving work. First, it involves learning to see the ways in which false images of God, ourselves, and the world have bound us and taken away the life God intends for us. Second, it involves learning to know God as God is, as a healing God, and learning to know ourselves, individually and communally, as people who correspond with that God in whose image we are made. Third, it involves imagining a future that is consistent with the God we come to know.[9]

One of the questions I have addressed in this book, in light of Jesus' dying words in Mark's Gospel, is whether God can be trusted. In the religious community to which I belong the story of Ignatius Loyola figures significantly, and one of the most serious questions he faced was to what extent he really trusted God. Convinced that God was absolutely trustworthy, Ignatius undertook numerous experiments with poverty, exposing himself to unspeakable hardship in order to learn from experience that God stood by him. He refused, unconditionally, to allow his trust to rest on anything except divine Providence. While Ignatius' practice of poverty subsequently became more moderate, he nevertheless never changed his mind about the importance of poverty as a means of learning to trust God. Mark would have applauded Ignatius' efforts, because for Mark trusting Jesus was everything that mattered, although learning how to do so was by no means easy. Mark might have cautioned Ignatius that

---

[9] See Roberta C. Bondi, *Memories of God: Theological Reflections on a Life* (Nashville: Abingdon Press, 1995) 11.

being poor by choice and being poor by necessity were quite different things. As a disciple one chooses not so much to be poor but to walk with men and women who are poor because of circumstances they had nothing to say about. Still, Ignatius' burning need to teach himself to trust God in all things bears a strikingly Markan signature. It is a lesson that simply cannot be learned without paying a price. The memory of Ignatius has affected the way I think about the Gospel.[10]

Throughout the book I have used the masculine personal pronoun in referring to God, although I have tried to do so as infrequently as possible. All of us realize that the mystery of God transcends gender, but attempts to avoid the personal pronoun altogether (like the attempt to show reverence to the divine name by writing G-d or L-rd) can be both cumbersome for the writer and tiring for many readers, given the nature of biblical literature. I trust readers will not take this to be an indication of stylistic insensitivity on my part.[11]

I do not believe that Mark intended his Gospel to be read or heard just once in a single sitting, but repeatedly over years by the same individuals and communities. Built into its narrative structure is the intention that the story be continually retold. Mark did not write as if composing a Lectionary in our sense of the term, but the Gospel is certainly at home in a Lectionary format. This requires, however, that later passages have to be understood in terms of earlier ones, and that the early scenes need to be interpreted in terms of what the listener recalls comes later. There is even something kaleidoscopic about the Gospel. Theoretically, then, one could begin reading the Gospel at any point, assuming, of course, that a disciple will be living with Mark's text for the whole of his or her life, for Mark is someone who was able "to climb the mountain with him."[12] My parting wish for students as we reach the end of a semester is that when,

[10] Ignatius' Autobiography (or "Reminiscences") can be found in *Saint Ignatius Loyola: Personal Writings,* trans. Joseph A. Munitiz and Philip Endean (London: Penguin Books, 1996) 13–64.

[11] James L. Kugel makes this point with respect to translating the divine name. See *The Great Poems of the Bible: A Reader's Companion with New Translations* (New York: The Free Press, 1999) 18.

[12] The allusion is to Origen's *First Homily on Genesis* (see Hans Urs von Balthasar, *Origen: Spirit and Fire. A Thematic Anthology of His Writings,* trans. Robert J. Daly [Washington: The Catholic Univ. of America Press, 1984] 247). The accompanying passage from Augustine that I used to preface these pages comes from vol. 4 of *The Works of Saint Augustine: A Translation for the 21st Century,* trans. Edmund Hill, ed. John E. Rotelle (Brooklyn: New City Press, 1992) 245–46.

many years hence, they are preparing to meet God face-to-face, they will find themselves with their loved ones on one side and the text of Mark's Gospel on the other.

I am most grateful to John R. Donahue, S.J., Michael Downey, Daniel Harrington, S.J., Robert Manning, S.J., and Donald Senior, C.P., for their willingness to read the manuscript. I should also like to thank the members of the weekly Bible study class at Casa Maria. For months on end they have borne patiently with my probings into Mark, and their responsiveness has been a great stimulus: Emanuela, Ramonita and Carlos, Martin, Edith, Beatrice, Jorge and Maria, Margarita and Enrique, Sergio, Francisco, Emerita, Dolores, Venecia, Margada, Pedro, Elizabet, Felix and Isabel, Ermenegildo and Etelbina, Maria Geargina, and Lydia. I am grateful, too, to the associates at the Center for Religious Development in Cambridge, who over the years have helped me stay attentive to the vital connection between theological reflection and one's personal relatedness to God. And finally, I want to thank Fr. Michael Gillgannon, the staff, and students at the Pastoral Universitaria Arquidiocesana in La Paz for their invitations to visit. During my teaching trips there over the past few years the Bolivian altiplano gradually furnished the landscape in which I pictured the Galilean part of Mark's Gospel unfolding. The remembrance of colonialism, of the silver and tin mines, and of dictatorship supplied vivid images of Jesus' days in Jerusalem and his passion.

Introduction

The Theological Matters

While Jesus was teaching in the temple, he said, "How can the scribes say that the Messiah is the son of David? David himself, by the Holy Spirit, declared,

> *'The Lord said to my Lord,*
> *"Sit at my right hand,*
> *   until I put your enemies under your feet."'*

David himself calls him Lord; so how can he be his son?" And the large crowd was listening to him with delight (Mark 12:35-37).

The Gospel of Mark is not a prayer book. One can open a good prayer book at any spot and locate a meaningful prayer, or thumb through it in search of a prayer that matches one's mood or circumstances. But the individual verses of the Gospel derive their meaningfulness in large measure from the text as a whole. Chancing upon a severed limb would unsettle us, to say the least. Limbs belong appended to a body, and our sense of the body as something whole explains our shock and horror over dismemberment. I suspect an analogous rule applies to the way we approach the Gospel text. The parts—the individual passages and scenes—are organically connected to the "body" of the text. In listening to a part of the story, our minds and imaginations automatically supply the whole. Whenever we turn to a particular verse or episode, our imaginations are unconsciously invoking the entire narrative—the larger picture of Jesus—as the context for meditating on individual passages.

In the chapters that follow we shall be looking at a number of specific passages and issues from Mark's Gospel, but the purpose of this introduction is orientation to the body of the Gospel. We shall do this by highlighting some of the broad issues and concerns the evangelist sets before us. What are some of the Gospel's more striking characteristics and what questions does it prompt us to raise?

An Easter Story Without Resurrection Appearances

A most curious feature of Mark's Gospel is that he concluded his account of Jesus' ministry and death without providing any accounts of the Easter apparitions. For those we have to look to the other three evangelists. Most modern translations indicate that the author ended his account with verse 8 of chapter 16. Some ancient Christian readers, apparently dissatisfied with the abrupt and puzzling nature of Mark 16:8, attempted to round the Gospel out with what seemed to them a reasonable and tidy conclusion. But verses 9 through 20 sound so unlike the rest of the Gospel text that even the non-scholarly reader can detect another hand at work in the composition of the final verses. Oddly enough, the Church draws the Gospel reading for the feast of Saint Mark, which it celebrates on April 25, from the part of the Gospel he did not write.

Our sense of how a Gospel ought properly to end and begin has probably been determined by the other three Gospels. There we find the warm accounts of Jesus' resurrection appearances: his encounter with Mary Magdalene and the apostle Thomas, for example, in John's Gospel; the two disciples on the road to Emmaus in Luke; the risen Jesus' encounter with the women in Matthew. Even Paul mentions the apparitions of Jesus to his disciples, including at one point a remarkable appearance to more than five hundred of his sisters and brothers at the same time (1 Cor 15:3-10). Why then does Mark fail to tell us anything about what happened after Easter?

Matthew and Luke begin their accounts of Jesus with birth stories, something else that is missing from Mark. Once again caution is called for. We need to be careful not to read the first eighteen verses of the Fourth Gospel as if they were analogous to the infancy stories in Luke and Matthew. The opening verses of John's Gospel anticipate the whole story that is to follow. The Word becoming flesh is less a mystery of biology than of history, culture, social world, religion, and anthropology. The enfleshment of God's Word takes place in terms of the whole of Jesus' life, from his conception to his exaltation. And it was his being raised from the dead that made such an inspired reflection possible. Without Easter there would be no incarnation. That explains why, even though Mark shows little interest in the life of Jesus before his baptism in the river Jordan, his Gospel (like John's) is complete without birth stories. For Mark fully believes in Jesus' resurrection; the resurrection is the only logical starting point for thinking about Christian faith. In fact, one could argue that the idea of the incarnation represents a highly contemplative grasp of the resurrection's power to reach into human history in order to liberate and sanctify human beings and their communities. The incarnation is consummately paschal; it is the risen Jesus who remains the Word made flesh.

Two episodes in particular have the ring of the more conventional Easter appearances, namely, the story of Jesus' calming the sea in Mark 4 and the story of his walking toward the disciples over the water in Mark 6. It does not require much cleverness to recognize in those episodes the early community's faith in the power of the risen Jesus to rescue his followers from whatever storms threaten their safety and well-being. Jesus, Mark is reassuring us, is never absent. He may feel absent, or asleep, or we might not be aware of his being aware of us, watching us from a distance; but there should be no doubt about his presence, his concern, or his power to save. The reaction of the frightened disciples who believe a ghost is approaching them, and the assurance of Jesus that it is truly he who has drawn near, sound awfully close to some of the Easter scenes from the other Gospels.

Granted that the resurrection is central to the Gospel story and, even more critically, central to the Christian understanding of God, what exactly makes it so significant? It seems to me that the theological significance of the resurrection is that in raising Jesus from the dead the God of Israel has identified himself with the life and death of Jesus. What this implies remains to be seen. Yet this much can be said at the outset. God's identification with the life and death of Jesus is properly a mystery of faith. This mystery is not something that can be reversed, it challenges the mind as well as the heart, and it powerfully colors the way we understand human life and human history. The voice of divine approval we hear at the moments of Jesus' baptism (1:9-11) and transfiguration (9:2-8) rightfully belongs at the tomb on Easter morning, but no narrator could have placed it there; everyone knew that no one would have been at the site to hear those words. Nevertheless, the wonderful expression of divine solidarity with the person of Jesus, together with his preaching, encounters, healings, and exorcisms, reveals to us the deeper meaning of the resurrection itself. For the resurrection was not God's way of rewarding Jesus for service above and beyond the call of duty (Moses, Elijah, and John the Baptist would have merited that too).[1] Nor was it just a way of teaching

---

[1] The well-known hymn in Phil 2:5-11 states, "Therefore God also highly exalted him." I agree with those who find in these verses an implied contrast with Adam, God's first son, whose disobedience led to a fall from grace. The "exaltation" (that is, the resurrection and ascension or enthronement of Jesus) cannot represent his personal reward, since everything God does in Jesus is, as the Nicene Creed says, "for us and for our salvation." If Jesus is raised

Jesus' enemies how wrong they were about him. Judging from the way they treated the early Church (told to us by Luke in the Acts of the Apostles, and mentioned in various places by Paul), his adversaries appear to have remained as unconvinced after Easter as before. Neither Pilate nor Herod, neither the Pharisees as a group nor the high priest, had been struck with remorse.

The resurrection indicated more than God's approval of the message underlying Jesus' life and death; it revealed a lasting oneness with the crucified men and women of every time and place.[2] By "owning" Jesus' story, God had assumed the solidarity Jesus himself had lived so thoroughly and exemplified with such prophetic boldness. Like the haunting beauty of the desert, at once so barren and dangerous, so clarifying and captivating, the resurrection points the Christian soul in the direction of living the same solidarity. For divine solidarity with human beings is the beginning of their salvation. If God in Christ takes on the human, then all those who follow Jesus and share in the same Spirit will become partakers of the very life of God: holy, sinless, passionate, loving.

For the sake of his people, Jesus put his own life at risk in order to preach and enact the reign of God. The liberating nature of Jesus' ministry, which the New Testament and Christian catechesis often abbreviate (perhaps too much so) by means of the phrase "for the forgiveness of sins," is revealed to be the very content, the heart and soul, of human salvation. The God of Israel is and always has been a God who saves and delivers. Sometimes this is confessed on the basis of evidence, as when Moses led his people out of Egypt, or when they actually arrived in the Promised Land after forty years of wandering, or when they returned from the fifty-plus years of exile in Babylon, or on the occasions when they defeated their enemies. More often than not, however, Israel's confession about God sprang from its expectation and hope, its instinctive trust in the faithfulness of God.

Therefore, lifting burdens from the shoulders of men and women, identifying the roots of their oppression, and calling them to share in

---

or exalted, then that too is for our salvation. As head of the new humanity, Jesus' obedience has won for all of us the position Adam lost. The bending of knees and confessing of tongues (vv. 10, 11) are expressions of praise and thanksgiving for the gift of salvation, not of congratulations to Jesus because he worked hard for his crown.

[2] The idea of the crucified people is correlative to the title of Jürgen Moltmann's book *The Crucified God.* This idea finds expression in a number of similar titles, for example, Song, *Jesus, The Crucified People;* Boff, *Passion of Christ, Passion of the World;* Sobrino, *Principle of Mercy;* and Ellacuría, "Crucified People" in *Mysterium Liberationis,* 580–603.

God's saving work by opening themselves fully to the gospel (Mark refers to this as denying oneself for the sake of Jesus and the gospel) belong to the heart of Jesus' ministry. Everything Jesus did was consistent with what he believed about Israel's God. Jesus lived and died as he did because he had committed himself to living for the sake of his people. Indeed, perhaps this commitment was his own radical response to the preaching of John the Baptist. The baptism is the first instance we have in the Gospel of Jesus' solidarity with the men and women of Israel, a solidarity that was sacramentalized when John plunged him into the waters of the Jordan. In making Jesus' story his own, God took hold of human history in a decisive way, for God's saving design would extend not only to Israel but to all of us of every time and place. Jesus' ministry was focused on the sons and daughters of Abraham, the lost sheep of the house of Israel. But in raising Jesus from the dead so that he would henceforth and forever be found among the living, God had revealed that a new epoch in the history of human salvation had begun.

I am speaking, of course, from within the Christian story, that is, as a Christian. The way that people who are not Christian describe and interpret God's action in the world is not going to be identical to ours. Ecumenical sensitivity has become increasingly important today, not only as a result of the effort and vision of the Second Vatican Council but also as a moral attitude or virtue called forth by the globalization of the human spirit. Nevertheless, we do not speak the same way among ourselves as we do when we dialogue with the world; the way we speak with and relate to members of our own families is understandably different from the way we speak and relate to people outside our households. Mark was writing to fellow believers from within the household of faith. It would be unfair to hold him to metaphysical assertions about Jesus, despite sayings that circulated in the early Church such as: "The one who believes and is baptized will be saved; but the one who does not believe will be condemned" (16:16).

In other words, we should not read Mark, or any of the evangelists, in a way that would diminish or obscure the reality of the mysterious, wonderful action of the Spirit outside the Christian household, or even read them in ways that might construe that action as merely provisional. Whoever appended the extra verses in chapter 16 to Mark's text apparently believed that anyone who did not accept the Gospel would be sentenced to everlasting misery. But such language reflects a conviction born of personal commitment and affection; it does not spring from theological reason or pastoral sensitivity. Mark himself was quite aware that sometimes graced things happened outside the Jesus circle, as when Jesus reproved the two disciples who complained about the "foreign" exorcist (9:38). Or perhaps more to the point, despite the narrowly Jewish reach of Jesus' brief ministry, Mark was keenly sensitive to the fact that God had never intended the Gentiles to be excluded from the good news of the kingdom. The great sign of Jonah was nothing less than the repentance and conversion of the Gentiles, the godless Ninevites, the "dogs," after they heard the preaching of a prophet of Israel. According to Matthew and Luke, Jesus applied that memory to his own situation when large crowds of non-Jews assembled to hear him and even to be healed. For Mark, the missionary point about the sign of Jonah is implied by the faith of the Syrophoenician woman (7:24-30), the deaf man in the region of the Decapolis (7:31-37), and the feeding of the four thousand in territory presumed to be Gentile (8:1-10).

Neither Mark nor any other New Testament author would have been able to envision all the questions that future generations of Christians would have to face. There was no other option, as far as Mark was concerned, but to trust in the guidance of the risen Jesus: the Jesus who, by virtue of his being raised from the dead, had already begun to transcend his own time and place, his ethnicity and religious background, even his maleness and his own determinate social situation. In this sense, the Church could not become fixated on the historical figure Jesus of Nazareth in a fundamentalistic way. Had it done so, the early communities might never have welcomed Gentiles. In the end, the story of Jesus turned into a story about God's relationship with the whole human race.

A Gospel Without Birth Stories

I have already suggested that the ancient disciple who composed the Prologue to John's Gospel caught the same insight that links Jesus' story with God when he wrote, "And the Word became flesh" (John 1:14). The process of meditation that led to that formulation could not have been set in motion apart from the resurrection. The basis for all reflection on the person and mission of Jesus, and even for understanding the mystery of God itself, has to take as its starting point the raising of Jesus from the dead. The doctrine of the incarnation, summing up as it does the silent, wonderful, unbreakable communion of God with human nature, is essentially an effort to plumb, interpret, and express the paschal mystery. Some theologians have suggested that the enfleshment of God's Word was not complete *until* the resurrection. The biological level of this mystery, like the literal meaning of biblical texts for ancient commentators, is the least interesting. There is nothing in the text of the Prologue to the Fourth

Gospel requiring us to teach that the incarnation is another way of referring to the conception of Jesus. That the beginning of a Gospel should tell
us something about Jesus' birth is an expectation we acquired from reading Luke and Matthew. Mark, of course, opens with the story of Jesus' baptism. Reading Matthew and Luke, however, perhaps primes or predisposes
our minds to anticipate an infancy motif in the first fourteen verses of
John's Gospel. And that would be a mistake. The mysterious oneness of
God with the human story that lies behind John 1:14 is ultimately an expression of Easter faith. God owned the life and death of Jesus in raising
him from the dead. Yet it was not the human condition as such that God
owned; God owned the particular enfleshment or enactment of the human
condition that we observe in the story of Jesus' ministry. Jesus was not
human life in the abstract; he was not each and every one of us in some
transcendental, romantic, but basically nondescript way.

A major drawback in the way the Church's teaching about the incarnation is often presented is that it obscures the more fundamental
place of Easter within both the Gospel narrative and the structure of
Christian faith. Divine solidarity *with human nature* may be both consoling and uplifting, and it may indeed lead us to seek moral and spiritual
perfection: God becomes human so that human beings might become
God, that is, sharers in the divine nature. But when divine solidarity is
specified in terms of solidarity *with the poor, the excluded, the crucified ones
of this world,* then the mystery before us is truly wondrous and intensely
challenging. Wondrous because God has joined the history of suffering so
intimately; challenging because we now have to make some important
choices and engage in careful, maybe even painful discernment. Just as we
need to know the whole of Jesus' life before we can understand why exactly he was crucified (and thus appreciate precisely what God was raising
from the dead), so also we need to know the whole of Jesus' story before
we can begin to grasp exactly what was becoming flesh. In short, the Prologue of John's Gospel could be viewed as an Easter meditation. It presupposes that we already know the whole of Jesus' story even before we
set about reading the Gospel text.

The Gospel of Mark is as theologically and spiritually sophisticated
as any of the other three, although because of its brevity and somewhat
fragmentary character, Mark's narrative strikes many readers as clumsy
and even incomplete. The way in which Mark has stitched together memories and sayings of Jesus can leave the impression that he ought to have
hired an editor possessed of sharp theological as well as literary skills.
Nevertheless, in this Gospel we do find a coherent account of the one

Mark firmly believed to be the Son of God, someone who was all the more deserving of that title because of his faith, his fidelity under temptation, his obedience and humility, and his solidarity with his people in their suffering and in their hope.

The Gospel as Disclosive of the Evangelist's Inner Life

It is plausible to think that Mark knew more about Jesus than he recorded in his Gospel, just as Paul must have known a lot more about the historical figure of Jesus than one might guess from his letters. The Jesus of Mark is every bit as much Son of God as the Jesus of the Fourth Gospel, without the overtones of preexistence, privileged insight into the Father's mind, foreknowledge, and Word mysticism. While the cross looms large in all of the Gospels, not to mention its supreme prominence in Paul's writings, it does not always carry the same message. Some have explained Mark's emphasis upon the way of the cross in terms of the situation of persecution in which his readers were living. Mark could have been highlighting the necessity of suffering in following Jesus in order to encourage and console the people for whom he was writing.

Yet it is not impossible that the catechesis Mark himself had received was already stamped heavily with the fact and mystery of Jesus' death by crucifixion; maybe the voice of Paul in some churches had already given shape to the way Mark himself was instructed about the Gospel. Whatever the explanation, Mark's approach to the cross is different, say, from John's. His approach is different, too, from the way some preachers and commentators today choose to present the cross. While a liberationist approach to Jesus is thoroughly consistent with (and perhaps for us today even required by) the Gospels, I think that Mark's understanding of the cross was pretty much framed by the Suffering Servant motif of Second Isaiah. Mark, or the tradition he was drawing on, needed a metaphor to make sense of the suffering and death of Jesus, and Second Isaiah was ready to hand; history without metaphor is lifeless. A metaphor, however, is not the reality. Or to put the matter another way, the fact that Mark did not think in liberationist terms hardly means that a liberationist metaphor for understanding the cross is unfaithful to the subversive memory Mark has passed along to us.

The cross represents the fate of a prophet whose message had placed him on a collision course with the powers that be, but it further expresses a realized solidarity with the poor and the powerless in their daily struggle to survive and even to surmount their oppression. Jesus did not have to accept the Lord's yoke; he did not have to bind himself so radically to the life and history of his people. Jesus might well have been a poor tradesman from Nazareth with just a rudimentary education. He was most certainly Jewish, and like everyone else in Galilee and Judea, his political and social life was ultimately governed by the Romans. In that sense Jesus, like so many other Jews, did not *become* poor; he was born poor: not destitute perhaps, but poor. His *becoming* poor (to pick up on a verse from Paul's second letter to the Corinthians) had to do with his willingly taking on the Lord's yoke and allowing his own life to be replaced henceforth by the life of his people.

When, at the narrative's end, Mark places the words of Psalm 22 on the lips of the crucified Jesus, the reader needs to recall that Mark knew quite well that Jesus was not the first believer to utter those words, nor would he be the last. The verses of Psalm 22 carry within themselves the historical and spiritual experience of generations of God's faithful ones. Indeed, with the resurrection those words acquired a new resonance because they had been prayed by the Son of God. Still, the dominant resonance in that prayer remains above all the thousands of voices that were crying out through Jesus in that final hour of his life. And along the same line, the tradition's appropriation of the figure of the Suffering Servant provided more than a metaphor. The Servant was, if not the whole nation of Israel, then at least a faithful remnant. Associating Jesus with a group of righteous sufferers effectively projected his story against the background of the wider story of Israel's tragic past. In other words, Jesus could not be adequately understood unless his life was visualized in connection with the entire suffering people of God.

At the close of his Gospel Mark tells us about the messenger who directed the women to inform Jesus' other disciples about what they have seen and heard. "He is going ahead of you to Galilee," Mark writes; "there you will see him, just as he told you" (16:7). The instruction then is to return to Galilee, and for the reader of the Gospel that of course is exactly where we must direct our attention: back to Galilee, back to the very beginning of Jesus' ministry, in order to hear the story afresh with Easter hearing and Easter sight. To contemplate the resurrection from the vantage point of Mark's Gospel requires returning to the beginning, to the point where the ministry started, and to hear how the story now sounds from the perspective of an empty tomb.

Mark's listeners would have recognized the conclusion of Jesus' story in the rugged confidence that breaks through in the opening verse: "The beginning of the good news of Jesus Christ, the Son of God" (1:1). The words resound with a sense of triumph and vindication that they have already known and experienced. There is hardly a scene in the Gospel that is not informed by Easter faith. The failure to appreciate this theological feature may explain why some readers become confused by what Jesus does or says, or by the arrangement and sequencing of various episodes. The Jesus who acts in the story, the reader naturally presumes, is the historical figure Jesus of Nazareth, but was that Mark's presumption as well? The companion fact is that Mark wrote as an Easter disciple. We may not find him so expansive or effusive about his faith in the risen Jesus as Paul becomes when he shares with us the dimensions of his own religious experience. Mark does not reveal himself to us so directly. Yet we do come to know a lot about him: not about his biography, but about what really mattered to him.

In the final analysis, we can reasonably guess, Mark found faith to be the greatest challenge of a person's life. Either you believe or you don't: there is simply no middle ground, no room for half-measures. His story opens with Jesus plainly immersed in a profound religious moment. The baptism and temptation scenes are not charades, and we have absolutely no reason to presume that Mark believed them unnecessary to the overall purpose of Jesus' mission. Mark gives no indication that Jesus did not need to hear the preaching of John the Baptist before being anointed by the Spirit for his own mission. And if John's baptism signified repentance and conversion, solidarity with the people, oneness with the tradition, historical suffering and destiny of Israel, and recommitment to the great promise lying at the heart of Israel's hope, then Jesus needed to go through all of that. We would never conclude, when Mark notes on several occasions that Jesus went off and prayed (1:35, 6:46), that Jesus did not really need to pray, any more than we would suggest that he did not really need to eat and sleep. All believers need moments of renewal. Frequently they need to be reawakened by the word and example of powerful religious witness. We do Jesus no disservice by suggesting that he, too, experienced and responded to the divine call to renewal symbolized by John at the Jordan.

Mark gives us no reason to infer that Jesus was merely pretending to want to hear John and join in the renewal of Israel, or that a radical turning toward God would have been superfluous in Jesus' case. If that had been the case, then Mark should never have left the words of Psalm 22 on Jesus' lips, and he ought further to have suppressed the memories of Jesus being tested in the wilderness and his praying in the garden of Gethsemane. The slightest hint of pretense would have meant that Jesus could not relate personally to large portions of the Psalms and that he never really shared the experience and religious desires of his people as they begged God for mercy, forgiveness, and strength.

As I remarked, Mark tells us a considerable amount about himself *as a person of faith*. Not only is faith the dominant motif in the opening scenes; it is the dramatic note on which the story ends. Jesus' preaching begins with the enthusiastic announcement of the reign of God and concludes with what appears to be a shocking experience of divine abandonment. The unsettling question that the ending forces upon the reader is, *Can* I really trust God? *Should* I trust God unconditionally? What will happen if I put my life in God's hands as fully as Jesus did? Was this what the letter to the Hebrews had in mind when it warned that it is a terrible thing to fall into the hands of the living God (Heb 10:31)?

Before we rush to answer yes, that we can and will trust God, Mark brings us back to the note of fear that runs through the whole story like a menacing undercurrent. The women at the very end are afraid, as the disciples are shown to be on numerous occasions. One can be a believer and still be afraid at times. Jesus' reassurance, like the word of the messenger about not fearing, normally does not erase the reality that prompted the fear in the first place. Eventually one learns not to surrender to the things that can terrify us or steal our peace, but that lesson too belongs to the process of discipleship.

Mark, I would conclude, knew what fear was all about, and not just the daily anxiety that afflicts all of us in various circumstances and encounters. After all, fear can be a healthy defense mechanism. The fear that crops up in a believer's life is more, too, than the fear of death. Jesus, one could reasonably believe, was also afraid to die, especially under circumstances that he must have foreseen fairly well. The great fear that attacks faith, or that might be an indispensable condition for coming to deep, tested faith, is the fear that God will not stand by us to the end, or that God's power is not so strong as that of human beings whose hearts have been hardened. Jesus' words to his disciples about not fearing, no matter where these occur in the narrative, could well reflect a lesson the evangelist himself had learned. God can be trusted, even if death comes before we see the light of God's justice and wisdom. Mark, I am led to guess, probably identified with the reaction of the disciples at many points within the narrative.

What sort of believer might Mark have been before he encountered the Jesus community? This is obviously a speculative question, for apart from a few references to a certain Mark or John Mark elsewhere in the

New Testament (who might or might not have been the Gospel writer), the figure of the first evangelist never comes into view. He appears to have been a Gentile convert. If he had been Jewish and then come to believe in Jesus, Mark would already have possessed an understanding of God. He would already have been part of a religious tradition that was conversant with notions about God's sovereignty as Creator and as Lord of history, as covenant maker, and as faithful. Thus a prominent feature of Paul's writing is his theology of God. Paul situates the death and resurrection of Jesus within the wider context of God's dealings with the human race, and above all with the people of Israel, since the beginning of time.

Mark, however, does not possess that sort of vision, or at least if he does, then that wider vision of salvation history and the God who stands behind it is not evident. In the Gospel, Jesus feels far more immediate than God, even though God is certainly the principal mover in Jesus' life. The voice of God calls Jesus "Son" at the baptism and transfiguration scenes; God is the one to whom Jesus would have addressed himself whenever he prayed (as in the garden); and God is the one who raised Jesus from the dead. But the narrative spotlight belongs to Jesus. This could be explained by supposing that Mark understood and believed a great deal more about God than he could communicate in his text. It could also be explained by recalling that if Mark had been a Gentile convert the good news about Jesus could easily have been his first serious encounter with the mystery of God, his awakening to the life of faith, and his first real experience of salvation. He would have moved into the mystery of God through Jesus, whereas Saint Paul would have moved into the mystery of Jesus through his zealous pursuit of the God of Israel. The contrast may not be a neat one, but it might help us appreciate why God seems less directly present to Mark's Gospel than, say, to John or Matthew. Mark is a thoroughly Jesus-oriented person.

The Gospel Is About the Present, Not the Past

Many readers of the New Testament today are familiar with the scholarly distinction between the historical figure who was Jesus of Nazareth and the stories about him that the early Church collected, developed, and passed along. Inspired by their faith in Jesus risen, the evangelists assembled the traditions, memories, and sayings of Jesus that were available to them. They then reworked that material into a narrative. In this process they were guided not only by their faith but also by their particular historical moment. Mark, after all, was hardly interested in writing a narrative that would edify the first disciples; by the time he wrote his Gospel the original followers of Jesus would almost certainly have been dead. As a result, each of the Gospels bears deep traces of the social and cultural conditions of the early communities from which these documents emerged.

In crafting his Gospel Mark was naturally concerned to address the spiritual needs and circumstances of the readership or listeners who passed before his mind's eye. Mark was less likely to be concerned about creating a document that could be reliably handed on to future generations of Christians, whose historical, social, political, and religious circumstances he was hardly able to foresee, and more likely to be speaking to the men and women who made up his church or community. This point is terribly important but easily overlooked; it is sometimes even discounted altogether by Christians who believe the Gospel text is addressed to them in an unmediated, unhistorical fashion. It is always the *present* historical moment that determines the way we appropriate our faith and tell our story, and the same rule held for Mark. The Gospel narrative, therefore, was not ultimately about past events, although the past obviously provided the literary, imaginative, and religious landscape of the Gospel scenes. In reality, the message of the Gospel was addressed to the Markan present. And just as Mark's point of departure was his faith in the presence of the risen Jesus within his community, that same conviction has to be the starting point of prayerful reflection on the Gospel for future generations.

Maybe we ought to be grateful that Mark could not reach back in time, for the message he bequeathed to the Church was that no one historical situation is to be canonized above every other, not even the situation or context of Jesus himself. The world is much too large and history much too open-ended for Mark to write a Gospel that obsessed over a past so hard to retrieve. Live in the present, he seems to be saying, for the present is the only place where we shall meet Jesus risen. Our own religious imaginations may have been forever formed and transformed by the Gospel narratives, but the world we live and work in and in which we practice our faith and pray is the world of the late-twentieth- and early-twenty-first century.

To put the point another way, perhaps we could say that just as Mark was "inspired" as he wrote his account of the Jesus story, his readers need to be equally inspired if they are going to encounter the risen Jesus in and through Mark's text. They need inspiration if they are to recognize the features of the one who walks ahead of them into their everyday Galilees, and they need to be inspired if they are to discern the saving action of God in the signs of their times. For the gift of inspiration extends not only to the composition and interpretation of the Gospel; it also extends to the actual living out of the story. Inspiration thus includes our being able to take the enormous risk of joining Jesus, symbolically, imaginatively, in our own time and place, along the Jerusalem road. Only through first living the story of Jesus was Mark able to write his Gospel, and only through living the gospel tirelessly and uncompromisingly have subsequent generations been able to make sense of Mark's great paschal narrative.

A Fragmentary Narrative

Coming to Mark's text for the first time, readers may find themselves more confident about their own perceptions once they are assured that Mark's narrative style is indeed fragmentary, even at times abrupt. The awkwardness of Mark's transitions and the clumsy way in which sayings of Jesus are occasionally stitched together are not imagined. Whatever the explanation for this might be, that fragmentary and episodic character seems particularly appropriate for us. Philosophically speaking, reality for many men and women today has become exceedingly disparate and unconnected. There is no grand conceptual synthesis linking together and integrating the various dimensions of our existence, no bedrock truth that can securely anchor us against the tides of rapid change, the breakdown of communities and traditional values, and the shortness of historical memory. Even the earth shows itself to be an increasingly fragile ground for human life. And modern life seems to have grown increasingly episodic, as our attention constantly shifts from one crisis to another. The truth is that the human mind—even an evangelist's—is simply incapable of attending to everything at once, yet our modern technology and instantaneous communication foster the myth of universal awareness.

The First Gospel lacks the conceptual smoothness of the other three, for Mark does not seem to have an overall theology of salvation history beyond his belief in the fulfillment of Scripture. He makes no pretense at being a systematic theologian; his text betrays no unifying cosmology. There is certainly an ordered movement within the Gospel as Jesus makes his way from Galilee to Jerusalem, but the Gospel's sense of direction may derive more from the Christian's prior knowledge of the course of Jesus' life than from the text itself. Scenes and events within the narrative could be rearranged rather freely without disturbing the fundamental logic that Jesus' prophetic life was the direct cause of his arrest and execution. In the end the historical intentionality of the story was not compromised by Mark's literary or catechetical creativity.

Mark's story is certainly about discipleship, although it is not really about the disciples themselves. The disciples' reactions range from their un-hesitating response to Jesus' call at the beginning, to the various outbursts of misunderstanding and fear, and to their abandoning Jesus at the hour of his death. I do not think we can reconcile these different reactions to Jesus. On the one hand, the disciples dropped everything to follow Jesus; even Levi abandoned his tax station to become a disciple. What did they see or perceive about Jesus that would have led them to modify their lives so quickly and to make such an astonishing act of faith? Mark does not explain it to us in so many words, perhaps because he thinks the reason should be fairly obvious to Christian readers. They already know that Jesus is the Son of God, and that specialness ought logically to have been discernible to the ones Jesus would call to follow him. As I remarked, the influence of Easter faith breaks into the story very early. Nevertheless, their initial response to Jesus stands in sharp contrast to what comes later in the narrative when Mark portrays the disciples as stumbling along the way, missing important points, in need of special instruction, and downright scared.

Clearly, Jesus would not have been so deliberate about selecting the Twelve (Mark pictures Jesus as first having spent a night at prayer) if the ones he was about to choose to be such close companions had been un-teachable. Thus we are dealing with Mark's peculiar way of presenting the disciples, not with how the disciples had behaved historically, what their actual motives and qualifications were, and so forth. Yet perhaps in this Mark has revealed a little more about the nature of his own inner struggle. The contrast between the disciples' initial response and what comes later may be reflecting a tension within the story to which Mark himself was keenly sensitive. Jesus' ministry begins with the enthusiastic, confident announcement of the kingdom's arrival, and it fairly concludes with death by crucifixion. The twenty-second Psalm served as Mark's gloss on that horrifying moment. By the time Mark composed his Gospel, he knew full well that the kingdom had not come as Jesus had announced. Thus an im-portant element of his mission remained unfulfilled, and that realization had led some of his followers to conclude that Jesus would return fairly soon to finish what had been started in Galilee. How could redemption be complete when so many men and women were still oppressed, locked in their sinfulness, or overtaken by demons?

Mark must have believed that the risen Jesus actually did return to Galilee, otherwise the message to the women would have been pointless, and Mark would never have included it. Why then should the evangelist have been fearful? Having become Christian, did he find himself facing opposition and even persecution (4:17; 10:30)? Or was he fearful because such is the nature of the faith experience? Nothing is ever absolutely sure and predictable in one's life when a person opens himself or herself to God's mysterious plan for the world. Mark may have shared some of the fear that comes from realizing that one's existence is in jeopardy, that one could be killed for believing in God as totally as Jesus did. Or he might have been afraid that in the end the most basic of all temptations a believer ever has to endure is the one that asks, "Can God really be trusted? Is God reliable when it comes to an actual salvation and liberation *in this world?*" Did the evangelist himself pass through a dark night of the soul? The question is speculative, but I think it points us in the right direction.

And this, of course, is the great question that echoes so hauntingly in the Psalms and elsewhere in Scripture. This question was the driving force behind Job's engagement with a God whose justice seemed anything but reliable, while only in light of this question does one grasp why Second Isaiah wrestled so mightily with the suffering of the innocent Servant. There are probably many more of us who have related to those sentiments of doubt, questioning, and complaint than to the happier stories, say, of deliverance in Exodus or the return from exile in Ezra. The mighty actions surrounding Israel's deliverance from Egypt, recalled and celebrated so often throughout Scripture, when God brought the people out "with a mighty hand and an outstretched arm" (Deut 26:8) sound awfully close to fantasy. Where was God, we wonder, at the time of the killing fields of Cambodia, the massacres of indigenous people in Guatemala and El Salvador, during the nightmarish years of the dirty war in Argentina, in Chechnya, or among the despondent, emaciated refugees fleeing African genocides?

We could add to this list interminably, but the same question keeps returning: Where do we find evidence of the mighty deliverance memorialized in the book of Exodus? Or was that event a once-for-all display of divine energy and passion, a fluke of divine providence? And might it have been the case that by the time of his final Passover meal Jesus too had begun to succumb? The temptation so effortlessly overcome in the wilderness (or so it appears) could have come back with a vengeance. Luke's addition of "until an opportune time" (Luke 4:13) reflects an important insight into the nature of the devil's testing of Jesus. Those were not temporary, discrete episodes of being put to the test. They belonged, rather, to a pattern of struggle with the most severe assaults against Jesus' confidence in God. Jesus had thrown in his lot with God, much against the tempter's counsel (if we allow ourselves to follow the scenes in the wilderness re-created by Luke and Matthew). On the eve of their arrival into the

Promised Land Moses had told the Israelites: "He humbled you by letting you hunger, then by feeding you with manna, with which neither you nor your ancestors were acquainted, in order to make you understand that one does not live by bread alone, but by every word that comes from the mouth of the LORD" (Deut 8:3). But unless Jesus could turn stones into bread, he was going to discover that biblical words alone were incapable of keeping hungry people alive.

In the end, Jesus' immersion into the life of his people and his walking the way of faith was going to cost him his life. Mark almost certainly had realized for himself that faith is a fearful thing; and where fear is involved, people need to be free to choose. He leaves us with *his* story of Jesus, never pressuring anyone to embrace it, since that would have been asking too much of people. Once having chosen to stand with Jesus, the disciple could never escape the wrestling with God that inevitably follows. Easter, Mark knew, does not spare us anything. Thus the women ran from the tomb, scared practically witless.

Jesus' Spirituality Was Not New

In order to avoid becoming either complacent or presumptuous about our spiritual lives, it is salutary to remind ourselves occasionally that no matter how firmly attached we are to our Christian faith and tradition, Christians enjoy no divinely guaranteed corner on the religious experiences of the world. The biblical notions of "election," "chosen race," and "Promised Land" may have misled us as much as they misled Israel. It has taken us centuries to acknowledge that the way we once defined truth had blinded us to the saving presence of God outside the Christian religion. Humbly admitting this fact does not land us on a greasy chute to religious relativism, but it might make us more mannered about our religious claims and maybe even sincerely interested in the religious traditions and spiritual well-being of the rest of the world.

For us, Jesus is the cornerstone of a new temple, our point of contact with the mystery of God. Yet Jesus by no means invented religion, and he obviously was not preaching to men and women who were religious illiterates. Jesus was a devout Jew. Given the memory that he attended Sabbath services regularly, we ought to assume that he kept company with other devout men and women. They already knew the commandments and how to worship God. They paid the tithes prescribed by the Law and practiced good works, such as almsgiving, fasting, and pilgrimages to the Temple in Jerusalem. They would have offered the appropriate sacrifices, and they experienced the need for deeper conversion and renewal, as in the case of those who were drawn to hear John the Baptist by the Jordan. Despite the negative view the Gospel writers generally adopted toward people like the Pharisees and teachers of the Law, there is no reason to assume that religious belief and practice in first-century Palestine had entered a dark age.

To be sure, Jesus called sinners to repentance, but is it realistic to think the majority of those who followed him were terrible sinners who had suddenly experienced the grace of conversion after listening to Jesus? Is it not more likely that the majority were God-seeking people who heard in Jesus' preaching not so much the call to individual repentance for personal, private sins but a call upon the nation as a whole to reimagine its future in light of its past? Is it not more satisfying to think of Jesus as another Isaiah than as a second Jonah, someone capable of envisioning a world made new, a possibility for universal salvation, a possibility to be made actual through the instrumentality of Israel as God's servant? Jesus was not calling a pagan nation to faith but an already believing people to appropriate its own historical experience anew. Jesus, then, did not create Jewish faith or its spirituality; he inherited it.

The kingdom of God was not just a matter of words; it was an immediate possibility waiting to be realized. As Christian missioners and evangelists later traversed the globe to preach the gospel, the Spirit of God had already preceded them. Unfortunately, missioners not uncommonly failed to notice and thus to appreciate the rich significance of this fact. In some cases people were already in possession of a native religiosity and spirituality. Whatever "corrections" Christians thought they had to make, an interior life existed in those men and women long before the missioners arrived on the scene. Mark has given us the intriguing account of the demon-infested man of Gerasa who had terrorized the countryside. In that episode, the Gospel breaks into a Gentile world with an explosive power that proved to be so frightfully liberating that the startled villagers begged Jesus to depart. They were not ready for the new wine of Jesus' preaching. They needed time and they needed to hear voices that would sensitize them to the things of God and prepare them for the eventual arrival of Jesus' apostles. The Gospel is not a document one would place in the hands of a person who had not already been awakened to the things of the Spirit. It is not a beginner's manual but a text for those who have already made some progress along the way of God.

Given their experience of living in the shadow of demons and their resistance to having Jesus in their midst, the villagers of Gerasa undoubtedly needed to be instructed about prayer, moral practice, and the nature of God. But this would not have been true of everybody in the Gospel who was non-Jewish. I do not mean to imply that the Gospel was some kind of religious superfluity the world could just as easily have done without. After all, even today we witness what happens when large numbers of people remain both unchurched and unevangelized, or even worse, when they seem to be completely impervious to the religious dimension of human experience. Today all of us are aware, although in different ways and to different degrees, of the creeping, globalizing materialism and individualism that have been transplanting themselves into the marrow of our humanity, atomizing whatever hope we harbor of a just and reconciled world.

The early Christian missionaries certainly encountered ignorance and resistance to their lifegiving message whenever they traveled outside worlds untouched by Jewish faith or outside societies that had acquired some sense of the transcendent. Nevertheless (and notwithstanding the opening chapter of Paul's letter to the Romans), spirituality was resident in the human world long before Christian apostles set about their work, because spirituality is a constitutive feature of human life to the degree that men and women are in touch with their deepest human desiring. Peoples and cultures manifest their interior life in the emergence of popular wisdom traditions, in rituals and practices that celebrate and attempt to restore balance and harmony within human society and in the world at large, and in the prayerful rhythms that add texture to their everyday existence.

Now, what does this have to do with Mark? Perhaps the most obvious point to make is that Mark has not given us a comprehensive tract on Christian asceticism. A person looking for advice on methods of prayer, spiritual pointers for conducting interreligious dialogue, or an examination of mystical experiences, should not turn to Mark. The evangelist supposes, in other words, that there is more to religious experience than he has incorporated into his narrative. Christians seeking to deepen their interior lives will certainly steep themselves in the Gospels and other New Testament writings, but those writings do not forbid them from drawing on the insight and wisdom of the wider human community.

For Mark the ministry of Jesus amounted to offering new wine, which therefore required new wineskins. "New wineskins" was a metaphor for a change of heart, a new way of thinking and of looking at the world. What Jesus embodied was a model of holiness and faith that did not quite fit the expectations and presuppositions either of the ordinary people or of the religious elites. He was not so much proffering a new spirituality as enfleshing the traditional spirituality of his people in a strikingly different way.

Holy people could keep the company of those considered unclean. They could compassionately touch a leper without defiling themselves, thereby requiring a ritual of purification. For Jesus, religion does not abet social stratification; it dismantles it. Holy men and women do not necessarily have to practice rigorous or even regular fasting; they could eat and drink together as people enacting God's own banquet. While they certainly pray, holy men and women never make a show of prayer; praying fits into their routine naturally, unobtrusively, as in the case of Jesus. While it is Matthew who draws this point out (Matt 6:5-15), Mark's Jesus (in contrast to Luke's) is a man of prayer without being a person who prays at every turn or who might be attracted to spending his life in the Temple or in the wilderness.

The scenes in Mark where Jesus actually prays are probably too concentrated or stylized to serve conveniently as examples or patterns for most of his followers: leaving the house early in the morning and seeking out a deserted place (1:35); a late-afternoon prayer up on a mountain (6:46-47); the messianic prayer of surrender after the Last Supper and before his arrest (14:35ff.); and Jesus' final prayer as he was dying (15:34). The naturalness with which Jesus prayed from day to day is perhaps better hinted at in Mark 11:25, when he says, "Whenever you stand praying, forgive, if you have anything against anyone; so that your Father in heaven may also forgive you your trespasses." The phrasing "whenever you stand praying" suggests routine action, something one takes for granted as an integral, normal part of daily existence. Since at the moment he states these words Jesus is in Jerusalem at the Temple precincts, one might conjecture that for him the forgiveness prayer is supposed to be the principal prayer one makes in the house of God. And one might conjecture further that the words "if you have *anything* against anyone" apply not just to insults and grievances, no matter how serious or slight, but to debts of any kind, including financial and social ones. This was hardly a novel sort of prayer for anyone nurtured on the Prophets and the Psalms.

Negatively, the metaphor of new wineskins meant that religious experts should not impart a spiritual doctrine that effectively cheats the majority of people. Holiness is not the preserve of a few but the promise intended for everyone. Poor widows, for example, ought not to be thinking that in contributing their last penny to the Temple treasury they are doing what God wants. A Jesus who multiplies loaves and fishes, not just once but twice, in order that people should not leave his company hungry; who instructs overjoyed parents to give their young girl something to eat; who celebrates Levi's conversion by joining him for a meal; or who defends hungry disciples as they pluck grains of wheat on a Sabbath, is not a Jesus who is going to nod approvingly at a piety that leads to chronic hunger. In relating the wilderness scene, Mark never mentions that Jesus fasted; the ministering angels may have been providing him with food the whole time! The poor widow of chapter 12 had been badly instructed. Coming to God's house, she did not find the protection and security celebrated in Psalm 68:5: "Father of orphans and protector of widows is God in his holy habitation." She departed God's house more impoverished than when she arrived.

The point bears repeating: Jesus did not invent Jewish spirituality. Nearly everything he does or teaches has its parallel in the Scriptures of Israel. But he does impress upon that spirituality, as Mark envisions Jesus' historical moment, a new form, decisively revealed through the cross and resurrection. Jesus' teaching and practice constituted a robust new wine, and only new wineskins could contain it. In attempting to gain some insight into how Jesus prayed or what he might have prayed about, we would probably be well advised to examine the psalms carefully. With good reason the Church found the voice of the risen Jesus throughout those prayers, for Jesus himself had surely prayed them. We are likely to find a lot more there to satisfy our heart's curiosity than in speculating about Jesus' use of *Abba* to address God. We can imagine, for instance, that Psalm 10 took on fresh urgency for Jesus once he learned the news of John's arrest, and it is nearly inconceivable that Jesus would not have prayed fervently to God on John's behalf.

Similarly, it would be hard to believe that Jesus did not pray regularly on behalf of and in union with all the other figures who appear in the Gospel story: the lepers; the demon-possessed; the people looking so much like sheep without a shepherd; the families of his closest followers and friends; not to mention the countless others whom he encountered among the towns and villages of Galilee. Mark has not incorporated these individuals and groups into his narrative merely as literary props or pieces of staging in Jesus' ministry. They are in the story because they figured first in Jesus' own life and imagination, his prayer and concern. Apart from them there would have been no divine call, no need for a baptism, no anointing Spirit from heaven. Jesus saw them, he touched them, he would have carried memories of them in his heart as he journeyed and probably prayed for them before falling asleep.

The people who appear within the story were not simply characters invented so Jesus could display his power or his compassion; they were the ones who evoked from Jesus the substance and style of his prophetic mission. This point could not have escaped Mark's attention. The evangelist surely recognized counterpoints to those Gospel figures in his own world and even among his own community. Mark's Gospel is hardly a wistful re-membrance of Jesus' ministry; rather, it is a road map for disciples of an-other generation. He wrote about that newness of life he had seen and experienced in his own day with the same depth of conviction as had the author of the first letter of John when he said, "We declare to you . . . what we have heard, what we have seen with our eyes, what we have looked at and touched with our hands" (1 John 1:1).

Why Put So Much Stress upon Faith?

The recurring call to faith within the Gospel story seems such a fa-miliar and natural element of the narrative that one could easily overlook the motive for Jesus' insistence. As we have already noted, it is hardly likely that Jesus' listeners did not believe in God. The fact that we find Jesus teaching at Sabbath assemblies so regularly tells us that those who heard him were already believers, and probably committed ones at that.

Mark portrays Jesus preeminently as a teacher. The assembly in the synagogue found his instruction refreshing because he taught with au-thority (1:27), while the crowds at the Temple listened to him with de-light not because he was so amusing but because they followed his religious critique (12:37). Given that Jesus' listeners were already daugh-ters and sons of Abraham, Jesus must have been teaching them something beyond what they already knew and believed, something that left many of them surprised, amazed, and glorifying God and others of them con-fused, suspicious, and angry. Since Mark fails to give us much informa-tion about the content of Jesus' instruction, we have to surmise through the actions of Jesus (which we today might call his audio-visuals) what the teaching might have consisted of. To repeat a point, Mark was not being neglectful by not drawing together the things he knew Jesus had taught, the way the evangelist Matthew did by means of the Sermon on the Mount. Mark may have realized that his audience was already conversant with the core contents of Jesus' message and thus that there was no rea-son to make his narrative longer. Or perhaps Mark, being a skilled story-teller, envisioned his Gospel being read in communities with frequent pauses during which the catechist elaborated on some detail or other, or suggested practical applications, or engaged in some imaginative recon-figuring of a Gospel scene. For the evangelist, the Gospel text was not supposed to be a document that was to be preserved unchanged for pos-terity. He would not have thought of himself as composing the authorized version of a canonical text. If that were how the early Church had understood Mark's Gospel, then it would be hard to account for the liberty Matthew and Luke took, for example, in fleshing out the scene of Jesus in the wilderness or, for that matter, to account for any of the other modifications they made of Mark.

In what ways the miracles point backwards to the teaching of Jesus will need to be looked at later. But we can at least say this much now: the miracles confirm Jesus' understanding of the will of God in our regard. God wills wholeness; reintegration of marginalized members into family and village life; the physical and moral healing of communities and of society itself; liberation from oppressive, dehumanizing forces (graphically symbolized by the presence of demons). Yet why does Jesus ask people who already believe in God to have faith? One reason might have been that Jesus was calling for faith in his message, even as Mark was beckoning his listeners to deeper faith in Jesus. Another reason may have been that the faith of many people was more habitual and cultural than vibrant and integrated into the everyday. If a person was an Israelite he or she automatically thought of himself or herself as a believer, perhaps in much the same way that many Christians recite unthinkingly the words of the Creed. The weekly profession of faith may not have sunk all that deeply into our daily lives and routine, our habits of thinking and behaving, our politics, the way we spend money, or our relationship with the physical world. Maybe Jesus' call to faith was essentially a call to hear fully, with all one's heart and mind, the great commandment found in Deut 6:4-5.

Mark did not believe, however, that Jesus' activity as teacher amounted to little more than conducting Jewish revival meetings. Jesus did not teach purely for the satisfaction of instructing others (although he undoubtedly found teaching a consolation; otherwise he would not have been nearly so effective) but for the sake of the kingdom of God. Or rather, his teaching was preparatory; it anticipated the arrival of God's rule. Jesus had been asking his followers to take with utmost seriousness that God acts in history (this much would have been evident from the Scriptures) and that the God of Israel was about to accomplish something extraordinary. God, Jesus believed, was about to bring Israel's age-old hope for a definitive, lasting liberation to fulfillment, to make good on an ancient promise sworn to the patriarchs and their families. And that fulfillment concerned a great deal more than real estate and the recovery of national sovereignty! The reign of God was really and truly at hand. Jesus felt the closeness of the reign of God in his bones; it had totally seized his imagination and transformed his prayer. Jesus could see and even taste the imminence of that reality, which, in God's providence, he had been called to usher in.

Yet Mark was no religious romantic. He could also see that what Jesus had proclaimed still had not been realized some forty years later. *In his heart,* Mark also knew that Jesus ultimately was not wrong to have believed and hoped the way he did. The failure of the kingdom to arrive in Jesus' lifetime or even in the lifetime of the first generation of his followers, who had been led to believe that their master's return was just around the corner, had not dissuaded Mark from becoming a Christian. And why not? Perhaps because Mark had discerned the mystery—the secrecy—surrounding the reign of God. It will surely arrive, Mark believed, in God's good time; not even the Son had been privileged to know for sure when exactly that moment would come. Jesus may have been more sure of the kingdom's imminence at the outset of his ministry than toward the end, although the ending of the story becomes all the more theologically problematic (and interesting) if Jesus saw himself facing death with little evidence that his mission had been successful. The notion that Jesus may have been wrong about the kingdom does not appear to have bothered Mark. He reset the apocalypticism of Jesus in terms of two time frames, one that anticipated the destruction of the Temple and another that gazed into a distant future. Mark shared the apocalyptic mind-set of the early communities, but he was much more taken by Jesus' fidelity to God's will despite the obstacles and resistances he had encountered along the way. The necessity of being tested so as to become immersed as deeply as possible in the mystery of God is central to the dynamics of faith. Since Jesus was above all a person of faith—a true Son of God—Jesus' route to God had to cross the same terrain as the rest of us.

It is uncomfortable for most of us to entertain the idea of Jesus having been wrong about anything. That the Son of God should have made a mistake strikes us as profoundly irreverent. We admit more or less readily that Jesus had to cope with the same physical limitations as everybody else. He needed to sleep and eat, for example. Long journeys would have tired him, he would need to grieve over the death of loved ones, he needed human companionship, he had to pray, and so on. Jesus' strong emotional reactions in several situations is a notable feature of Mark's Gospel. Sometimes the reader needs to linger over various words or expressions in order to let their emotional tone or energy sink in. Nevertheless, having emotions is no indication of being wrong any more than being subject to the cultural and social constraints intrinsic to the human condition or being born in a particular time and place. There are many things about the physical world that Jesus could never have known as a first-century person. Neither would he have known who had actually authored, say, the book of Genesis. Matters pertaining to business, farming, history, even interpersonal skills he had to learn, for discovery and learning are major ingredients of human development. Jesus would have been a singularly poor teacher if he had never had to undergo the process of questioning, thinking, discovering, assimilating, and talking with others. That, after all, was exactly what his followers would have to do in the course of their time with him.

That the Son of God should have been wrong about anything would likewise have been for Mark an irreverent thought. The few instances where Jesus is depicted as either not knowing (13:32) or not being able to perform mighty deeds (6:5) have to be read from the more comprehensive perspective of Jesus as believer and Mark's faith in Jesus as the Son of God precisely because Jesus was the person of faith. That Jesus might have been mistaken about the kingdom's timing really did not bother Mark because Mark knew on the basis of his own experience that the reality Jesus had preached and represented was unfolding before his very eyes. Mark may not have been able to work everything out systematically and coherently, but he had no doubt whatsoever that a divine plan had been at work throughout the life of Jesus and that it was continuing to guide the course of human history through the faith and practice of Jesus' disciples of Mark's own generation.

In the end, it is perhaps best to conclude that Jesus' emphasis on faith once again reveals an aspect of the evangelist's own spirituality and religious experience. Mark knew the difference between life as a believer and life as a non-believer. The ambiguity and suffering of human existence resolved themselves in terms of surrender to the mystery of God under the sign of the cross. For Mark, one surrendered to that holy mystery by following Jesus.

Conflict as Suffering

Although the negative view of the religious leadership given us by the evangelists would probably not correspond neatly to the historical situation of Jesus' day, for Mark Jesus' conflict with the official teachers, practitioners, and guides became an important element for understanding the factors that led to his being arrested and killed. Yet I think we have to understand also that in his portrayal of the religious elites as Jesus' adversaries the evangelist was not just reaching blindly for a historical explanation. Mark saw the history of Jesus as a story about conflict on various levels: conflicts between Jesus as God's anointed and the power of Satan, conflicts between

Jesus and those charged with shepherding God's people, conflicts between Jesus and civil authorities. For Mark, reality was conflictual. As soon as the seed is sown, birds try to eat it, the thorns and weeds grab it, the scorching heat kills it. If the scribes and Pharisees had never existed, for example, Mark would have had to highlight some other adversaries, because it was of the very nature of things that the Gospel would have its enemies. And if Mark, as we have been insisting, writes a story about Jesus in which being Son of God above all means being a person of tested faith, then perhaps Mark's way of presenting the religious leaders reflects by way of analogy the degree to which the evangelist found himself and his community in the thick of controversy, tension, and persecution.

Mark's attitude toward the groups that opposed Jesus probably indicates that the Church of his day experienced hostility, not faulty historical information. The fact that religious people could arrive at the conclusion that Jesus was a demon-possessed man (3:22) reveals something about the way *Mark* had heard and responded to the Gospel. Indeed, there could not have been a crucifixion unless certain individuals within Jewish society had determined that Jesus was a dangerous man, not a divinely appointed prophet. But in Mark's view the precise nature of their decision apparently had to do with the insider/outsider problem. Mark as a Gentile had come to Christian faith from the outside and had embraced the idea of the new family of which Jesus spoke, a family composed of those who opened themselves up to God and made doing God's will the most important value in their lives. The excessive nationalism and exclusiveness of Jesus' religious opponents, as Mark understood them, would certainly have put them on a collision course with Jesus. Easter disclosed, among other things, that the God of Israel was truly the God of the nations. Israel's faith, as embodied in the person of Jesus, was going to be the instrument of the world's salvation. For Mark, then, Jesus was neither crazed nor demon possessed. Through Jesus Mark had experienced a brand new life inside the community of disciples.

Where Is Love in Mark's Gospel?

That the world has been created out of love is a basic element of Christian belief. The only conceivable motive for God's having created the heavens and the earth had to be love; the world came into existence because God is good. The goodness God saw in the world after its creation reflected the goodness of the divine mystery itself. The intuition underlying this basic element can be found in much of our civilization's art, literature, ritual, and sacred narratives.

Conviction about divine love is not a uniquely Christian belief. The theme of divine love runs throughout the Hebrew Scriptures, however bewildering the literary character of God sometimes appears in those writings. Yet among the New Testament writings, the Gospel and letters of John as well as the letters of Paul draw special attention to the mystery of divine love, a mystery rendered all the more stunning in light of the extent and heavy weight of human sinfulness. How can God love humankind in the stark depravity of its disobedience?

Since we have learned that love is the premier divine attribute, a reader could be disappointed with Mark's Gospel because it does not attend sufficiently to God's love. Nevertheless, love is truly there. N. T. Wright's comment about the justice of God points us in the right direction. "God's justice," he writes, "is his love in action, to right the wrongs of a suffering world by taking their weight upon himself."[3] *Taking their weight upon himself* expresses the essence of divine solidarity, which is above all a matter of love. This love was concretely reflected in the attitude and response of Jesus on countless occasions: in his compassion, in his healing and exorcising, in his fidelity to his mission.

Mark does not depict Jesus the way Luke does, as the model of compassion on the cross. Nor does he anywhere say, as Paul and John would, that Jesus died out of love for us. The only time in Mark's Gospel that Jesus is presented as expressly loving someone is in the case of the rich man in chapter 10, who actually turned away from Jesus. We can presume, of course, that Jesus sincerely loved the children who were brought to him by their parents for a blessing, that he really loved his companions and was not merely bound to them by the formality of a teacher/disciple agreement, that he truly loved the wavering father who brought him his epileptic son, and that he really loved the woman who anointed him in the home of Simon the leper. When Jesus replied to the lawyer's question about the greatest commandment, we have to suppose (as Mark did) that Jesus himself lived that command fully, that he absolutely loved God with all his heart, mind, and strength, and that he sincerely loved his neighbor as he loved himself. If love was the Law's command, then Jesus practiced it, and not out of sheer obligation, either, but in the Spirit, freely and eagerly.

We can be equally confident that many people loved Jesus. The Twelve would have; so too the other disciples and the many women who

---

[3] Wright, *What Saint Paul Really Said*, 110. Solidarity does not imply vicarious suffering, as if God lifts suffering off human shoulders and places it on those of Jesus. Solidarity involves suffering *with* and *alongside of,* not suffering in place of another.

had accompanied him to the end. Mark singles out three of them, presumably because of their special affection toward Jesus: Mary Magdalene; another Mary who was the mother of James the younger and Joses; and Salome (15:40). Perhaps we should also include here Jesus' mother and family. While their motive could have been one of safeguarding the family name from further disgrace (3:21),[4] it is also quite possible that Jesus' family traveled to Capernaum to bring him back to the safety of Nazareth because they cared for him. Again, we have to infer that all these people would have loved Jesus, since Mark is quiet about such things. Affection shows itself above all in deeds, and the reality is that people did things for Jesus.

Only once, at the scene of the first multiplication of loaves and fishes, does Mark describe Jesus as reacting the way a shepherd would (6:34). Yet the fact that he expressly makes this comparison only once does not mean that Mark did not consistently think of Jesus as caring. The imagery is not so developed as we find in John 10, to be sure. And Mark does not gloss Jesus' healing activity the way Matthew does in quoting Isaiah: "He took our infirmities and bore our diseases" (Matt 8:17). It would be pointless to attempt to figure out why the love motif does not appear so prominently in Mark as it does in the Last Supper discourse of the Fourth Gospel. For Mark Jesus is love in action; the works of Jesus throughout the narrative draw attention to Jesus himself as a person of great feeling and compassion and to his closeness to God.

Even more to the point, Mark presents us with a picture of Jesus in which Jesus' first love is the kingdom of God. And lest this sound abstract and detached from everyday life, I should add that to imagine Jesus dedicating himself to the kingdom of God without at the same time committing himself fully and irreversibly to his people would make absolutely no sense. Jesus did not die for some abstract theological purpose, no matter how high or noble. The shedding of his blood symbolized as dramatically as anyone ever can in this world that Jesus' life was spent wholly for others: "to give his life a ransom for many" (10:45). I am not altogether sure how to read Mark's preoccupation with Jesus' attentiveness to his disciples, teaching and explaining everything to them, given their obtuseness. One would think that if God had planned the events of salvation history as carefully as Mark believed, then God could have arranged things differently. Why not a few more disciples with the zeal and theological acumen of Paul or the understanding and humility of Stephen? Apart from John and perhaps Peter the figures of the original Twelve fade

---

[4] See Malina and Rohrbaugh, *Social-Science Commentary,* 199.

from view, and the truly effective apostolic voice emerges in someone who had not been an eyewitness.

Two things may need to be said. First, Mark could have considered the full message about the cross so hard to comprehend that he had no choice but to portray the disciples as steadily losing their bearings the more Jesus spoke of his destiny in Jerusalem. Second, Mark's way of presenting the relation between Jesus and his closest followers was intended to signal the way Jesus continued to relate to his disciples in the early Christian communities. That relationship would have been marked by fidelity and love. We catch a glimpse of this when Jesus addressed the paralytic as "son" (2:5) and the woman with the chronic menstrual flow as "daughter" (5:34). These warm addresses surely tell us something about how Mark himself experienced the presence of the risen Lord. Faithfulness and love are what we need to hear in the great commandment, which Jesus cited in chapter 12. As we already noted, Jesus would never have cited a commandment he himself did not sincerely practice. The same faithfulness and love provide the affective resonance within which the eucharistic words of Mark 14:22-24 have to be heard.

Having looked at some of the theological landscape of this Gospel, we shall turn our attention in the chapters that follow to some of its contours and narrative detail. In chapter 1 we shall look at several features of the story of Jesus' baptism that make it so rich theologically. For it is with the baptism that Mark first presents us with Jesus in solidarity with the people of Israel. Standing in the Jordan was a moment of prayer and faith, Jesus' point of insertion in the historical drama of human salvation.

Recommended Reading

There are numerous titles to which one could reliably turn in order to learn more about the historical figure of Jesus and his times. I have found the following works particularly helpful:

Marcus J. Borg, *Meeting Jesus Again for the First Time* (New York: HarperCollins, 1994); John P. Meier, *Rethinking the Historical Jesus,* vol. 2: *Mentor, Message, and Miracles* (New York: Doubleday, 1994); Frederick J. Murphy, *The Religious World of Jesus* (Nashville: Abingdon Press, 1991); John Riches, *The World of Jesus* (Cambridge: Cambridge Univ. Press, 1990); E. P. Sanders, *The Historical Figure of Jesus* (London: Penguin Books, 1993); N. T. Wright, *Jesus and the Victory of God* (Minneapolis: Augsburg Fortress Press, 1996).

1

A Believer from the Beginning

And a voice came from heaven, "You are my Son, the Beloved; with you I am well pleased" (Mark 1:11).

What's in a Title?

Mark's Gospel is not an apologetic tract. It does not read like a pamphlet a catechist might place in the hands of a non-believer to urge devout consideration of the Christian faith, or even to answer questions from those who find themselves doubtful or skeptical about Christian claims. Mark does not set out to *prove* anything about Jesus but to proclaim and share his story.[1] Although Mark's Jesus clearly has adversaries among his own people, there is no anti-Jewish polemic in his writing and no anti-Jewish theological legacy. This point must be firmly stated and grasped, because in the course of the narrative the Temple in Jerusalem emerges as the institutional embodiment of everything that stands in the way of the rule and presence of God within Israel, a grotesque distortion of its mission to be a house of prayer for all the nations.

Yet Mark's Jesus is indelibly imprinted with the faith of Israel. When Mark announces "The beginning of the good news of Jesus Christ, the Son of God" (1:1), he presupposes that his listeners have already been introduced to that news and that they already know that Jesus of Nazareth, the Messiah of Israel, is indeed the Son of God. One cannot consistently

---

[1] Mary Ann Tolbert suggests: "[Mark] was written to individuals, not to groups, and individuals in primarily two general categories: individual Christians experiencing persecutions because of their faith who were in need of encouragement and individuals interested in Christianity but not yet fully committed who needed to be persuaded. Mark's rhetorical goals are exhortation and proselytizing." See *Sowing the Gospel*, 304.

acknowledge Jesus as Son of God and ignore or separate oneself from the religious tradition in which Jesus stands.

There is a twofold problem here. First, the title "Son of God," which appears in the opening verse, is liable to misunderstanding outside the thought-world of the Hebrew Scriptures. A Gentile could easily misinterpret the phrase, and thus Gentile converts would need to be particularly careful not to import notions of divine-human relations from the Greco-Roman culture to which they belonged. One recalls the reaction of the crowds at Lystra after witnessing a miracle worked by Paul: "The gods have come down to us in human form!" (Acts 14:11). Yet even those inside the community of faith sometimes needed to be schooled further about the mystery and paradox involved in Jesus' life as Son of God.

The second difficulty is that the expression "Son of God" is metaphorical, in the same way that the biblical portrayal of Israel as Yahweh's betrothed is metaphorical. Literally speaking, God neither begets nor marries, since God is spirit. On the one hand, because the word "son" normally implies a biological relationship between an individual and his mother or father (although there are clear exceptions, as in the case of adoptive parents or foster parents), the phrase "Son of God" becomes a metaphor. On the other hand, if God is understood as the parent of everyone by virtue of creation (Paul says as much in Acts 17:28-29), then all of us are truly children of God *first,* and our human parents bear the title "father" or "mother" derivatively or analogously. Normal linguistic usage is turned upside down in this radical faith perspective, a perspective that was demonstrated by Jesus in Mark 3:35 and by the author of the letter to the Ephesians: "I bow my knees before the Father, from whom every family [all fatherhood] in heaven and on earth takes its name" (Eph 3:14-15). The same radical faith was illustrated earlier in Mark when James and John "left their father Zebedee in the boat with the hired men, and followed him" (1:20). Their true parent, in other words, was God; they proved this by the fact that, like Abraham, they were ready to forsake their kinfolk in order to do God's will.[2]

Mark gives no indication that "Son of God" implied any physical relationship between Jesus and God, nor did he believe that human beings, whether carpenters, children of carpenters, or emperors, should arrogate this title to themselves. Historically, Jesus never did so, at least not in the exclusive sense in which the Church eventually came to employ the title

---

[2] Also relevant is the text of Malachi: "If then I am a father, where is the honor due me?" (Mal 1:6b). And again: "Have we not all one father? Has not one God created us?" (Mal 2:10).

in its creeds. The active presence of God within a human life, which made the attribution of the title "Son of God" appropriate, was first and foremost a work of the Spirit. In the eyes of the early Christian community, by raising Jesus from the dead God had revealed that from beginning to end the whole of Jesus' life had been exactly that, namely, a product of the Spirit, and therefore that the title "Son of God" most fittingly could be predicated of him.

From a narrative viewpoint Mark could not logically have placed the heavenly voice declaring Jesus to be Son of God at the tomb, although from a theological standpoint this would have been a truly appropriate place; the voice would have interpreted the event of Jesus' being raised from the dead. But since everyone knew that there had been no witnesses standing by at the burial site, Mark scripted the voice into the scene of the baptism. Furthermore, the reader realizes that the voice is not merely *approving* Jesus' life up to that point as if to confirm that Jesus had been since his youth a person filled with holiness and wisdom (the way Luke does). Rather, the voice reaches forward to the story's end, for it was in light of the whole story that the title had been invoked by the early Church as a shorthand expression for everything it believed and confessed about Jesus.

A Biblical Phrase

Within the Hebrew Scriptures the idea of God's "son" applied above all to the nation of Israel, as in the book of Exodus:

> Then you are to say to Pharaoh:
> Thus says YHWH:
> My son, my firstborn, is Israel!
> I said to you: Send free my son, that he may serve me,
> but you have refused to send him free,
> (so) here: I will kill your son, your firstborn![3]

The prophets Isaiah and Hosea had beautifully echoed this idea:

> I will say to the north, "Give them up,"
>   and to the south, "Do not withhold;
> bring my sons from far away
>   and my daughters from the end of the earth—
> everyone who is called by my name,
>   whom I created for my glory,
>   whom I formed and made" (Isa 43:6-7).

---

[3] Exod 4:22-23. Translation is from Fox, *Five Books of Moses*.

> When Israel was a child, I loved him,
>> and out of Egypt I called my son (Hos 11:1).

"Son of God" also came to refer to the king, as in Ps 2:7 and 2 Sam 7:14; the expression thus took on the note of royalty, although not many of Israel's kings measured up to how a son of God was expected to behave. The title further referred to one who faithfully carried out God's will even to the point of death in the wonderfully suggestive passage from the second chapter of The Wisdom of Solomon, composed some thirty years before the birth of Jesus. It deserves to be quoted, so suggestive is it of the Jesus story:

> Let us lie in wait for the righteous man,
> because he is inconvenient to us and opposes our actions;
> he reproaches us for sins against the law,
> and accuses us of sins against our training.
> He professes to have knowledge of God,
> and calls himself a child of the Lord.
> He became to us a reproof of our thoughts;
> the very sight of him is a burden to us,
> because his manner of life is unlike that of others,
> and his ways are strange.
> We are considered by him as something base,
> and he avoids our ways as unclean;
> he calls the last end of the righteous happy,
> and boasts that God is his father.
> Let us see if his words are true,
> and let us test what will happen at the end of his life;
> for if the righteous man is God's child, he will help him,
> and will deliver him from the hand of his adversaries (Wis 2:12-18).

The text of Isa 42:1, which also appears to lie behind the divine address in Mark 1:11, clearly affirms the idea that "son of God" means being enrolled in God's service, a service that involves "bring[ing] forth justice to the nations." The conjunction of royalty and servant motifs, therefore, represents a uniquely Christian insight into the mission of Jesus. Kings ordinarily do not belong to the serving class, and servants do not rule. One can imagine how Davidic monarchs might have discovered the moral legitimacy of their social and political power in the claim that the king has been adopted or begotten by God. In the case of Jesus, however, the social and political aspects simply do not fit. If God, the sovereign Lord of heaven and earth, is his father, then Jesus is royalty. And if the idea that flows from this sense of his being royal means anything, it is not that Jesus is being thought of as an earthly monarch in his own right but as one who represents before human beings the one and only Sovereign of the universe.

Luke referred to Adam as son of God in his genealogical account of Jesus (Luke 3:38), while Jesus himself found the expression suitable for describing peacemakers (Matt 5:9), people of forgiveness (Matt 5:48; the point is made indirectly), as well as all those who lovingly do the will of God (Mark 3:33-35; again indirectly). Those sitting around Jesus are his brothers and sisters, for they, like him, listen attentively to God as daughters and sons. Throughout the New Testament the idea of our being a son, a child, or children of God occurs frequently. I think its prominence points first to Jesus' prophetic preaching and instruction and second to a penetrating, joyous, and transformative experience of God as "merciful closeness," to use Karl Rahner's expression.

As used in the passage from The Wisdom of Solomon, the concept "son of God" appears to be more descriptive than explanatory; any judgment about a person's holiness and closeness to God is more securely (and deservedly) rendered at the end of the individual's life and testing, not at the beginning. It is toward this usage that Mark leans. To claim that Jesus is the Son of God is to describe his manner of living, choosing, working, praying, and dying. This descriptive sense was elaborated by the letter to the Hebrews: "Although he was a Son, he learned obedience through what he suffered" (Heb 5:8). What being Son meant concretely was spelled out in the preceding verse: "In the days of his flesh, Jesus offered up prayers and supplications, with loud cries and tears, to the one who was able to save him from death, and he was heard because of his reverent submission." Here, Jesus' being Son is demonstrated through the intensity of his prayer and the depth of his faith, measured in terms of humility and obedience. Phenomenologically speaking, a son or daughter of God is above all a person of faith. And the first instance in which this is demonstrated in the Gospel is Jesus' baptism.

The passage from Exodus 4 cited earlier moves, however, in a different direction. The people of Israel are thought of collectively as firstborn son of God. They are apparently named this way not on the basis of their fidelity and holiness but on the basis of divine purpose and election. God chose them. Their sonship thus goes back to Abraham's call. We are going to get nowhere speculating on whether the appropriate metaphor here is "begotten" or "adopted," or whether it was election itself that constituted the people as God's son, or whether it was Abraham's great faith that forever constituted them (in God's eyes) as a holy and specially loved nation. The point is that in this passage "son" is the title with which God designates the people. The divine motive is not altogether clear. What exactly it is about

the people of Israel that calls forth a filial relationship with God is left unexplained—not arbitrary, but unexplained. In the Exodus text sonship involves divine election, or adoption, or even generation ("my firstborn son").
Therefore, when the title is applied to Jesus, it automatically carries with it
the idea that Jesus has been chosen, adopted, or begotten by God. But it
further conveys the idea that Jesus and the people are inseparable. Jesus represents the whole history of Israel; he becomes the people. We shall be
looking at some of the facets of this idea in subsequent chapters. My point
here is that in the Hebrew Scriptures, much like the word "servant" in Second Isaiah, the concept "son of God," while sounding singular, does not
refer to a holy though unnamed individual but to a group.

If Jesus is identified as Son of God, therefore, then something is
being claimed about his relationship with the people and not just about
his relationship with God. Even the "righteous one" in the passage from
The Wisdom of Solomon does not appear to have been a single individual. The righteous one was probably a group of devout Jews living outside their homeland and struggling to follow their laws and customs
faithfully amidst a hostile, idolatrous, and morally corrupt people. And
what would a king of Israel be apart from his people? If the psalmist
thinks of the king as a son of God, it cannot be for the sake of the king
himself. The ruler stands for and with his people. In the same way God's
house in Jerusalem is not celebrated for its own sake but for what it says
about Israel's relationship with God.[4]

The identity of the Son of God, one may reasonably conclude, is inseparable from his identification with his people. And the reason for this
identification must be located in divine purpose. For what reason does
God call any individual, or any group, or any one people, if not for the
sake of saving others? "Son of God" embodies not a timeless essence but
a mission, a saving purpose: to rescue slaves, to redeem captives, to un-
lock prisons and open dungeons, to drive out demons, to open blind eyes
and deaf ears, to lead those threatened with destruction to safety. These
are manifestly the works of salvation. Some of the most penetrating reflections in the Hebrew Scriptures revolve around the historical experience of suffering and bad fortune. Why would God permit that Israel, the
chosen people, should undergo such humiliation and oppression? While
punishment for infidelity was an easy and obvious answer, the more
durable insight came in the reflection of Second Isaiah, where the Lord's
servant was seen as the instrument of deliverance for the many. A son of

---

[4] See Hooker, *Gospel According to Saint Mark,* 47.

God will necessarily be led into suffering, but that suffering always serves a purpose, and the historical form of that suffering is determined by what a son of God does to lift burdens off the shoulders of his sisters and brothers. Likewise, some of the most penetrating reflections in the Christian Scriptures were driven by the desire to know why being Son of God had to entail rejection, humiliation, and such an ignominious death.

Son of God on Roman Lips

The centurion who identified the crucified Jesus as Son of God was evidently moved by the prayer of the dying Jesus. If he had been accompanying the execution party since Pilate's judgment hall, it could well be that Mark was imagining the centurion's reaction to be a culmination of all he had observed as the soldiers and their prisoners made their way along that fateful road leading outside the city. At any rate, a Roman centurion would hardly have been sufficiently conversant with the Hebrew Bible to draw a connection at that moment between the dying Jesus and the phrase "Son of God." He could indeed have learned that this was an expression some had used of Jesus, or he might have heard the Temple leadership shouting the title disparagingly at Jesus as he passed by them. Nevertheless, the title would not have received its full meaning before Easter. The Church adopted the expression and redefined it so that "Son of God" would ever after apply preeminently to Jesus. Mark's placing this christological confession on Roman lips clearly served a theological, not a historical purpose.

A similar point could be made with the several instances in the story when demons declare Jesus as Son of God. From one point of view it could be argued that the demons possessed some insight into the true identity of Jesus (just as the reader does). Mark mentions this in 1:34: "And he would not permit the demons to speak, because they knew him." But their disclosures make it appear that who Jesus was could stand independently of what he would actually do in living and dying, fully obedient to God. The identity of Jesus, however, is linked to his life and death. In a salvation-history sense, Jesus could not be *fully* Son of God until the cross and resurrection. Strictly speaking, the demons have not yet seen this revelation. Their reaction to Jesus, therefore, is anticipatory. So too Jesus' reply to the high priest's question in the trial scene. Theologically speaking, the title "Son of God" in its full Christian sense would not have been appropriate to Jesus prior to the cross. Historically speaking, it would have been practically impossible.[5]

---

[5] Donahue, *Are You the Christ?*, 139–87.

Although "Son of God" would never take on even the slightest physical connotation, the title would be broadened to include a oneness with God so thoroughgoing and irrevocable that Jesus could also be viewed as God with us and Word made flesh. While Mark does not use this imagery, he clearly does connect God and Jesus: the disciples are as safe with Jesus as they are with God. One has only to read the account of the crossing of the lake in Mark 4:35-41 alongside Ps 107:23-32 to grasp this reconfiguring of Jewish faith along Christian lines.

A person could be called a child of God without necessarily being thought of as divine, unless one elects to understand divinity in participatory terms: the holy person participates in the very life of God. If Jesus is Son of God, then he must be divine; but what then does divinity mean? Divinity is not Mark's category. Mark would not claim that Jesus is God pure and simple, for he records Jesus' saying, "Why do you call me good? No one is good but God alone" (Mark 10:18). He believes that the categories of humility, obedience, service, and poverty are more descriptive of the expression "Son of God" than the all-too-human categories of power, influence, majesty, and wealth.

The real difficulty is that the Christian reader, enlightened by faith, already knows who Jesus is, and then frequently assumes that some figures (or at least Jesus himself) likewise possessed this knowledge in advance. Surely, they reason, Jesus must have known who he was from the very outset of his ministry if not even earlier. That Jesus would have thought of himself as a son of God in the sense of being a true son of Israel is altogether plausible. The parable of the vineyard in Mark 12, especially verse 6 ("He still had one other, a beloved son") may be reflecting such self-understanding; so too the way God is addressed in the Gethsemane prayer (14:36). That Jesus' experience and understanding of God never underwent any change, development, or transformation is simply unrealistic. It is hard to suppose that God could have been the same for Jesus at the Jordan where the story opens and at Golgotha where his life ends.

From one point of view all of us are children of God by virtue of our having been created, but our actually appropriating this truth and growing in it takes a lifetime. Thus from a slightly different perspective we are always in the process of becoming God's daughters and sons. And turning the perspective a few degrees more, it might be argued that we are never fully God's children until we become definitively one with God after we die and are "raised up." In the same way, Jesus can be called "Son of God" at his baptism, and modifying the perspective, it could be argued that Jesus does not become Son of God fully until the resurrection. There is nothing adoptionist about this way of putting things, at least as far as the Gospel of Mark is concerned.[6] What should govern our linguistic usage is the dynamics of growth in the Spirit, a process that underlies the life of Jesus as much as it underlies the life of any person of faith, any true child of Israel. The precision given to the title "Son of God" by the early Church must have been the consequence of Easter. Finally and most fully, "Son of God" refers to one whom God has raised from the dead for the purpose of being the bearer of salvation.

An Easter Lion

Christian iconography adopted the figure of a lion with wings to symbolize the evangelist Mark. The reason for choosing to associate Mark with the lion may have been that this Gospel practically roars its way into the Church's sacred texts. In the opening chapter John the Baptist is the voice that roars out of the wilderness, although his is by no means the only shouting to be heard in this Gospel. Demons cry out, like the wild dogs and hyenas that yelp fearfully and then retreat when a lion approaches. We observe this behavior in the inaugural exorcism in chapter 1, and then three more times:

> Whenever the unclean spirits saw him, they fell down before him and shouted, "You are the Son of God!" (3:11).

> [A]nd he shouted at the top of his voice, "What have you to do with me, Jesus, Son of the Most High God? I adjure you by God, do not torment me" (5:7).

> And after crying out and convulsing him terribly, [the unclean spirit] came out, and the boy was like a corpse, so that most of them said, "He is dead" (9:26).

The Markan Jesus, we recall, practically roared at Peter for his utter lack of insight in 8:33. In order to be heard the blind Bartimaeus was forced to roar above the tumult of the crowd in 10:47-48, and Jesus' dying words could arguably be heard as a desperate roar against the paralysis of the heavens. The frightened women react as if they had encountered a lion at the tomb, not a heavenly messenger. What better way for that ancient Christian iconographer to symbolize the triumph of God than to connect

---

[6] What cannot be found in Mark's understanding of Jesus as Son of God (or in his use of the title "Son of Man") is any firm idea of preexistence. See the arguments in Kuschel, *Born Before All Time?* 231–34, 309–16.

(even if unconsciously) the proud roaring of a lion with the empty tomb! Hosea had written:

> They shall go after the LORD,
>   who roars like a lion;
> when he roars, his children shall come trembling from the west (Hos 11:10).

With the resurrection begins the long-awaited homecoming of the scattered people of God.[7]

Yet however important and colorful the wilderness and its wild beasts beyond the Jordan were as a backdrop for the Gospel's opening scene, the rest of the story unfolds elsewhere. Landscape plays a colorful role in the way Mark casts the action of Jesus; it provides depth and dimension to a fast-paced narrative. There are numerous mentions of Jesus' being in solitary places, sometimes alone, sometimes with his disciples, and sometimes with large crowds. It has been suggested that these movements to out-of-the-way places might be informing us that Jesus was eminently arrestable and that at times he was prudently avoiding capture by Herod's police. But that would not account for his frequent appearances in towns and villages or for the enormous crowds that Mark tells us kept pursuing Jesus and finding him.

Whatever the historical record may have been, perhaps for Mark Jesus' movement in and out of strange or deserted territory simply mirrored the movements of colorful prophets like Elijah and Elisha or, more proximately, John the Baptist. John crosses into civilization, but temperamentally he does not permanently belong there. Wilderness suggests untamed power, the terrain of spirits and demons, the place where human beings can feel the heart's thirst for God with unrelieved intensity, the place where human beings are not in control, and even the place where the prophetic voice may be forced to take refuge, as the letter to the Hebrews tells us: "They wandered in deserts and mountains, and in caves and holes in the ground" (11:38). As a group the prophets seem to stand in a different religious space from the rest of us, and occasionally that is how the Jesus in Mark's Gospel strikes the reader.

Nevertheless, this trait of heading to out-of-the-way places lies at odds with another feature of Jesus' ministry, namely, his being fully at ease in the everyday life of his people. And the parables of Jesus confirm this. The parables are not merely pedagogical instruments; they are reflections

---

[7] The image of homecoming and return from exile is deployed throughout Wright's *Jesus and the Victory of God.* See also the first volume of Wright's study, *The New Testament and the People of God* (Minneapolis: Augsburg Fortress Press, 1992) 268–79.

of an imagination that understands, appreciates, and even cherishes the ordinariness of human life experienced by the vast majority of men and women. On this score, the Gospel leaves the reader with another narrative tension. Was Jesus the warm teacher and healer who was very much at home in the human world, or was he the prophet who looked for God in the wilderness and was more comfortable with rocks and wild animals than, say, with kitchens and children and hard-working parents?

One thing is certain. Jesus was not John the Baptist. That Jesus was indebted to John's preaching for his own prophetic awakening seems reasonable. That some of the things Jesus said and did made it possible for people to think he was the Baptist come back to life is exactly the point behind Herod's verdict in Mark 6:16. Yet Jesus did not fast, he did not pitch his tent by the Jordan River, and he had spent most of his life in a small village working alongside family and friends. One might not immediately think of a connection between Jesus the carpenter and Amos the shepherd, but the words of Amos are poignant: "I am no prophet, nor a prophet's son; but I am a herdsman, and a dresser of sycamore trees, and the LORD took me from following the flock, and the LORD said to me, 'Go, prophesy to my people Israel'" (Amos 7:14-15).

One could imagine Jesus identifying with these words in the days or weeks following his baptism. It is much more of a stretch, however, to imagine Jesus identifying with Elijah or Elisha. Elijah appears too much like a ninth-century Merlin. How anyone could honestly have associated the two is difficult to figure out, unless for the early Christian communities Elijah represented the prophetic type, the prophet par excellence, because he spoke and acted with such decisiveness before rulers who were religious and political midgets. Having inherited double the spirit of Elijah, the exploits of Elisha sound more sensational than revelatory. Still, Elijah was lion-like, and so was his muscled apprentice.

Mark's interest, however, was not biographical profile. Jesus goes out to solitary places because that is what Mark may have thought prophets did. When, at the end of the story, Mark reports that Jesus was going ahead of his followers back to Galilee (16:7), he means into its cities and towns, not a retreat to deserted places. Wilderness sometimes functions as prophetic landscape for the Markan story, bearing the symbolic resonances of Israel's encounters with God in the desert; but it really is not the abode of the Son of God. Nevertheless, there is a key wilderness scene yet to consider in order for us to form a fuller picture of what "Son of God" means for Mark. For in the wilderness one not only encounters silence; one is also stepping into the territory of wild animals and demons.

Put to the Test

The brief account of Jesus' testing in the wilderness is theologically one of the most tantalizing scenes in the whole story. There should be no doubt that Mark intended the baptism and testing episodes to be taken together. The same Spirit that gently descended upon him in the waters of the Jordan immediately afterwards rushed him forcefully into the wilderness to face the tempter. Both episodes underscore the reality of Jesus as a believer, a son of Israel, a person of faith. Each episode underscores in its own way the humanness of Jesus. Just because Jesus is Son of God, Mark appears to be saying, one ought not think he was above the desire to hear John's preaching and the need to express his inner response to God's word in a gesture of repentance, conversion, and dedication. Because he was Son of God, Mark is saying, Jesus was by no means immune to the assaults of Satan, whatever their guise or whatever their origin.

Nevertheless, I do not believe Mark's narrative purpose here is to teach us about Jesus' humanness, although susceptibility to temptation is certainly a human characteristic. That Jesus underwent temptation would almost certainly make us feel better about ourselves, but in thinking about Jesus Mark does not appear to be interested in the ordinary temptations human beings face or in making us feel better about our own humanity. The truly significant temptation is the eschatological one, fidelity to and at the end. Thus the episode has a lot to do with being Son of God. Both Matthew and Luke caught that point, since in their elaboration of Mark's two verses the devil is made to ask not once but twice, "*If* you are the Son of God" (Luke 4:3, 9; Matt 4:3, 6). As far as Mark is concerned such a question would be pointless; the devil does know who Jesus is, as we see in the first synagogue scene: "I know who you are, the Holy One of God" (Mark 1:24). Jesus' identity—who the evangelist believes Jesus is—and Jesus' mission—what he does on behalf of his people—have to be thought of together. Mark is explicit about some of the things Jesus does in reporting his healings, exorcisms, and some of his teaching. Mark conveys the rest of what he thinks Jesus has done implicitly. For here the title "Son of God" points back to function, and some of the function is to be divined from verses even so cryptic as these:

> And the Spirit immediately drove him out into the wilderness. He was in the wilderness forty days, tempted by Satan; and he was with the wild beasts; and the angels waited on him (Mark 1:12-13).

The Demons

Mark believed in the existence of demons. Many people today do not, at least not in the form of fallen spirits who have invaded and infested the human world. Demons provided Mark with a category for accounting for some unfortunate conditions that we today would explain in biological, psychological, or even social terms.[8] We do not attribute epilepsy (9:14ff.) or unnamed childhood diseases (7:25ff.) or severe behavioral disorders (5:1ff.) to the presence of unclean spirits. Whenever we spot irrational behavior our first impulse is to suspect mental disorder and to seek medical expertise or clinical assistance. Truly pathological behavior, we know, can turn deadly. For the protection of society, some individuals need to be securely hospitalized and heavily medicated.

Yet for all the advances in our scientific knowledge we cannot insulate ourselves against the crushing assaults of human wickedness and depravity. No one who has followed the stories over the past ten or twenty years of panic-stricken refugees from places like Rwanda, Angola, or Sudan could have failed to reflect on the staggering enormity of human suffering and the stark, gruesome sinfulness that has been responsible for so much of it.

Africa, of course, hardly stands alone. The religious hatred that has pitted Muslims against Hindus in India and that continues to destabilize relations between India and Pakistan; the bigotry that has pitted Catholics against Protestants in Northern Ireland; the grave economic injustices that led to tens of thousands being massacred in Mexico, El Salvador, Guatemala, Chile, Brazil, Argentina, and Paraguay; Israel's treatment of Palestinians; Indonesia's incursion into East Timor; Iraq's war against the Kurds; the killing fields of Cambodia—indeed, the list grows very long. In each instance do we not run headlong into the cement wall of human stupidity, arrogance, and greed? Do we not keep coming face-to-face with humanity's dark side, which, like the side of the moon that the earth never sees, seems to remain absolutely impermeable to scrutiny?

Saint Paul's somber description of the human scene in the opening chapter of his letter to the Romans would probably be too depressing to read if he were composing that chapter in light of our times. As the apostle reflected back to us what he had been observing, say, over the past thirty years of the twentieth century, his account would sound so horrendous, so bleak, that we would have to pause in our reading, compose our

---

[8] See Best, "Exorcism in the New Testament and Today," in his *Interpreting Christ*, 114–25.

unsettled nerves, and draw a slow, prayerful breath. Mark would have depicted all the hostile forces arrayed against humanity as, collectively, the power of the demons. And he knew two things in this regard.

First, Mark realized that this power was no fiction; it existed, as anyone with eyes and ears could readily attest. And second, he knew that this power had to be confronted and broken. All human suffering, even ordinary diseases and infirmities, bore witness to the awful destructive energy behind sin, which, like a vicious hurricane or tornado, will strike the innocent and the guilty with blind intent. Pick up the most insignificant, run-of-the-mill thread of human weakness and eventually one will be led to the source, to the center, from which all evil proceeds.

That Jesus once stood within that center and had destroyed sin at its root was something Mark, as a Christian, firmly believed. That no one after Jesus would ever again have to stand in that center would have struck Mark as untrue to experience. The descent into hell (not Mark's phrasing) belongs to the Christian religious experience. Others besides Jesus would have to descend there and face the enemy of our human nature, but they would never have to make that descent and face that demon alone. The cosmic battle to the death with evil did not take place in the wilderness around the Jordan River but at the cross, and the cross was destined to be as integral to the lives of his disciples as it was to the mission of Jesus himself.

The necessity, the inevitability of tempting and testing—this is one of the most difficult elements of the Gospel story to grasp. Difficult, because to speak about Jesus' contest with the power of sin and with evil of cosmic proportions sounds as if one has entered the world of virtual reality. It requires some skill to describe Jesus' struggle to death in a way that does not make him into a mythical hero engaged in a first-century equivalent of *Star Wars*. The only way to prevent such misunderstanding is to begin with our own present-day experience of evil and to see how that evil stares at us—cold, unmoving, and terrifying in its defiant irrationality. The demonic will not politely disappear. After we have taken into account Mark's obvious cosmological and medical limitations, the fact remains that his portrayal of Jesus' conflict with Satan, however understated, has the ring of great truth. The combat with evil is the most serious, the most deadly, and in the long run the most consequential engagement in an individual's life as well as in the life of a people.

One does not have to wait for the one big encounter in order to understand the nature of our enemy. Flights to the wilderness where one might be tested on barren mountain heights and asked to attempt impossible feats are the stuff of pious imagination. Most of our exposure to sin comes in everyday forms and simple challenges. We face ordinary temptations and deal with them, sometimes over months or years; we uncover the uglier sides of ourselves and slowly awaken to how much of us still remains unmade. In the end, sin does not reside cosmically on spheres untouched by the sun; when unmasked its real face is not that of dragons and monsters or even the squealing of two thousand frenzied pigs. Instead, sin is the cumulative effect of many small denials, acts of running away, infidelities, and fears. As these countless small particles drift closer to one another, pulled by the gravitational field of human insecurity, they can ignite in a fire storm. Individual greed coalesces into a structural nightmare.

It would be next to impossible to determine whether Jesus ultimately interpreted his own death as the result of a Spirit-driven conflict with cosmic powers, as N. T. Wright suggests.[9] Besides, cosmological thinking is difficult for men and women of our time to relate to, even if it resonated with the cultural world of first-century Galileans. Certainly we do not inhabit a symbolic universe where we are engaged in mortal combat with the unseen powers and rulers of the present age (Eph 6:12). The actual historical reality into which Jesus was pulled was the network of events, decisions, vanity, and greed that leave their heavy impress on human history and the daily skirmishes and conflicts that in the end made Jesus' arrest and crucifixion inevitable. The Son of God, for Mark, had to be someone who lifts crippling burdens off human lives. But the Son of God only does so genuinely and credibly if he has felt the backbreaking weight of history's sin within his own heart and life.

In What Way Was Jesus Sinless?[10]

The fuller form of this question ought perhaps to be, How could Jesus honestly live in the deepest solidarity with his people and not share in their sinfulness? But that way of phrasing the question perhaps also points to the proper answer. Solidarity by no means implies complicity in sin, and it goes far beyond superficial identification with the human race. The Church's conviction about the sinlessness of Jesus should not be

[9] Wright, *Jesus and the Victory of God,* 450–61. Even if Jesus had viewed the prospect of his own death in cosmological categories, contemporary readers are more likely to grasp the tension in Jesus' ministry when explained in historical categories. In canonizing the New Testament writings, the Church was not canonizing Jesus' first-century worldview.

[10] The section that follows first appeared in *The Living Light* 33:2 (1996) 66–73. I have made a number of changes here.

allowed either to undercut his humanness or to reduce his baptism to an edifying gesture.[11]

Mark tells us that John the Baptist preached a baptism of repentance for the forgiveness of sins (1:4), that people came forward "confessing their sins" (1:5), and that Jesus likewise accepted baptism at John's hands. But Mark was not intimating, even unintentionally, that Jesus had committed sins during his lifetime prior to undertaking his mission or that he shared in the moral vulnerability of human nature.

Nevertheless, aware of the potential for scandal in this episode, Matthew qualifies it by pointing out that Jesus actually had no need of John's baptism (Matt 3:13-15). Luke differentiates Jesus from the rest of the people and turns the moment into a time for prayer and the Spirit (Luke 3:21-22). Not only does the Fourth Gospel make no mention whatsoever of Jesus' being baptized, it also lets us know that Jesus is "the Lamb of God *who takes away* the sin of the world" (John 1:29).

The fact that Mark immediately includes a heavenly voice that declares "with you I am well pleased" (1:11) suggests that Jesus is *already* righteous in God's sight and therefore legitimately deserves to be called a "son of God." Nevertheless, the unwary reader might not spot that connection. The first objection that St. Thomas cited against the fittingness of Jesus being baptized by John makes the difficulty clear: "John's baptism was a baptism of penance. But penance is unbecoming to Christ, because he had no sin. Therefore, it would seem that he should not have been baptized with John's baptism."

Following several patristic writers, the reasons Thomas offered to account for why Jesus was baptized were (1) to show his approval of John's practice of baptizing, (2) to sanctify baptism, and thus (3) to set an example for subsequent sacramental practice. Thomas was convinced that Jesus did not need either the remission of sins or the conferral of grace and that at the Jordan he could not have been baptized in the Spirit because he was filled with the Spirit since his conception.[12]

Commenting on Mark 1:9, Morna Hooker notes:

[11] The baptism of Jesus can also be viewed on the level of religious symbol as theological mystery. See McDonnell, "Jesus' Baptism in the Jordan," 209–36. For a discussion of its significance for understanding Jesus' own religious experience see Dunn, *Baptism in the Holy Spirit*, 23–37. Schillebeeckx refers to the baptism as "Jesus' first prophetic act" (*Jesus: An Experiment in Christology*, 136). For a recent study of the significance of John's baptism see Kazmierski, *John the Baptist*.

[12] *Summa Theologiae*, Samuel Parsons and Albert Pinheiro, trans. (New York: McGraw-Hill Book Company, 1971) vol. 53:25–27 (IIIa, q. 39, a. 2).

Mark is apparently unembarrassed by the problems raised by this story which troubled later writers. Matthew's description of John's hesitation regarding the propriety of baptizing Jesus (Matt 3:14f.) and even more the account in *The Gospel according to the Hebrews,* which stresses the sinlessness of Jesus, both demonstrate the difficulties which were felt regarding Jesus' submission to baptism at the hands of an inferior. . . . The problems perhaps arise from a misunderstanding of Mark's narrative, together with an emphasis on the negative aspect of repentance. It is unnecessary, and indeed unwarranted, to explain the baptism of Jesus . . . as a vicarious act of repentance, or an identification with sinners. If John's baptism was . . . the rite which gathered together a holy people of God who affirmed in this committal that they were ready for his coming, then it was natural for Jesus . . . to join those who by baptism showed that they looked for the coming Kingdom of God.[13]

Yet the very fact that Mark features the baptism so prominently at the outset of his narrative reveals that, at least for this evangelist, the baptism both historically and theologically played a major role in the development of Jesus' mission. Jesus' baptism was, after all, the moment that defined for the apostles the beginning of their association with the Jesus movement (see Acts 1:21-22). Moved and set afire by the preaching of John, one might imagine, Jesus underwent what could be regarded as a conversion experience or religious awakening. This awakening would have consisted of that profound sense of being claimed by God and sent forth that was experienced by Israel's greatest prophets and that we naturally associate with deep prayer and the Spirit (following Luke).[14] The Jesus who journeyed to the Jordan from Nazareth seems to have been remarkably different from the prophet who returned there some time later. Mark writes:

On the sabbath he began to teach in the synagogue, and many who heard him were astounded. They said, "Where did this man get all this? What is this wisdom that has been given to him? What deeds of power are being done by his hands! Is not this the carpenter, the son of Mary and brother of James and Joses and Judas and Simon, and are not his sisters here with

[13] Hooker, *Mark,* 44. By the "negative aspect of repentance" I suppose her to mean the action of turning away from sin. The *positive* aspect would then refer to the action of turning wholeheartedly toward God in love. Nothing presumably would prevent Jesus from experiencing this second moment.

[14] Jesus could have experienced the inadequacy and incompleteness of the creature before its Creator without ever having committed moral fault. If this were not the case, then it becomes difficult to conceive how Jesus could have entered meaningfully into the sentiments expressed in many of the Psalms of Israel. I have developed this idea further in *Talking About Jesus Today,* 39–43.

us?" And they took offense at him. Then Jesus said to them, "Prophets are not without honor except in their hometown, and among their own kin, and in their own house" (6:2-4).

Sinlessness Does Not Contradict Humanness

Some people find the New Testament's claim that Jesus was sinless (e.g., Heb 4:15; 7:26; 2 Cor 5:21) hard to reconcile with an equally strong belief in the fullness of his humanity. What might have prompted the early Christians to elevate the category of sinlessness so conspicuously? One possible explanation might be that Jesus *had* to be sinless in order to be able to take away the sins of the world. The sinlessness of Jesus would thus have become a christological first principle premised on the conviction that a sacrifice or sin offering had to be pure and unblemished in order to be acceptable to God. How could Jesus take away sin if he himself were a sinner? The symbolism appears essentially cultic; the holocaust requirement was "a male without blemish" (Lev 1:3, 10). Similarly: "No descendant of Aaron the priest who has a blemish shall come near to offer the LORD's offerings by fire" (Lev 21:21).[15]

By the same token, the category of sinlessness enabled the ancient Christian tradition to express its belief in the holiness of Jesus; a person uniquely close to God must almost by definition be regarded as sinless. Jesus' holiness is refracted in the sayings, miracles stories, encounters, and parables of his ministry. Luke, for example, presents Jesus as a person of prayer (that is, of faith) and blessed from his conception with the Spirit of holiness (Luke 1:35). John portrays Jesus as joined in heart, mind, and soul to the Father. The Jesus of the Fourth Gospel could therefore say, "The Father and I are one" (John 10:30). Paul, the earliest New Testament writer, thinks of Jesus as the second Adam, the human being who is truly "whole," whose response to God was one of filial obedience (Phil 2:7-8). Needless to say, the concepts of sinfulness and holiness need not be mutually exclusive. There are numerous earnest, devout Christians who manifest profound sanctity while remaining conscious of being sinners daily in need of divine mercy and grace.[16]

[15] I do not mean to imply that the cultic sacrifice of Israel could not embrace repentance for social sin, for such inability would have driven a wedge between worship and covenant. See Brueggemann, *Social Reading of the Old Testament,* 43–69.

[16] Ancient Christian ascetical tradition connected sinlessness with uninterrupted contemplation and constant attentiveness to the things of God, a practically unachievable feat. To say the least, this was a lopsided view of contemplation. In his introduction to

That to be human is to be sinful is a widely shared, understandable assumption. If Jesus was truly human, some people might conclude, then he had to have been a sinner, unless he possessed a special moral or spiritual protection that the rest of us do not enjoy. Whenever Jesus becomes exceptional, however, he becomes increasingly distant from the rest of humanity. How can we meaningfully relate to someone who was by nature morally and spiritually superior to us? The more exalted, other-worldly, and exempt from the human condition Jesus is believed to be, the more removed he becomes from us and the less likely we are to take his example with the seriousness of realistically committed disciples. To expect, let alone demand, perfection of people who are by nature sinful and weak is not realistic. If we set ourselves alongside a human being who was supposed to be morally and spiritually flawless, we shall inevitably come off poorly. Disciples might also find themselves experiencing a low-grade yet incurable guilt because they simply do not measure up to God's high expectations of them: "Be perfect, therefore, as your heavenly Father is perfect" (Matt 5:48).

Perhaps the answer to this difficulty has to be worked out in two steps. First, we have constantly to monitor the tendency to assume that sinfulness is the proper place to *start* in describing the human condition. For the bottom-line theological assertion about us is that we have been called into existence by God's love, and it is that totally unmerited love that becomes the first word about human beings.

Second, being human is not a once-for-all achievement but a process of growth and development that requires effort, vigilance, prayer, and considerable patience. When applied to Jesus the notion of sinlessness may be much too static; it connotes an already complete, once-for-all endowment rather than a quality or *freely chosen orientation* realized over time. If the incarnation can appropriately be viewed as the process of the Word becoming human and historical not only at the conception of Jesus but throughout every moment of his life up to and including the resurrection, then why not think of sinlessness along the same lines?[17]

"The Third Conference of Abba Theonas: On Sinlessness" Boniface Ramsey writes: "Very possibly there is a link between Cassian's insistence on the sinfulness of a lapse in contemplation with the view, typically Egyptian, that the original and hence archetypal sin was rejection of divine contemplation" (786). But if one were to argue that Jesus was sinless because he never suffered distractions, one would be claiming the unprovable. See Cassian: *Conferences,* 783–813.

[17] Jon Sobrino writes: "the Incarnation cannot be viewed in natural categories, as if the Son took on some human nature once and for all. It must be viewed in historical cate-

The Eschatological Aspect of Sinlessness

The first thing to recall, therefore, is that we were not created sinners; we were fashioned in the image and likeness of God. Consequently, the initial theological word about us is that we are first and last God's daughters and sons, even though human beings may not consistently think, react, and behave that way. Human beings do sin, of course; but sin does not belong to their nature, to the human essence. Thus we can conceive of someone being fully human, but without ever committing sins.

As a matter of fact, some human beings actually never commit sin, such as young children or people with certain mental disabilities. While these groups obviously do not have the capacity for moral choice (and thus are "exceptional"), we can also entertain the possibility of others who never do anything seriously or even slightly wrong from a moral standpoint. That does not mean they cannot feel inadequate before God or that they are totally unaware of their need for grace and strength. The human being's relationship with God is hardly exhausted by doing good and avoiding evil. The moral valence of our actions and thoughts is not the only concern that should enter into our conversation with God. Radical dependence upon God, so embedded in the psalms, is a far more substantial and prayer-worthy experience than our moral woundedness.

Nevertheless, the possibility that some individuals, lacking the requisite moral capacity, might never have committed sins would not render them "sinless" from a theological point of view. To be sinless from a theological or spiritual standpoint is consistently to choose God over oneself. The clearest Gospel illustrations of Jesus' sinlessness, therefore, would have to be the temptation episode and the later scene in Gethsemane. Furthermore, our fervent hope that the entire people of God will one day be as free from sin as Mary was suggests that the notion of sinlessness contains a strong eschatological dimension.[18]

Human spirituality draws on other basic experiences, such as the sense of being incomplete, not fully created or not fully made, in need of "redemption," or even being "ransomed." These experiences often include

---

gories. Jesus became fully human in an ongoing process, and it is that process that serves to mediate his divine sonship." See *Christology at the Crossroads,* 268. Evans appears to move in a similar direction when he writes of the "historicity of the incarnational narrative," where "incarnational narrative" designates "the story of Jesus of Nazareth, taken from the New Testament as a whole." See *Historical Christ,* 2.

[18] One could figure this out by connecting chapters 5, 7, and 8 of the Second Vatican Council's Dogmatic Constitution on the Church *(Lumen gentium).*

a moral dimension, but the sense of being incomplete goes beyond our moral well being. While we should never underestimate either the reality or the power of sin in our world or in human history, neither should we settle for a facile identification of humanness with sinfulness. Jesus could experience the deep need for God that other human beings experience. He could even feel incomplete and inadequate standing before God, the Creator and Lord, and desire with all his heart to live out his radical dependence on God with great faith, hope, love, and gratitude. It is theoretically possible that some human beings might not share the moral fracture that characterizes the vast majority of human lives. The point is obviously speculative, but it is worth considering. The rich man who approached Jesus insisted that he had kept *all* of God's commandments *since his childhood,* and Jesus loved him for this (Mark 10:20-21). According to Christian tradition, Mary did not share that general brokenness either, yet she still needed redemption.[19] Even Jesus, although he was God's Son, needed God to save him from the awesome power of death:

> In the days of his flesh, Jesus offered up prayers and supplications, with loud cries and tears, to the one who was able to save him from death, and he was heard because of his reverent submission (Heb 5:7).

In short, the possibility that some human beings might not be sinful in the technical sense should not jeopardize Christian soteriology. But reducing the significance of Jesus' life and death to his replacing the role of Israel's cult in obtaining divine pardon would jeopardize it considerably.

The second point is that the word "human" normally serves as a simple designation of our nature as men and women; our "nature" is what differentiates us from all other life forms. But apart from its biological reference, "human" can also refer to what makes us *special,* namely, that we come from God and that God is our ultimate destiny. The crucial business of our lives, therefore, is that we own up to who we are and that we become, ever more really and truly, people of God.[20]

Becoming a man or woman of God takes a lifetime, and it involves all the aspects of our nature. From this perspective sin is not a sign of human fallenness from some primeval state of perfection but a sign of our incompleteness, of our not yet being fully made, of our love not being rightly centered. Some early Christian writers explained the matter this way:

---

[19] That Mary was redeemed is also the teaching of Vatican II. See Dogmatic Constitution on the Church, no. 53.

[20] The best presentation of this process view of Christian existence, from a Pauline perspective, is still Jerome Murphy-O'Connor, *Becoming Human Together.*

We have been made in the "image" of God, but over the course of our lives we come to put on the divine "likeness."[21]

Yet sin is not the only indication of our incompleteness. There are other aspects to our interior lives besides the moral dimension. Learning how to love, to share, and to forgive takes time. We do not master these lessons in an instant, from childhood. Not even Jesus could escape the conditions, limitations, and creative challenges so integral to our being human. Just as every failure in discipleship is not automatically a moral fault, neither are those points of tension where belief in God is pulled and stretched, where prayer becomes dark and even burdensome, or where the mind painfully learns that God's ways are not our ways. The point about Jesus being a believer, a person of faith, is predicated on the fact that in his case, as in ours, faith is a *life* that grows organically, follows certain patterns, endures questions, doubts, disappointments, and so forth. We need to picture Jesus, then, truly growing and developing as a believer, because he was human.

The question about whether Jesus was a sinner, then, may be basically misguided, for it distracts us from what was central to the Church's belief about him. To state things positively, Jesus behaved in every respect as one would expect a "son" of God to think and act. To talk meaningfully about Jesus' humanness does not require us to conclude that he must have sinned in the sense of deliberately violating God's word. To say that he is like us in all things *except* sin (see Heb 4:15) cannot be turned around to imply that he was fundamentally *unlike* us because he was unable to do wrong. Sin is an accidental, not an essential feature, of being human. The major question raised by his receiving John's baptism thereby becomes, Was Jesus in the fullest sense a person of prayer and faith?

If the notion of sinlessness is not going to sound spiritually static and unreal, then, as we have seen, we must learn to view it eschatologically, that is, as a description of our future state when we become definitively one with God. Sinlessness, like innocence, is something to be attained over a lifetime. Human holiness always has a history. While thinking of Jesus as

---

[21] "Thus when he said, 'In the image of God he created him' and said nothing more about the likeness, he is actually indicating that while the human being did indeed receive the dignity of God's image in the first creation, the dignity of his likeness is reserved for the consummation. This is so that human beings would work to acquire it by their own industrious effort to imitate God; for in the beginning only the possibility of perfection is given them by the dignity of the 'image,' while in the end they are to acquire for themselves the perfect 'likeness' by the carrying out of works." See Hans Urs von Balthasar, *Origen: Spirit and Fire,* 56.

a sinner is obviously inconsistent with Christian faith, it is understandable that Mark's audience would hear in the word "sinner" more than a deliberate choosing of what is contrary to "every word that comes from the mouth of God" (Matt 4:4). By placing him at the Jordan, the evangelist signaled Jesus' solidarity in human brokenness without compromising the community's belief in Jesus' holiness as God's beloved Son. Yet even Jesus' closeness to God must have had a history; he was not above or beyond the experience of learning obedience and the ways of the Spirit.

Sinlessness as Dedication to the Will of God

Perhaps the most important move we have to make in considering the sinlessness of Jesus is to let go of any view that defines sin exclusively as *personal* moral failure. Unless sin is also defined socially and economically in terms of the forces, structures, and relationships that destroy human life, we shall not have adequate categories within which to interpret the Church's belief that the life of Jesus could be summed up as the taking away of sin. We have already seen that cultic imagery and symbolism left an indelible imprint on the way the Church talked about the death of Jesus. But one does not place poverty, for example, on the back of a scapegoat. Evils such as systemic economic oppression, slavery, and exploitation are not carried into the wilderness by a sin offering, even if we were to imagine that burden being placed on the shoulders of Jesus.

Jesus lived in solidarity with broken humanity; he ritualized this solidarity at his baptism, even though the evangelist does not state the point in so many words. This solidarity meant that Jesus, too, felt the depressing weight of sin's destructive power in human lives. It also means, first, that Jesus had no part in the structures that brought evil on so many human beings; he was, they would say, "without sin." And second, it means that through his ministry he labored to transform society in the direction of justice and reconciliation. Jesus was not an accomplice in the reign of evil, which is why the demons immediately perceived his presence to be so threatening (see Mark 1:24), nor did he acquiesce to the sinful situation in which people were forced to live.[22] Perhaps the positive or obverse side to being sin*less* (since the word is basically a negative expression) is one's dedication to dislodging evil from human lives (Mark 3:23-27).

In other words, the Christian claim that Jesus was without sin might also be viewed positively as a statement of Jesus' mission; sinlessness was

---

[22] See Myers, *Binding the Strong Man,* 141–43.

not a mere personality trait of Jesus. "Sinless" characterizes Jesus' actions and preaching as essentially works of liberation or setting people free by "tying up the strong man" (Mark 3:27; also Luke 4:18-19; Lev 25). Jesus prophetically challenged business as usual in the society of his day. Would it be stretching things theologically to suggest that sinlessness might make better sense to us as an attitude, an orientation, or perhaps as living fully and unreservedly for others?[23]

A final point connected to the notion of sinlessness that complicates any effort to square the humanness of Jesus with his being sinless arises from one of the ways Christian thinkers have understood salvation. On the one hand, if Jesus is too much like us, then we have no model of that perfection that we are called and created to achieve as God's daughters and sons. In other words, if Jesus is a sinner like us, then why are we following him? On the other hand, if Jesus is too much unlike us, then following him is hopeless, for we can never expect to attain the degree of holiness that he exhibited throughout his life.

Behind this dilemma lie the dynamics of one of several possible experiences of salvation. In this view salvation consists of our becoming like God, of being joined through faith to the Son of God as he ascends to the Father. In order to mediate this divinization, Jesus obviously must be without sin. Otherwise, like a sick physician, how could he assist us? Jesus' being sinless, however, is therefore not actually the driving concern; the important matter is the real possibility of our becoming holy or "perfect." That is why, according to the Creed, the coming of the Son makes absolutely no theological sense unless it is linked with human salvation: "who for us and for our salvation came down from heaven."

We might say, therefore, that the Church's insistence upon Jesus' sinlessness amounts to an affirmation of the perfectibility of human beings *and their communities*. The communal aspect always has to be acknowledged. Salvation is hardly an exclusive, private affair between each individual and God. The early Church universalized Jesus' solidarity with the people of Israel, ritually expressed when he received John's baptism, in order to encompass the whole human story. Furthermore, that solidarity re-

---

[23] Commenting on Jesus' sinlessness, Gerald O'Collins writes: "[Jesus'] activity comes across as that of someone utterly oriented towards God and unconditionally committed to the cause of the kingdom. The more we agree that such an orientation and commitment accurately summarize the data, the more we should be inclined to accept that Jesus was sinless in principle" (270). O'Collins goes on to elucidate the connection between sinlessness and freedom. What I have suggested here, however, is that sinlessness might be more meaningfully described as the orientation itself. See O'Collins, *Christology*, 268–73.

vealed a divine purpose, namely, the redemption and transformation of the human world in all its dimensions.[24] The Gospel proclaims this great hope as the good news of the kingdom of God. Professing that Jesus was sinless can be viewed as a way of portraying his unconditional openness to the Spirit and his loving and complete dedication to the work of God in the world.

Jesus as Person of Faith

While Jesus as believer is thematic throughout Mark's Gospel, this feature is dramatically evident in his being baptized. That the moment was prayerful goes without saying. Jesus travels to the Jordan because he wants to hear the Baptist, he is moved by what he hears, and he enters the Jordan's waters in order to ritualize the desire he shares with others to cross over, once and for all, into the land of promise. As we have just seen, we must not allow the Church's belief about Jesus' sinlessness to obscure what is happening here. Jesus has just expressed, through sign and symbol, his oneness with the people of God. He shares with them their desire for divine mercy, for salvation, and for reconciliation with God and with one another. He does not stand above the people as if personally exempted from feeling the weight of the human condition. He does not make mental reservations when everyone else chants the psalms of Israel confessing guilt and pleading for forgiveness, saying to himself that he has no need to utter such prayers. Because he stands with and among them, he shares their thirst, their sense of inadequacy and unworthiness before God, their earnest pleas, and their determination to live henceforth as people of the covenant. Such sentiments, we should recall, are of themselves holy. In the end, the baptism marks Jesus' marriage to the people of God.

Morna Hooker notes in her commentary that some rabbinic writing occasionally viewed the dove as a symbol of Israel but then goes on to say that this does not appear to be Mark's thought in the baptismal scene.[25] While the text obviously reads more coherently if we take the descending spirit to be from God, the variant meaning of the dove raises an interesting prospect. The figure of the dove, perhaps representing Israel, appears in the Song of Songs, a writing much allegorized by early Christian writers; Christ becomes the lover, the beloved is the Church. But there is also another text:

[24] The notion of salvation must have social and historical features in addition to cosmic and personal ones. See Brackley, *Divine Revolution.*

[25] Hooker, *Mark,* 46.

> Do not deliver the soul of your dove to the wild animals;
>> do not forget the life of your poor forever (Ps 74:19).

In this text the dove appears to represent God's people, particularly the poor. It is tempting to draw a literary connection between the mention of the dove-like character of the Spirit and Jesus' being possessed by the poor people of God. In any event, to intimate that it was Israel that descended upon Jesus in the Jordan opens the scene to what may be its deepest mystery and significance, rendering it more like the call of a prophet than the anointing of a king. The people have claimed Jesus for themselves; the marriage is complete.

Having explored some of the issues raised by Jesus' baptism in the Jordan at the hands of John, we turn next to the calling of followers. The total, loving dedication to God above everything else that made Jesus the sinless one is a way of living to which others have been invited. For Mark relates the baptism story and everything else about Jesus for the sake of our salvation. If the people claim Jesus for themselves, then eventually they will also claim his followers.

2

Of Calling and Following

And Jesus said to them, "Follow me and I will make you fish for people." And immediately they left their nets and followed him (Mark 1:17-18).

All men and women have been created to praise, reverence, and serve God our Lord and by this means to save their souls.[1] Or as Deuteronomy puts it, "You shall love the LORD your God with all your heart, and with all your soul, and with all your might" (6:5). It could be argued, therefore, that every human being, having been loved into existence by God, has received a call from the Creator to lead a life worthy of his or her nature. Vocation is intrinsic to our being.

Calls of a religious type, however, tend to be more focused, more specific. And few religious experiences are so freighted with consequences as the experience of feeling or hearing oneself called by God for some special purpose or mission. In Scripture some are called to be prophets, others to be kings; some to be nation founders, others to be priests; some to be disciples and others to be apostles.

This special calling can come to men and women in a wide variety of circumstances, both sacral and everyday, as Scripture makes abundantly clear. The young Samuel was lying down in the Temple of the Lord when he heard God's call; Moses was tending his father-in-law's flock in the wilderness; and likewise Amos: "I am no prophet, nor a prophet's son; but I am a herdsman, and a dresser of sycamore trees" (Amos 7:14). Mary was simply at home in Nazareth, Saul was in the middle of tracking down fellow Jews turned Christian, and Lydia might well have been doing her

---

[1] The formulation of this (for a Christian) self-evident truth is that of the Principle and Foundation given by Ignatius Loyola at the beginning of the *Spiritual Exercises* (no. 23).

laundry along with some other women from Thyatira when Paul dropped into her life (Acts 16:13-15). Paul's instruction to the Corinthians that they remember the sociocultural condition they occupied when they were called (1 Cor 7:24) could be broadened: never forget where you were and what you were doing at the time when the Spirit of Jesus reached into your life.

The typical biblical response to the sense of being called is a profound awareness of one's unreadiness and unworthiness, an awareness that might persist through the whole of a person's life. While the Gospels do not reveal much more about John the Baptist's call than we might be able to discern from the brief text of Luke "In the fifteenth year of the reign of the Emperor Tiberius . . . the word of God came to John son of Zechariah in the wilderness" (Luke 3:1-2), they do report that John felt himself unworthy in the presence of the one who would be baptizing with the Holy Spirit. If part of John's mission was to prepare the people for the one yet to come, then he must have lived for some time with the realization that he was only the precursor, doubly unworthy: unworthy to stand in the other's presence, unworthy to have been called by God to undertake even that humble role in the long history of Israel's salvation. Isaiah's moving, memorable response to the seraph, "Woe is me! I am lost, for I am a man of unclean lips, and I live among a people of unclean lips" (Isa 6:5), typifies that awareness of unworthiness intrinsic not only to the prophetic vocation but also to discipleship: "Go away from me, Lord, for I am a sinful man!" (Luke 5:8), and even to Mary's calling to be the Savior's mother: "Here am I, the servant of the Lord" (Luke 1:38).

Paul never fully recovered from his experience of being overwhelmed by the fact that the Father had called him to be an apostle of Christ Jesus, and he urged his communities always to remember their calling: the moral, social, spiritual, and intellectual conditions in which they were living when God reached into their lives, lest they fall into boasting (see 1 Cor 1:26-31). The sense of unworthiness prompted by the experience of being called by God is itself an enduring grace. We probably ought to assume the presence of this grace in the call stories of the Gospels even when the evangelists neglect to underscore it.

Disciples First, Apostles Later

Mark, like Paul before him, would have assumed that the people for whom he was writing had been called by God to be followers and companions of Jesus. He was not preoccupied with special or exclusive calls except in the sense that every disciple's call to follow Jesus was special and distinct. That explains why the selection of twelve from the wider group of disciples does not occur at the very beginning of the narrative and why the spiritual line between disciples and apostles had to be so fluid. Many readers have grown so used to interpreting the Gospel references to Jesus and his disciples as meaning Jesus and the Twelve that they fail to appreciate what the texts literally say.

There are three stories in the early part of Mark's Gospel in which Jesus invites others to follow him. The first, consisting of two scenes, occurs in the first chapter when Jesus calls the four fishermen. In the first scene he calls two brothers (Peter and Andrew) to join him, and in the next scene he invites a second set of brothers (James and John).

The second call story appears in chapter 2 when Jesus passes by Levi at his tax-collector's station along the shore—a place from which he could probably observe the vessels laden with fish and levy a toll on the catch. Like the first four, Levi (we must suppose) left "everything" when he "got up and followed him"; in a dramatic reversal of life and work, Levi had joined Jesus. The "everything" here does not mean that Levi had suddenly embraced a life of voluntary poverty but that he had undergone a thoroughgoing conversion in much the same way the famous tax collector of Jericho would in Luke's Gospel.

The third story, more composite in form, is found in chapter 3. Mark does not give us any details about the time and place for the calling of the remaining disciples, who would later constitute the group of twelve. He simply writes:

> He went up the mountain and called to him those whom he wanted, and they came to him. And he appointed twelve, whom he also named apostles, to be with him, and to be sent out to proclaim the message, and to have authority to cast out demons. So he appointed the twelve . . . (3:13-16).

This scene appears to be a call within a call: the first call was to be a follower, and the second call was to be one of the Twelve who would be with him and would be sent out. Being with Jesus and being sent out by him, personally, on a mission might accurately spell the essential ingredients of the experience of apostleship. Later, in chapter 6, we find the same pattern: "He called the twelve and began to send them out two by two." Calling and sending—or rather, since Mark was drawing upon remembrances ultimately from the apostles themselves, the experience of having been called and of having been sent—are thus connected. For the apostles these two experiences might aptly describe the impact of having encountered Jesus. The symbolism of the number twelve does not introduce a new level of responsibility into the disciples' lives; it does not offer additional insight into their mission, although the number's association with the historic tribes of Israel does tell us something about the way Jesus viewed his mission. Jesus had started a renewal movement that anticipated the full restoration of Israel, the moment when at last Israel would visibly express in its historical existence its nature or essence as the beloved child of God.

Needless to say, the fact that Mark recounts the initial calling of only four of the future twelve apostles does not necessarily mean that he was unfamiliar with at least some of the other stories. Furthermore, although Jesus called Levi, his name does not appear in the listing of the Twelve in Mark 3:16-19. It is unlikely that Mark would have made a mistake here. Either Mark and his readers took for granted that one of the Twelve went by two names (Mark mentions a James who was the son of Alphaeus, which was the same name as Levi's father) or, despite the proximity of this story to the call of the fishermen, Mark did not view the two stories as parallel. Recounting the call of Levi may have served another purpose. Indeed, maybe Alphaeus, like Zebedee, had more than one son.

If Mark did know more about the first encounters of the other apostles with Jesus, then evidently it was not to his purpose to include them the way the Fourth Gospel later would. Gospel readers may have become so accustomed to thinking the historical pattern of the events was, first, Jesus' period by the Jordan, followed by, second, his calling of the twelve apostles, that they do not consider the significance of an intermediate stage in which Jesus invited many people to follow him and from whom he subsequently would appoint twelve for a special purpose.

Since Mark does differentiate the first callings from a later, more solemn summons to apostleship—being with *and* being sent out—it would not be unreasonable to think that in some way what had happened to four of the future twelve was also happening to others, like Levi. In fact, Mark 3:13 presupposes that this had been the case. Jesus' calling ordinary working people to follow him (as in the case of Simon and Andrew, James and John, and Levi) occurred far more frequently than we usually think. If Jesus lured the brothers by telling them that they would soon be fishing for people, what image might he have used in calling farmers, or shepherds, or artisans, or housewives, or even tax gatherers? Would he have told villagers from the Galilean countryside that he would teach them how to harvest people, or shepherds that they would learn how to pastor men and women, or tax gatherers how to collect human lives, or bakers how to make living bread? Indeed, if Jesus could invite a married man like Simon to discipleship and expect that he readily would follow him, what would have prevented him from calling a married woman? The *first* call obviously did not entail renouncing home and family, for shortly afterwards we find Jesus relaxing with Peter's family in his home. Indeed, although Mark has not elaborated the point, how could Peter's call to follow Jesus not involve Peter's wife and family?

Thus not all who were first called wound up among the Twelve. It does not follow, however, that their calls were any less special or that their responses were any less complete. To be sure, some people whom Jesus called must have declined the offer (the rich man of chapter 10 does), or after an initial enthusiastic response must have changed their minds later, or just lost interest entirely as time went on (could this be what happened to Judas?). The parable of the sower enables us to conjecture along these lines. But others did respond generously and joyously. In fact, from one point of view every figure in the story was in the position of responding to Jesus' call in one way or another. Calling men and women to discipleship was a basic part of Jesus' preaching; he could no more easily neglect that than he could fail to talk about the kingdom of God. In short, the Twelve were not more exemplary of discipleship than Levi (and his household?), or the woman who responded to Jesus' message so curiously in chapter 5 when she reached for his cloak (she had, after all, been literally following him), or the blind Bartimaeus of chapter 10, or the demon-cleansed man of chapter 5 who is paradoxically sent out but not permitted to remain with Jesus, or the unnamed but touchingly faithful woman who anointed Jesus in chapter 14. Discipleship is unfolding all through the narrative in one form or another. Men and women want to be with Jesus; they are prepared to follow him even into deserted places.

That the Twelve have a distinctive profile in the story is obvious, but being with Jesus was by no means their exclusive prerogative. Consider the Last Supper. In 14:12 some disciples ask Jesus about Passover preparations. In 14:17 Jesus arrives with the Twelve, but unless we suppose that some of Jesus' other disciples had located the designated house, set the table, procured and cooked the food, bought the wine, and then withdrew, we have to conclude that there were certainly more than thirteen people in the room. Who would have been doing the serving? The men? Mark nowhere claims that only Jesus and the Twelve were present for the Last Supper. For if Jesus had guessed that particular Passover was to be his final meal, it is not at all implausible to think he would have wanted as many of his followers to be around him as physically possible. Jesus had foreseen that the room would be large and furnished (14:15), and he entrusted those particular disciples: "Make preparations for us [Jesus and the Twelve] there." This is a small example, but it serves to remind us that Jesus and the Twelve moved within a larger group of followers. What distinguished the Twelve from the rest was not that they were spiritually closer to Jesus, for the line between apostle and disciple, between being one of the *twelve* disciples and being a disciple, was not fixed in such a way as to create a new insider/outsider category. To say that Jesus' approach to community—to the renewed Israel, the new people of God—was not hierarchical is to speak anachronistically. Nevertheless, the Gospel makes it clear that for Jesus the conventional markers of holiness and righteousness were simply too rigid to accommodate the new wine of his teaching. The Twelve did not stand on a higher spiritual plane than the rest, at least not in Jesus' mind.

The Story of Levi: The Miracle of the Needle's Eye

It seems to me that the call of Levi is recounted not because he was one of the Twelve and Mark fortunately had inherited the story of his call to be an apostle but because Levi's change of heart was so dramatic. Like that of Zacchaeus in chapter 19 of Luke's Gospel, Levi's turnaround defied normal expectations and challenged everyone—ordinary people in the fishing village of Capernaum and religious leaders alike—to rethink their assumptions about who the kingdom of God was for. What we have in Levi's case, as in the case of every specific healing story and exorcism, is a class-action moment. Within the call and conversion of Levi, Mark has invited us to envision the call and conversion of every public sinner, of everyone who collaborates with a system of oppression, of everyone viewed by his or her contemporaries to be beyond righteousness and thus beyond redemption. Levi is more than an isolated instance; he represents a gospel type, as does the paralytic of chapter 2 whose sins were forgiven, the man with the withered hand in chapter 3, and the father of the epileptic boy in chapter 9. Gospel readers have implicitly acknowledged this for centuries, since otherwise we would not be able to relate to their stories or put ourselves in their places. Levi not only can be us; he *must* be us in some respect in order for the story to work on our imaginations and lead us into prayer.

The actual story is told quickly. All we know is that Levi was a toll collector and that he was at work when Jesus paused in front of his booth. It does not require detailed historical background regarding how Herod's administration collected taxes to figure out that Levi's profession was not one that would have endeared him to the townsfolk of Capernaum. And given Herod's connection with the Roman emperor (who had appointed him), Levi represented more than just a local nuisance and a regional politics of oppression. The tax collector ultimately stood in the shadow of Rome, the very Rome that would besiege and destroy Jerusalem and deliver a devastating blow to Jewish nationalist hopes in the year 70. The Gospel reader would logically understand that imperial Rome was no friend of Israel and that through a kind of reverse guilt by association Levi and his associates had to have been both conspirators and traitors. What the tax collectors were historically and what they signified in the narrative world of the evangelist were probably different. But Mark needed the sharpness of their outsider status to illumine the true content and radicalness of Jesus' teaching about the kingdom.

It makes little sense to speculate about what was going on within Levi's psyche. Nevertheless, if this scene is genuinely a class-action moment, then we ought to consider it in the wider context of what Jesus might have been teaching just before he called Levi. In Mark once more an action becomes the lens through which we look back into the teaching of Jesus. Just as it would be reasonable to think that something in what Jesus had been talking about provoked the reaction of the demon-possessed man in chapter 1, so also here Mark may be implying a connection between message and action. For he says:

> Jesus went out again beside the sea; the whole crowd gathered around him, and he taught them. As he was walking along, he saw Levi son of Alphaeus sitting at the tax booth, and he said to him, "Follow me." And he got up and followed him (Mark 2:13-14).

What had Jesus been teaching to the crowd? In a general way he must have been talking about the kingdom of God. One major feature of the kingdom, however, was that it would be inclusive, that those whom respectable people would have dismissed as ritually unclean, immoral, sinful, and *beyond change* would have a place in it. Including the story of Levi would make eminent narrative sense if we could anticipate the reaction of the people. Yes, indeed, it was good news, hearing that ordinary men and women would have a place in the kingdom. Yet realistically they could have objected—some Israelites were simply beyond redemption. Camels do not slip through the eyes of needles; bloodsucking tax collectors were not about to surrender their perks. The call and conversion of Levi becomes all the more forceful once we consider how improbable it would have sounded to the crowd when Jesus announced that even tax collectors were being summoned to be part of the new Israel. With God, we believe, all things are possible. But to be honest, there appear to be some men and women in every age who are simply too compromised by the means they used to get where they are; their souls are not salvageable.

Levi's response to Jesus had proved the truthfulness of Jesus' teaching. Some of his audience would have been scandalized; others would have been as astonished as if they had witnessed a great miracle. The small band of followers may have felt uncomfortable. Was Jesus suggesting that they and Levi had something in common? To the religious elites Jesus' behavior would have looked like madness. Still, Levi had proved a lesson about divine possibilities that must have been an important part of Jesus' proclamation. Levi had done the unthinkable. He had let go of his post (and presumably the source of his income). Or maybe something even more unthinkable: Levi might have continued being a tax collector but now with a social conscience. After all, John the Baptist had directed the tax collectors who came to him, "Collect no more than the amount prescribed for you" (Luke 3:13), while Zacchaeus, though eager to pay restitution and give enormous alms, mentions nothing about retiring. And later still we learn that a royal official together with his household (John 4:53), and even some members of the emperor's household (Phil 4:22), would be drawn to the gospel, although they do not appear to have given up their employment. Jesus' words "Follow me" did not automatically refer to a career change for everybody who responded to him, except of course in those cases where the career was a career in sin.

Since New Testament times some of Jesus' followers have always been drawn to dedicate themselves in a focused, intense, all-or-nothing manner to preaching, living, exemplifying, and explaining the gospel. The assembling of the Twelve from a much larger group of followers may have furnished a measure of biblical grounding for this specialized service to the word. The selection of the Twelve, furthermore, has sometimes been viewed as supplying the rudiments of early church structure. Whatever their merits, neither of these ideas appears to have been on the evangelist's mind, however. Mark locates a renewed call to discipleship in 8:34, a clarification of what can be expected in following Jesus, and it is plainly addressed to many more than the Twelve. Are *all* of Jesus' listeners, he is asking, prepared to deny themselves, pick up *their* cross (Mark does not say their share in Jesus' cross), and come after Jesus?

The prospect of further suffering would hardly have appealed to men and women who had already experienced a considerable amount of struggle and desperation in their lives. Is it likely, therefore, that Jesus was inviting people to continue shouldering their burdens, meekly conforming themselves to circumstances that could not be changed? Or was he urging them to take up the cross of prophetic resistance? At this stage of Mark's narrative, taking up their cross implies a bold determination on the part of his followers to bring their suffering to Jerusalem and, alongside Jesus, to lay their case before God in the house of God's justice. That someone like Levi should have been among their number is nothing short of astonishing. What more vivid way to demonstrate how effective and inclusive Jesus' practice was than to include a converted tax-collector or two in the entourage heading toward the Holy City!

Who Is It That Calls?

The most obvious answer to this question would have to be God or the Spirit; who else could it be? But divine action in our lives is always mediated in some way. We "hear" God speaking to us through Scripture, or even in other forms of religious and non-religious literature. We "see" God in the signs of our times, in the circumstances and events that make up our lives. We even "feel" God in the encounters and relationships that define us, the people who need us, the other men and women of faith whose example inspires and steadies us. Theologically speaking, ultimately it is God who calls; anthropologically speaking, God addresses us through people, circumstances, and events. Theologically speaking, the word of God "comes" to a prophet; anthropologically speaking, the process of receiving God's word is a lot more complex than it sounds.

When the first disciples responded to Jesus' invitation to follow him, they were answering the voice of Jesus, not the voice of God directly. Mark's way of telling the story could suggest that it was the force of Jesus' person that swayed the fishermen to drop their nets and come after him. But I doubt that charisma had anything to do with it. The response of the brothers only makes sense after it dawns on us that it is *the reader's* knowledge of who Jesus is that allows the scene to slide by. How could one refuse the Son of God? Nevertheless, if we are to avoid doing a serious disservice both to the disciples and to ourselves, we probably ought to infer a few additional details. Either they had previously met Jesus at the Jordan, or else they had already heard his preaching about the kingdom by the time he encountered them at the Sea of Galilee. They would have needed at least some time to hear, to reflect, and to become inwardly ready to do something; after all, we do. Thus they had to have been disposed to make a change in their lives for the sake of the deliverance and peace of their people. They would have needed to connect the preaching and invitation of Jesus with the mysterious action of God in their lives to sense in Jesus' words and presence the will of God for them at that moment. In short, the disciples could not have responded to Jesus with such alacrity without some adult understanding of what they were embarking upon. They would not have followed Jesus unless the Spirit of God had moved them to do so.

The same line of reasoning would apply to any of the Bible's famous call stories, however truncated for the sake of narrative effect the accounts may be. Divine calls require human mediation; otherwise the one who feels himself or herself called might fairly be suspected of self-deception. Anyone claiming "God told me" risks offending not just human intelligence but the whole sacramental, symbolic, linguistic, and social process that God created and by means of which we reach insight and judgment. Individuals who believe themselves called to deliver a message to others need to be aware, as well as the men and women to whom they speak, of how they reached the conclusion that God was directing them. Human beings cannot be faulted for questioning any claims about privileged communications from God. Too much mischief has been worked by those who have asked others to suspend their intelligence in the name of blind faith. No believing community, therefore, can take a detour around its responsibility to discern spirits. Signs and wonders may alert human reason to hitherto unnoticed dimensions of existence, even stunning the intellect into pondering further the Spirit's action in the human world. But miracles become nothing more than irrationality's trump cards when divorced from discerning faith. We do not believe in God because we have witnessed miracles. Miracles, rather, are what faith perceives in the ordinary and everyday unfolding of our lives. In Mark's Gospel the disciples followed Jesus on the basis of hearing what he said, not because they had first witnessed a miracle.

Nevertheless, it was not simply Jesus who had called the fishermen and their families; they must have detected or perceived in Jesus' words the voice of the people. Or to put things another way, they became Jesus' followers not because they wanted to pursue their own individual salvation but because they earnestly sought life and freedom for all the sons and daughters of Israel.[2] The salvation of the individual apart from the

---

[2] In his book *God's Long Summer: Stories of Faith and Civil Rights* (Princeton: Princeton Univ. Press, 1997), Charles Marsh relates the very different stories of Sam Bowers and Fannie Lou Hamer. Both experienced calls, but Bowers' story shows the devastating consequences of a perceived call from God that is not intrinsically connected with the life of the poor. Mrs. Hamer's story demonstrates the exact opposite.

restoration and deliverance of the community would have been unthinkable for Jesus. It must have been equally inconceivable for those whom he
wanted to work with him in proclaiming the kingdom of God.

This point is extremely important for understanding the nature and
purpose of God's calling us. What sort of figure would Moses be without
the people, or Isaiah, or Amos, or Jeremiah, or John the Baptist? Indeed,
the overriding concern of Jesus' ministry was the people of God, for
whom his blood—every ounce of his life—would be poured out (Mark
14:24). At some point in examining the Gospel story we have to recognize that every genuine call includes a communal, social, or ecclesiological dimension. The divine call emerges from the heart of the people, that
is, from the depths of their historical experience. The voice of the people
is what John heard when the word of the Lord came to him in the wilderness. Their voice, too, is what Jesus apprehended in the preaching of the
Baptist and what the disciples perceived in the message of Jesus. Once
again, divine call is mediated through human instrumentality.

An individual cannot function as a prophet unless enabled by people
who in their hearts have cried out to God for protection and deliverance.
For all practical purposes this means the poor, the downtrodden, the
voiceless ones of history, since *ordinarily* the rich and powerful neither
want nor readily tolerate prophets from God. A prophet who is marginalized from the people of God is a contradiction. The same idea might be
applied to teachers. One cannot instruct if people resist or refuse being
taught. Students and disciples for their part have to give permission to
their teachers and masters; otherwise learning is absolutely impossible.
The reaction of the people at the synagogue service in Capernaum,
"What is this? A new teaching—with authority!" (Mark 1:27), reflects not
the magisterial tone or manner of Jesus but the way in which he appealed
to the everyday experience of his listeners. Thus his authority probably
came from the bottom, not from the top. Jesus did not enjoy the authority and approval conferred by a heavenly voice, by a connection with the
religious establishment, or by the working of mighty wonders, as Moses
once did. The people had been struck not by his footnotes but by his
rootedness in the everyday world. They listened to him with pleasure.

Similarly, Paul would have been utterly frustrated if virtually no one
had been open to his apostolic endeavors. It is always the people who call
out: enslaved Israelites crying for deliverance (Exod 3:7-9), the Macedonian
calling to Paul in a vision to come "and help us" (Acts 16:9), the Gentiles
patiently waiting in darkness for a great light (Isa 9:1-2), the Gerasenes on
the other side of the lake whose land was infested by Legion. Curiously, in

this last case the people decided that they did not want Jesus to remain among them. He had "heard" their need but they refused him permission to stay, and thus he could do nothing else for them. In many cases (including this wonderful tale in Mark 5) real human need calls forth a messenger from God, even though the people do not explicitly ask for one. Their need for salvation becomes in effect the apostle's, or the prophet's, or the evangelist's call. The Ninevites, for instance, had not petitioned God for a prophet; but their need for conversion summoned one, and they listened wholeheartedly to Jonah's preaching. Their openness to conversion is what enabled Jonah to preach.

As for Mark, Jesus could do little for people unless they opened themselves to God, which in effect meant paying attention to God's homegrown messenger. Jesus thus left Nazareth for the second time, amazed at the lack of faith (Mark 6:5-6), incapable of doing any powerful deeds there. The villagers of Nazareth were unteachable, as were the Pharisees, most of the scribes, and the religious elite that managed the Temple.

Now while it is easy to appreciate the role played by the voice of the people in the calling of a prophet or an apostle, can we see the same dynamic operative in the calling of men and women to be disciples? It is doubtlessly true that every Christian, by virtue of following the prophet Jesus, shares in his prophetic work. The baptismal anointing, in fact, makes it abundantly clear that each of us is a member of Christ who is Priest, Prophet, and King.[3] And it is equally the case that each of us shares in the Church's apostolic consciousness, for we are all sent forth to bear courageous witness to what we profess. But most of us as followers and close friends of Jesus are perhaps more comfortable with the designation "disciple." Does the summons to be a disciple rest upon one's being called by the people, or is it purely a matter of being called by God as we discern the voice of Jesus addressing us from within the Christian story?

The answer lies on the side of human mediation. Jesus invites men and women to be his followers today through the Christian story as proclaimed and lived by faithful communities. He also invites them through their engagement with the world, from within the signs and circumstances of their times. Or to put the matter as concretely as possible, our invitation to walk with Jesus frequently comes through human beings desperately in need of redemption, forgiveness, and support. We endeavor so hard to follow Jesus faithfully because so many struggling human beings, like Paul's Macedonian, are begging us to do so. In the final analysis, a

---

[3] See the Rite of Baptism in Bouley, *Catholic Rites Today,* 157.

prophet's message to those of high estate derives its force and its credibility from the fact that the prophet has accompanied the voiceless poor and learned from them what sort of salvation they look for from God. The same holds true for the message announced by ordinary disciples.

Religious calls, to elaborate for a moment, may be perceived suddenly and evoke an immediate, spontaneous response. A number of scriptural stories read that way, although one suspects that such accounts tend to be condensed and their supernatural sense heightened in order to capture our interest and excite our desires. But call, like the correlative reality of conversion, may more typically unfold over a period of time. Just as the mind considers and deliberates before reaching an assent, so too does the human spirit have its preparatory moments. The Jesus story works over our memories, desires, thinking, and imagination like leaven in a batch of dough, gradually transforming us both inwardly and outwardly into a different kind of people. The story works its way in and out of the hundreds of details and concerns that constitute daily life, eventually disclosing to us the mystery of grace that has been unfolding beneath and around us.

To claim that the call to discipleship is mediated by the Church is hardly to state anything startling. But this ecclesiological fact should be framed more precisely, and I ask the reader's patience while I explain. However unaware of the dynamics of solidarity we may be, I believe that it is the people of God, particularly the poor, who actually invite us to be followers of Jesus. Out of their poverty they speak as Jesus would, urging us to let go of everything for the sake of the kingdom of God. They call us to know and follow him not simply for our own sake but for the sake of their salvation and enduring peace. Countless millions of human beings need us to be faithful disciples of Jesus, although they will never vocalize the urgency of this plea. The voice of the Jesus who speaks to us by the lake is none other than the voice of the one who abides among God's children; in them we hear his invitation.

The preceding reflection is not all that removed from what Marcus Borg has written about renewal movements:

> Religious renewal movements are spawned by a perceived difference between how things are and how they ought to be. They are thus shaped by two factors: loyalty to an inherited tradition . . . and contemporary circumstances which call for change. Sometimes a third factor enters as well, the religious experience of the leader and/or adherents. When this is the case, the perceived difference may be between what is disclosed by that religious experience and the present state of affairs. In any event, contemporary

circumstances are the medium within which renewal movements grow and the conditions to which they must respond, directly or indirectly.[4]

The way things ought to be, for Jesus, would have been expressed as the kingdom of God. The contemporary state of affairs were the political, social, economic, and cultural circumstances of Galilee around the year 30; or more precisely, the state of affairs was the people themselves as circumscribed by the conditions in which they found themselves. The renewal movement that Jesus led was not an abstraction, for the situation in which he preached and healed always bore a human face. And it was those faces that drew his mission from the depths of his soul.

Fishing for Human Lives

Jesus' preaching about the kingdom was considerably more detailed than Mark's brief formula. The first followers, we can be reasonably confident, had discovered a happy congruence between his message and their longing. The way in which Jesus interpreted what was happening throughout Palestine and in the daily life of their villages resonated with their experience. Thus they followed with insight, not blindly; not by a leap in the dark, but as people prompted by the Spirit. Jesus assured them that they would be casting their nets to bring human beings into the kingdom of God. They followed Jesus because they cared for the people of Israel.

However we picture the call stories in our imaginations, it is best not to picture Jesus as recruiting an itinerant teaching faculty to conduct spirituality seminars for the peasantry. Present-day academic models do not serve us here. Besides, such a representation can too easily become the basis of defining a community in terms of authorized teachers and perpetual learners. By definition, however, a disciple is always learning. There will never be a moment in our lives when we can declare that there is nothing else to learn about the mystery of God in our world or in our own hearts. At the same time, being a disciple involves assuming responsibility for teaching others by word and by deed so that they in turn will become instructors as well.

The fishing metaphor, like the shepherding one, ought not be pressed too far. Human beings are neither fish nor sheep. The crux of the metaphor is the action of casting the net, the drawing of as many men and women as possible into the reign of God. This is something Simon and Andrew, James and John, are being called to, but not these individuals alone together with a few other hand-picked figures. *Active* discipleship is

---

[4] Borg, *Conflict, Holiness, and Politics,* 43.

the only form of following Jesus the gospel knows; there can be no stay-at-home disciples in the sense of sitting forever on the student side of the teaching platform. Thus the call stories let none of us off the hook. We cannot say to Simon and his companions, "You go, we'll stay here." The mentality of Mark is that all of us go. All of us have to step away from our nets and our fathers and be prepared to take a leave of absence from our routine ways of thinking about God, ourselves, and one another.

In calling his followers Jesus was scarcely interested in breaking up families and splitting households. Quite the contrary. The ministry of reconciliation (to use Paul's expression) had to reach into the heart of communal and family life; what would reconciliation mean otherwise? What credible evidence would there be that the kingdom of God was at hand if husbands and wives were warring with one another, if children were treated as of no account, if divorce were forcing women from their homes, or if like leprosy petty debts ate away at village life? That Peter's own family did not break apart when he decided to follow Jesus is abundantly clear, for within a scene or two Jesus will be at Peter's home. When Paul was reminding the Corinthians that he enjoyed the right of taking a wife along with him on his missionary journeys (1 Cor 9:5), he appealed to the practice of Peter and the other apostles. If Peter had traveled with his wife on missionary journeys after Easter, the idea of doing so must have seemed the most natural thing in the world even before Easter, while Jesus still walked among them, unless Peter's children were too young at the time. In any event, Peter and his wife had not separated in order to allow him greater freedom to spend time with Jesus casting nets to rescue human lives. Once again we recall that couples and families were called to be disciples, not just individuals. And what was true then holds equally true today. But hearing Jesus in the voice of his people, that may be the great mystery of Christian vocation.

After narrating the story of Jesus' baptism and the summoning of disciples, Mark moves on to a number of healing stories and conflict scenes. One of these is the story of a paralyzed man who is brought to Jesus for healing but curiously is greeted with a word of forgiveness. Having looked at the relationship between God's call and the call from God's people, therefore, we shall explore in the following chapter the theme of forgiveness. What is surprising about the story of the paralytic's being forgiven is the way Jesus desacralizes the granting of divine pardon. Why does Jesus do that? And if forgiving sins is so important, why does Mark devote only one story to it?

3

The Authority to Forgive

"But so that you may know that the Son of Man has authority on earth to forgive sins"—he said to the paralytic—"I say to you, stand up, take your mat and go to your home" (Mark 2:10-11).

Locating Forgiveness in Mark

Nothing seems more natural to a Christian than to connect the death of Jesus with the forgiveness of sins. Matthew's account of the Last Supper, for example, makes the association clear: "[F]or this is my blood of the covenant, which is poured out for many for the forgiveness of sins" (Matt 26:28). And nothing would seem more obvious to a Christian than to think of the whole of Jesus' ministry as a mission of assuring human beings of divine forgiveness. Stories such as that of the sinful woman who approached Jesus while he was dining at a Pharisee's house (Luke 7:36-50), or the woman surprised in the act of adultery (John 8:1-11), or the parables of the lost sheep and prodigal son (Luke 15), confirm an overall impression that Jesus' mission was to seek out and to save what was lost (Luke 19:10). But what strikes the Christian as obvious may distract us from a major point of biblical faith. Forgiveness and compassion belong to the divine nature. Thus the forgiveness of sins was an essential component of Jewish faith long before Jesus arrived on the scene. Consequently, summing up the life of Jesus in terms of the forgiveness of sins is not all that clarifying; the expression requires elaboration. To argue that the death of Jesus replaced the sacramentals of Jewish worship for obtaining divine forgiveness does not carry us very far. The cross is not merely the substitution of one saving instrument for another. And any intimation that forgiveness was not readily available before the death of Jesus to the one who repents has to be rejected outright.

Some ten to fifteen years before Mark began composing his Gospel Paul had spoken of being entrusted with the ministry of reconciliation in a way that suggested that reconciliation was the principal work of God in Christ (2 Cor 5:18-21). Indeed, in the effort to sum up Jesus' life the word "reconciliation" may be more serviceable catechetically than "forgiveness." Paul's graphic description of human beings in the state of alienation from God in the first chapter of his letter to the Romans set the stage for his presentation of life according to the Spirit. With life in the Spirit, every trace of alienation between the Creator and the creature is so completely erased that men and women come to know and address God as intimately as Jesus did. The theme of reconciliation would reappear beautifully and richly in the second chapter of the letter to the Ephesians, where the writer celebrates the end of alienation between Gentiles and Jews: "For he is our peace; in his flesh he has made both groups into one and has broken down the dividing wall, that is, the hostility between us" (Eph 2:14).

Is it not curious, therefore, to discover only one explicit forgiveness story in all of Mark's Gospel? To be sure, Mark relates the fundamental disposition that was supposed to precede and penetrate every prayer Jesus' disciples would ever make: "*Whenever you stand praying,* forgive, if you have anything against anyone; so that your Father in heaven may also forgive you your trespasses" (Mark 11:25). But the saying itself does not appear to be thematically woven into the rest of the Gospel narrative, and given the words of Jesus that precede it the instruction sounds out of place. Forgiveness is mentioned in Mark 3:28 with amazing matter-of-factness: "[P]eople will be forgiven for their sins and whatever blasphemies they utter." The single exception appears in the following verse; blasphemy against the Holy Spirit—maliciously closing one's eyes and ears to the presence of the Spirit in the ministry of Jesus—constitutes an unforgivable and eternal sin (see also 4:12). But the theme of forgiveness is tangential here; the main point concerns the colossally hateful allegation that Jesus is in league with Satan. Even the Gospel's sole forgiveness story in chapter 2 appears to be less about the reception of forgiveness than about the authority to forgive.

The case could be made, of course, that there are actually multiple forgiveness stories in Mark, and even that at one level the entire story is about forgiveness. John the Baptist introduces the narrative as the messenger who offered the people forgiveness of their sins as they immersed themselves in the waters of the Jordan. Jesus' eating at Levi's house presupposes the tax collector's change of heart and his determination to follow Jesus. Jesus' crossing into Gentile territory in chapter 5 might be read as an outreach on Jesus' part that would one day bear fruit in terms of the repentance and conversion of the nations. So too the episode of the second multiplication of the loaves and Jesus' journeying through the cities of the Decapolis with their heavy Gentile presence. Intrinsic to breaking bread together is the openness of individuals to forgiving and being forgiven, and thus the two feeding stories could be read (among other things) as expressions of communal reconciliation. Finally, the reader assumes that the disciples of Jesus who behaved so cowardly at the time of his arrest were subsequently invited to forgiveness and reconciliation; otherwise the instruction about returning to Galilee makes little sense.

At any rate, the fact that Mark narrates only one story specifically about forgiveness makes the forgiveness motif no less significant. Mark writes:

> When he returned to Capernaum after some days, it was reported that he was at home. So many were gathered around that there was no longer room for them, not even in front of the door; and he was speaking the word to them. Then some people came, bringing to him a paralyzed man, carried by four of them. And when they could not bring him to Jesus because of the crowd, they removed the roof above him; and after having dug through it, they let down the mat on which the paralytic lay. When Jesus saw their faith, he said to the paralytic, "Son, your sins are forgiven." Now some of the scribes were sitting there, questioning in their hearts, "Why does this fellow speak in this way? It is blasphemy! Who can forgive sins but God alone?" At once Jesus perceived in his spirit that they were discussing these questions among themselves; and he said to them, "Why do you raise such questions in your hearts? Which is easier, to say to the paralytic, 'Your sins are forgiven,' or to say, 'Stand up and take your mat and walk'? But so that you may know that the Son of man has authority on earth to forgive sins"— he said to the paralytic—"I say to you, stand up, take your mat and go to your home." And he stood up, and immediately took the mat and went out before all of them; so that they were all amazed and glorified God, saying, "We have never seen anything like this!" (2:1-12).

I do not believe that the evangelist intended to suggest that the man's physical condition was the result of his having sinned. Paralysis might well be symbolic of what sin does to human beings, but it is not only paralytics who feel its crippling weight. The same could be said of the other physical conditions that Jesus heals. Cumulatively they tell us something about how seriously Mark views the woundedness that runs so deeply in individual lives, in families, and in communities; but Mark does not view them as punishment. If anything, Mark would have attributed such suffering to the stranglehold that demons exert on human lives. Moreover, there is simply no indication in Mark that social scourges such as poverty, financial indebtedness, chronic hunger, and exploitation were things that sinful men and women brought upon themselves and their children. Once again, the demonic structures that so imprisoned and ate away at human dignity would have been for Mark the work of Beelzebul.

Jesus did not believe that suffering was a penalty for sin any more than Mark did. The lifting away of physical burdens through the power of the Spirit discloses a major feature of Jesus' teaching about the kingdom of God. God does *not* will that human beings suffer, even as punishment for their moral offenses; otherwise Jesus would not have been empowered to heal and to cast out demons. The message of Jesus must itself have been profoundly liberating for those who opened their hearts in faith. What more effective way to portray the redemptive power of Jesus' teaching than to show him restoring people to wholeness? The healings are hardly incidental accompaniments of Jesus' message; they do not serve as theological condiments to awaken the tastebuds of the spirit but as manifestations of divine purpose.

Obviously the healings did not move everyone to believe in Jesus; indeed, moving people to faith may never have been their intent. There were many who witnessed the healings and exorcisms but still walked away in disbelief, or even in downright anger (as we see in Mark 3:1-6). The healing episodes are in effect the message of Jesus turned inside out, and they undoubtedly deliver a confirmatory message about divine compassion. But since no child of Israel would have doubted that God was compassionate, perhaps even more importantly the healings point to the wholeness God wills for human beings and their communities. The healings and exorcisms might even be viewed as the Spirit's protest against the dehumanizing forces and destructive elements so rampant in the everyday world.[1]

While neither Jesus nor the evangelist would have believed that physical affliction was a sign of divine chastisement, it is quite probable that many of those around Jesus did share this belief. After all, the logic of blessing and curse, so central to what Moses presented to the people as God's

---

[1] Morna Hooker argues that the variant reading of Mark 1:41 is probably correct. If so, then Jesus' reaction at the sight of the leper ought to be read as his being *angry* with everything that had shredded away the man's life: the disease itself, enforced separation from family and village life, poverty, and exclusion from assemblies of worship. If Jesus has been moved with anger, then the miracle is his protest against the evil that could reduce human life to such an awful state. She writes: "Anger is an appropriate emotion when one is confronted with the devastating effects of disease" (*Gospel According to Saint Mark*, 80).

law, implied that if one did not have children, a long life, and family land holdings, then that individual must have violated one of the precepts or ordinances of the Lord. Although called into question by the book of Job, this logic was reaffirmed in a number of the psalms: "For the LORD watches over the way of the righteous, / but the way of the wicked will perish" (Ps 1:6).

We know that the Jesus of the Fourth Gospel explicitly rejected the connection between a man's blindness and the moral state both of the man himself and of his parents (John 9:1-3), while the Jesus of Matthew urged his followers to imitate the compassion of God, who "makes his sun rise on the evil and on the good, and sends rain on the righteous and on the unrighteous" (Matt 5:45). Mark does not address this issue so pointedly, although he obviously was engaged in theological reflection about the mystery of suffering as it touched upon Jesus himself. How shall we account for the suffering borne by God's holy ones, and above all by God's Son? The place where Scripture perhaps wrestled with this issue most intensely was Second Isaiah. In the end, therefore, even if a number of Jesus' contemporaries had linked bad fortune with personal sinfulness, Mark does not appear to be attempting to correct that particular mistake through the story of the paralytic. Nothing Jesus says there challenged that unfortunate assumption, which was so corrosive of one's relationship with God.

The Restoration of a Parent's Confidence in God

Before looking at the theological significance of the scene with Jesus and the paralyzed man, it would be worth our while to glance ahead to the story of the desperate father in Mark 9:14-29. In that case the boy's condition was attributed to a "spirit," which Jesus ordered to depart from the boy *and never enter him again!* The actual healing in the form of an exorcism is a forgone conclusion, almost anticlimactic after the conversation that took place between Jesus and the father. As the story unfolds and the father relates to Jesus the entire history of the boy's condition and, presumably, the family's valiant efforts over the years to prevent him from hurting himself, we are drawn to see that not only was the life of the child in jeopardy. The emotional and religious life of the father had been placed under severe strain, just about to the breaking point. The desperation behind the father's plea should come as no surprise: "Immediately the father of the child cried out, 'I believe; help my unbelief!'" (Mark 9:24).[2]

---

[2] *The King James Version* translates this verse a bit more elegantly: "And straightway the father of the child cried out, and said with tears, Lord, I believe; help thou mine unbelief."

The story makes no allusion whatsoever to the boy's physical state as a result of anyone's having sinned, although in the Markan story failures to believe are tantamount to manifestations of sin's power over us. The demonic assault, however, was not only against the boy; the spirit had also assaulted, day by day over many years, the father's faith and nearly vanquished it. The poor father needed healing too; and from one point of view, he may have needed forgiveness for his greatly weakened confidence in God's providential love. In contrast to the disciples, whose faith had not yet been fully tested, Jesus understood the situation of the father's soul; he knew what it was like to wrestle with powerful, relentless doubts. Whenever Jesus exclaimed, "If you are able!—All things can be done for the one who believes," he was speaking from conviction, from experience, from having learned for himself that one can emerge from being tested by demons with seasoned faith. For that reason Jesus replied to his disciples that this kind of spirit can only be driven out through prayer (Mark 9:29)—not the spirit that had infested the boy (his physical condition was not objectively worse than that of the paralytic or the crazed man who lived among the tombs) but the spirit that had begun to take up residence in the father's soul. What we may have in this scene, therefore, is a deeply moving story about forgiveness, understood in this instance as the rebuilding of shattered hope. In a profoundly Christian sense, only someone who has died and been raised up, who has experienced divine abandonment and then fallen into the hands of God, is able to mediate the healing of crippled faith.

The allusion to resurrection is important. Easter, we have noted, pervades the story. There are numerous instances in the Gospel where someone figuratively dead is raised back to life. One first thinks of the leper who is healed in the opening chapter, and then of the demented individual in chapter 5 who made his dwelling among the tombs. The leper had died to his family and friends ("He shall live alone; his dwelling shall be outside the camp" [Lev 13:46]); the crazed man was dead to human contact as such. Both are brought back to life. The daughter of Jairus is another obvious example: "He took her by the hand and said to her, 'Talitha cum,' which means, 'Little girl, get up!'" (Mark 5:41).

The woman with the issue of blood is surely another. From the viewpoint of ritual holiness, her chronic condition would have rendered her unclean and thereby prevented her from participating, if she had wanted to, in Temple services in Jerusalem. Uncleanness, however, does not appear to be Mark's concern in recounting this story.[3] The details he

---

[3] Peter Chrysologus had noted that the poor woman received from Jesus both healing *and* forgiveness, for she knew that she was violating the holiness code in touching even

does stress are that she had been suffering for twelve years, that she had exhausted her resources, and that she persevered by pressing through the large crowd. In touching Jesus' cloak, the woman recovers her health and the drain on her resources is over. Figuratively, she has come back to life, and she knows it.

The scene with the epileptic boy furnishes one further example of someone being raised to life:

> After crying out and convulsing him terribly, it came out, *and the boy was like a corpse,* so that most of them said, "He is dead." But Jesus took him by the hand *and lifted him up,* and he was able to stand (Mark 9:26-27).

The near-helpless paralytic who stands up, picks up his mat, and "returns home" is likewise raised to life. What do we have in this scene and so many others, if not precursors of the resurrection itself? The restoration to life, to wholeness, and to community, which is so evident in the healings and exorcisms, prepares us for Easter. Those earlier stories dispose us to hear with understanding the great revelation underlying the whole life of Jesus.

Forgiveness as Liberation from Burdens

If the healings and exorcisms show Jesus releasing people from the grip of evil, then his being raised from the dead ought to demonstrate the definitive sign of God's will to reconcile us to one another and to himself. The lifting away of the weight of death, not just in the literal sense of physical mortality but in the symbolic though eminently real sense of being killed by sin, lies at the heart of the Christian mystery. Every instance of being raised back to life becomes a demonstration of the Spirit's power over sinful forces, institutions, social arrangements, and economic conditions. The reign of sin is constantly being checked and broken by the sheer fact of God's merciful, healing closeness. Forgiveness is without doubt knowing oneself pardoned and loved by God in such a way and to such a degree that one readily extends the same pardon and love to others, but this experience does not exhaust the mystery of reconciliation.

---

his clothing. See Oden, *Mark,* 74. Mary Rose D'Angelo points out that impurity does not appear to have been the issue at all. She explains: "No opponents call attention to the supposed breach of purity, the miracle effects no refutation of such objections, and no scornful or judgmental authorities are put to shame." See "(Re)Presentations of Women in the Gospels," 141. I am grateful to John Donahue for calling this article to my attention.

Courtroom proceedings do not issue in forgiveness but in settling the claims of justice, or at least of fairness. Financial forgiveness, on the other hand, is altogether different. One can imagine what it would be like to awaken each morning under the wearisome stress and constant worry of not being able to get oneself and one's family out of debt. One can imagine further how personal crises, fears, real or imaginary hurts, prejudices, pride, the inability to let go of resentments, envy, insecurity, and so on could weigh on people just as grievously as indebtedness. Human beings can be as imprisoned by the greed, the indifference, and the privileges of others as if they were locked inside jails.

To lift oppressive weights like these off the backs of men and women, however this might be done in practice, would be tantamount to forgiving or releasing them. For if the burden is to be taken away, someone must do the actual lifting. And if the last state of the person is not to be worse than the first, then the entire situation in which human beings are living will have to change. In this sense, forgiveness is disruptive; most demons do not yield easily. With respect to individuals we speak of conversion; with respect to institutions and structures we might speak of transformation. In either case, whatever causes paralysis both within individuals and communities has to change if forgiveness is to happen.

When the prophets appealed to the rich to act justly toward the poor, they were calling for social change: the rich would have to give up something if they canceled the debts of the poor. Within the world of the Gospel Jesus is always forgiving, insofar as he is constantly taking burdens off other men and women. This he does both by his practice and by his teaching, but in his teaching Jesus was showing why everyone without exception must engage in the business of forgiving. Assisting others to get up from their mats, to escape their isolation, and to rejoin their communities—all of which sacramentalizes their oneness with God—involves laboring for a world that is both just and humanizing. In other words, if Jesus forgives sins, he does so because he expects his followers to do the same. What reason would Mark have for narrating the episode in chapter 2 unless the story had some bearing on the life of the Church?

The question is not rhetorical. Guided by his faith in the presence of the risen Jesus, everything Mark wrote served to instruct, encourage, and inspire the Church. The community's own practice of extending God's peace to others was rooted in the memory of what Jesus had done and said. Forgiving sins, the scribes in the audience rightly noted, is a properly divine action: *divine* not because sin, being an offense against God, can only be forgiven by the One offended but *divine* because forgiveness is equivalent to remaking the human heart, and only God can breathe life into us. Besides, the real harm done by the sinner is directed to other human beings, to families and communities, and even to oneself. *We* are the casualties of our own spiritual blindness and moral failings, not God. In forgiving us God does not pat us gently on the head and with a smile send us blessedly on our way. Forgiving involves real healing, but before anyone can be forgiven the person has to face and admit the reality of his or her condition.

This point should be underlined several times. The individuals who approached Jesus knew exactly what they wanted: "If you choose, you can make me clean" (1:40); "Come and lay your hands on her, so that she may be made well, and live" (5:23); "If I but touch his clothes, I will be made well" (5:28); "She begged him to cast the demon out of her daughter" (7:26); "Teacher, I brought you my son; he has a spirit that makes him unable to speak" (9:17); "My teacher, let me see again" (10:51). The specificity and urgency of these requests stand in marked contrast to the vague expressions of a desire for wholeness that fall from many lips. Those expressions may be vague because people do not have sufficient self-knowledge to realize in what ways they are incomplete or the full extent of the incompleteness they do feel. Or the desire for wholeness may be weakly expressed because materially one is leading a fairly secure and undisturbed life. "Whatever Jesus is fussing about in the Gospel," one figures, "surely he has no need to be all that concerned about me." The Gospel story does not work when it falls on the ears of those with only a superficial sense of the world's woundedness. The Gospel's redemptive potential is frustrated wherever men and women do not want, with every ounce of spiritual, moral, and psychological energy at their disposal, to be whole human beings.

The paralytic, the reader realizes, certainly knew what he needed from Jesus. "But," Mark leads us to ask, "am I conscious of what my condition is? Do I realize that in lifting away my guilt, God is creating a space in my life for something that must replace it, something akin to that joyous defiance that led many whom Jesus healed to announce it far and wide? Do I realize that in taking away my sinfulness God is creating a vacuum in my soul into which the gospel will rush with all the force of newfound liberty and love?" If God alone can forgive sins, then in assuring the paralytic that his sins were forgiven Jesus could scarcely have been pretending to play God's role. Nevertheless, he was claiming to have been authorized by the Spirit to place the awesome responsibility of assuring fragile men and women of God's love into the hands of his disciples. And they were to exercise this responsibility within the parameters of daily life, for this scene takes place in Peter's home, not in the Temple, in the middle of a religious ceremony, or in the hallowed waters of the Jordan River. The assurance of forgiveness comes from the lips of a carpenter, a layperson, and not from a priest.

Jesus' disciples in any age seldom raise up paralytics impoverished by their bad fortune, and God does not mean them to feel guilty because they cannot work miracles. This one paralyzed man represents all paralyzed men and women, an entire class or group of afflicted people. The friends or relatives who carried him to Jesus draw our attention to the burden, however patiently undertaken, that such afflictions impose on families and communities. The tearing apart of the roof (presumably of Peter's house) alerts us to the fact that forgiveness has its disruptive side, for it not infrequently happens that one person's encounter with Jesus brings about dislocation, even turmoil, in the lives of others. Mark would not have recounted this story if he believed that forgiveness was reserved for only one poor individual. The reader can identify with the paralyzed man not because we too are physically constrained but because we recognize ourselves to be sinners in need of healing. In this case, forgiveness means something close to restoring a person's dead limbs to life; the man gets his physical freedom back. In every instance of forgiveness, freedom is the great treasure. In the case of financial indebtedness, the point is clear. But the same holds true with the exorcisms. The regaining of freedom becomes a way of describing forgiveness, or rather, each exorcism is a demonstration of what forgiveness means. Forgiveness means returning to family and friends, it means leaving places of exile, it means being liberated from external oppressors, it means being able to walk again on one's own.

Theologically, what enhances the richness of the story in Mark 2 is the context in which the expression "son of man" appears in chapter 7 of the book of Daniel. In that passage the seer has a vision of four terrible beasts coming out of the sea, an encoded message about God's judgment against the enemies and oppressors of his people. At one point Daniel beholds one "like a son of man" coming before the Ancient One:

> To him was given dominion
>   and glory and kingship,
> that all peoples, nations, and languages
>   should serve him.
> His dominion is an everlasting dominion
>   that shall not pass away,
> and his kingship is one
>   that shall never be destroyed (Dan 7:14).

Later the prophet is given an interpretation of the vision. The beasts are encrypted representations of ruthless, repressive regimes; but the one like a son of man turns out to be the holy people of God:

> The kingship and dominion
>> and the greatness of the kingdoms under the whole heaven
> shall be given to the people of the holy ones of the Most High;
> their kingdom shall be an everlasting kingdom,
>> and all dominions shall serve and obey them (Dan 7:27).

The usage here may be significant, for the saying of Jesus in Mark 2:10 could not have so narrow a reference that they exclude the possibility of others after Jesus extending forgiveness of sins to those who need it. To be sure, prophets *before* Jesus had mediated divine forgiveness. John the Baptist had preached a baptism of repentance for the forgiveness of sins, and Nathan assured David, who on hearing the prophet's parable immediately recognized his guilt: "Now the LORD has put away your sin" (2 Sam 12:13). Isaiah had proclaimed: "[T]hough your sins are like scarlet, they shall be like snow" (Isa 1:18). But these were prophetic *individuals.* Proclaiming, mediating, or assuring sinful Israel of divine forgiveness was hardly something new with Jesus. The novelty and thus the radicalness of what Jesus does in this scene has to be appreciated in terms of his overall message.

In other words, the activity of forgiving sins, of doing for others what strictly speaking only God can do, was a concrete manifestation that the kingdom of God—the everlasting dominion of God's holy ones—had arrived. Now if the prerequisite for engaging in the ministry of forgiving and reconciling was that the disciples themselves had to be morally perfect, then only Jesus could have forgiven sins. The great mystery here is not that the God of Israel is truly a God of forgiveness or that Jesus of Nazareth has been authorized by the Spirit to offer God's forgiveness to sinful men and women. Rather, the mystery is that ordinary, sinful men and women, once forgiven and set free, should become the bearers of forgiveness and freedom for others. In the eyes of some of Jesus' contemporaries, perhaps, grace had been cheapened. But what else could our being baptized with the Holy Spirit imply if not that we together must continue to do what Jesus did among us?

Thinking back at this point to the call stories, one might ask whether the disciples ever envisioned themselves being called to carry on a ministry of forgiveness. It is hard to imagine a group composed largely of Galilean peasants and assorted fishermen warming to the notion of roaming the world forgiving other men and women in Jesus' name. The very idea might have struck them as presumptuous; besides, who would have given them a hearing? It is possible, of course, that the movement around Jesus, like healing cults in some societies, drew its moral energy from being empowered apart from the official religious institutions and structures of the country. Forgiveness extended at the popular level could thus have posed a real challenge to the religious elites of Israel. But that would make sense only if people had felt themselves cut off from ready access to the mystery of God's love or impeded from receiving divine mercy and grace by the religious establishment itself. The one thing that seems clear is that any desire for personal or individual wholeness that does not at the same time seek wholeness just as earnestly for one's family, one's community, and the society in which one lives is not fully evangelical. In being entrusted with a mission to forgive, Jesus' apostles were being sent forth to teach how communities in their everyday interactions might be reconciled, healed, and strengthened. The Church was to be a living sign of this new social reality.

It is possible, too, that the disciples had to learn over time that forgiveness of sins, precisely as an indication of God's nearness, was just *one* of the things they would be called upon to proclaim. Mark devotes, after all, only one story to the forgiving of sins, and the central issue of the scene is more about authority than sin. Nevertheless, when forgiveness of sins is viewed as one expression of a ministry more comprehensively described as a ministry of reconciliation, then the disciples' initial calling comes into sharper relief. Jesus' words "Whenever you stand praying, forgive, *if you have anything against anyone*" most likely encompass all the things that separate and alienate human beings from one another. It is hard to imagine that Jesus, such a keen observer of the human scene, would have excluded from this rule the debts, large or small, that cost people their independence and paralyzed their hope.[4]

Jesus' mission was not primarily to forgive people's moral offenses but to proclaim the kingdom of God. And the indispensable condition for belonging to that kingdom was repentance and a change of heart. Jesus enabled the men and women who listened to him to resume their lives, to rebuild their families and communities. His overall aim was the restoration of Israel by redefining the boundaries of holiness and by prophetically befriending and defending Israel's poor. Whatever it was that caught the attention and the imagination of the disciples, we can be sure that it was something of moment. They would have seen themselves

---

[4] See Horsley, *Jesus and the Spiral of Violence*, 251–55.

as invited to play a role in the renewal of the nation, in the redemption of Israel from the hands of its enemies. The actual contours of that call might not have been clear from the start. They needed to spend time with Jesus before they would be able to grasp what the renewal of a nation demands.

A Theological Note on Mark 11:25

That we should not seek God's forgiveness while at the same time withholding forgiveness from anyone who may have offended us is ax-iomatic for Christian spirituality. This rule of religious etiquette is reaf-firmed in every recitation of the Lord's Prayer with the words "Forgive us our trespasses, as we forgive those who trespass against us."

There is, however, something anthropomorphic and even a bit mis-leading about this way of formulating our relationship with God. It prac-tically suggests a quid pro quo: first we forgive others and then God will extend forgiveness to us. The financial analogies drawn by the Gospels of Matthew (with the parable of the unforgiving servant in 18:23-35) and Luke (with the story of the sinful woman in 7:36-50) can throw us off in this regard. Releasing a client from debt costs a billionaire a great deal less than it would cost a small-time farmer to forgive a loan made to a poor neighbor. It is no doubt true that in God's eyes all are immensely in-debted, but that dependence includes multimillionaires and beggars alike, the unrighteous and the righteous equally. Yet if God is the billionaire, then God really has nothing to lose. What always needs to be highlighted, therefore, is *the experience of being completely in God's debt,* an experience that cuts across social and economic lines and goes straight to the heart of the human condition.

On the one hand, there is something profoundly irreverent and prideful about a person approaching God's presence while at the same time harboring resentment toward another human being. Such irrever-ence and failure in humility create a deadly block to the individual's ex-periencing the healing, saving power of God in his or her life. On the other hand, it seems far easier for God to forgive us than for us to forgive one another. After all, God is not susceptible to being hurt or offended by human sinfulness. Any talk about displeasing, insulting, or even wound-ing God by our sinfulness is plainly anthropomorphic. God does not re-deem us because we have caused him untold suffering but out of love.

Yet the very idea that forgiveness comes easier for God than for us is a sign that our thinking about God has gone offtrack. If the unwelcome

implication of our rhetoric about sin as indebtedness should be that forgiveness requires more of us than it does of God, then the saying of Jesus
in Mark 11:25 does not really serve us along the path of discipleship. A
suitable way to resolve the difficulty might be to view forgiveness as a
function of one's freedom. To the degree that our hearts are not free, that
we do not enjoy the liberty of the children of God, then the things we
refuse to let go of render us incapable of forgiving others. Conversely,
God forgives because God is freedom itself, not because God is incon-
ceivably rich and can write off bad debts.

The other side of knowing oneself totally indebted to God is the consoling experience of a liberty of spirit that lasts a lifetime. For being in-
debted to God belongs to our nature; it is a debt that can never be canceled
and is impossible to repay. "What do you have," Paul asks the Corinthians, "that you did not receive?" (1 Cor 4:7). Sporadic attempts to pay God
back may be well intentioned and understandable, but they are misplaced.
Divine gifts are not given in order to generate a sense of indebtedness, although from the human side there is no way around the fact that our indebtedness to God can never be escaped, no matter how hard we might try
to put some balance into our relationship by doomed efforts to pay God
back. Acknowledging our indebtedness is the beginning of wisdom and,
paradoxically, marks the real birth of human freedom.

It seems to me, then, that Jesus' instruction "Whenever you stand
praying, forgive, if you have anything against anyone so that your Father
in heaven may also forgive you your trespasses" should not be read
naively, either as a charge to imitate divine mercy or as giving something
in order to receive something. Divine mercy is not held in abeyance until
people demonstrate their worthiness. God does not act and react the way
human beings do. However healing the word of forgiveness and love can
be to the one who has committed an offense, *extending* forgiveness may
be even more important to people's spiritual well-being. The truly urgent
questions are, What sort of people do we want to become? and What sort
of communities do we want to create for ourselves and for our children?
Men and women who are unwilling or unable to forgive those who have
trespassed against them are destined to a life of spiritual illiteracy; they
have yet to acknowledge the extent of their indebtedness to God. Those
who have learned to forgive are men and women of a new creation where
the dead are raised to life.

We have seen, then, that Jesus envisioned forgiveness to be a regular
and pervasive feature of life in the renewed Israel. Furthermore, forgiveness as the lifting away of whatever burdens crush human lives displays

moral and spiritual, psychological and social, economic, political, and cultural dimensions. In the next chapter we turn our attention to Mark's sense of what God wills or ordains for human lives. And one thing that should become clear is that the will of God is not another of life's burdens but the ground of our hope.

4

What God Ordains

Then he began to teach them that the Son of Man must undergo great suffering, and be rejected by the elders, the chief priests, and the scribes, and be killed, and after three days rise again (Mark 8:31).

Although the precise phrase "the will of God" makes only a single appearance in Mark, the entire narrative is governed by the conviction that the life, death, and resurrection of Jesus reveal what the divine will in our regard is all about. The divine instruction "Listen to him!" (9:7b) reverberates throughout the whole Gospel. On a symbolic level, Jesus' steadfast orientation toward Jerusalem from the first passion prediction in 8:34 to his arrival in chapter 11 is Mark's way of indicating the intensity and fidelity with which Jesus pursued the will of God.

Early in the narrative Jesus indicated that anyone who does the will of God was his brother, sister, and mother (3:35). With the words "does the will of God" Jesus could simply have meant whoever obeys God's commandments, just as Moses and the prophets had directed. Taken in this sense, the will of God would have been revealed in the Mosaic instruction itself, an instruction that looked to practice, actions, or something to be done. And practice is absolutely vital to Mark's view of discipleship.

Yet the idea of doing the will of God can take us in a different direction. Human beings have been created in order to share the divine Spirit and to develop a joyous, penetrating, and liberating responsiveness to the slightest movement of that Spirit across the length and breadth of their lives. The Spirit of God is at work in one's prayer and worship, in one's thoughts and imagination, and in the multiplicity of ordinary events, circumstances, and encounters that make up our days. For Jesus, therefore, doing the will of God would not be just another way of referring to the need to observe Moses' instructions, as if the new family Jesus envisioned was going to be established *solely* on the basis of common practice or a solidarity of works. Doing the will of God additionally conveys the idea of leading a life built upon obedience to the Spirit; this, in a nutshell, is what faith means. One experiences oneself actually being drawn or led by the Spirit of God and at every moment surrendering to it. The difference between these two senses may sound subtle, but it is extremely important.[1]

This second sense of doing the will of God lies closer to Jesus' prayer in the garden. The words "yet, not what I want, but what you want" (14:36) express Jesus' determination to remain faithful to his experience of the God who had drawn him into solidarity with his people. The will of God in the Gethsemane prayer obviously refers to much more than keeping the commandments. And contrary to how many of us may have been accustomed to hear these words, there really is little reason to think that the prayer in the garden was one of passivity and resignation. Obedience, yes; surrender (following the spirit of the aged Simeon's prayer in Luke 2:29), no. There was nothing passive about Jesus throughout the course of his ministry or in his final days in Jerusalem. Why then should we think he suddenly adopted the attitude of abandonment to divine providence at the very end? In the end, fidelity to his prophetic experience of God proved very costly.

The words of Mark 14:36 point to the particular response to God that Jesus alone could make, to something that God wanted from him and from nobody else in precisely the same way. In this distinctiveness of life and mission, of course, Jesus is exactly like us. For though we are all children of God, each of us is irreducibly different, and our routes to God

---

[1] Occasionally one hears the question, "How do I find out what God's will is for me?" *Seeking* (as opposed to *doing*) the will of God becomes identified with making a vocational choice or deciding upon a concrete course of action. Important as these matters are, they are not Mark's concern. For Mark, one does not seek the will of God; one does it. Furthermore, equating the will of God with some particular choice that God wants us to make is spiritually dangerous. We risk turning prayer and discernment into a sophisticated effort to guess the divine mind. Biblical writers removed the need for guessing at the divine will by employing devices such as dreams, visions, and visitations by heavenly messengers. We are on more secure ground when we trust that all the circumstances of our lives will conspire to bring about the good that God wants for us (Rom 8:28). Thus every choice we make is contextualized by a pattern of thought and action, by a habit of prayerfulness and trust, that have developed over time. In short, the will of God is organic. No single moment stands in isolation unsupported by all the things that have made us who and what we are. It is unhelpful to think of the will of God as coming from outside or beyond what we already are. There is, we might say, a biography of grace. The will of God in our lives has a history.

are as distinctive as our thumbprints; each response is unique. The prayer reveals, therefore, the same lifelong openness to the Spirit that Jesus asked of his closest followers. It underscores his awareness that in all things one must seek the inner freedom to be led by God, no matter where that path will take us. And it presupposes that ultimately it is God who both fashions individual destinies and shapes the course of human history. *How* God directs our lives without controlling them and determining their outcome is something we may not be able to figure out, but the notion of divine providence is not intrinsically offensive to human reason. *That* God should be so much a part of daily life is, in the best of times, what accounts for the spirit of gratitude among us. In hard times it accounts for our perseverance. In the worst of times it accounts for why we refuse to yield to the demons of despair.

But what are we to make of the "great suffering" mentioned in Mark 8:31? Does God really want this for Jesus or for any of his followers?

Wrestling with Suffering

Central to the biblical understanding of God is the conviction that nothing happens in human history that God has not foreseen. Furthermore, the historical fortunes and destinies both of individuals and of nations unfold according to divine Wisdom. While God does not directly cause everything that happens to us, there is nothing about us that God does not already know. The whole of Psalm 139 declares this truth beautifully. In addition, the laws of nature itself, like the rhythms disclosed in historical process, reflect the Wisdom of God. This conviction is celebrated, for example, in Psalms 65 and 104.

This ancient Hebrew sensibility is also indelibly Christian. It is echoed, for instance, in Acts 17:24-28, where Paul describes God as the Creator, as the Lord of heaven and earth who allots nations "the times of their existence and the boundaries of the places where they would live." Indeed, God's ongoing, redemptive involvement in human history is the presupposition of the entire New Testament. And the mystery of that involvement has now been disclosed to us:

> With all wisdom and insight [God] has made known to us *the mystery of his will,* according to his good pleasure that he set forth in Christ, *as a plan* for the fullness of time, to gather up all things in him, things in heaven and things on earth (Eph 1:8b-10).

Nevertheless, the idea that God as Creator is all-powerful sits alongside the all-too-real fact of incalculable human suffering. Efforts to reconcile the idea of a wise Creator with abundant evidence of moral, political, and social chaos are an ongoing testimony to faith seeking understanding. The biblical writers were indeed thinkers, although they obviously cannot be classified as ancient philosophers. We are not going to find in Scripture speculative attempts to resolve the contradiction between God's power and love on the one hand and the presence of physical evil in the world on the other. Jesus himself, fully confident of God's care, never offered a theological apology for the tragedies that typically beset human beings. To draw on Luke for a moment, innocent pilgrims, caught in the wrong place at the wrong time, could be slaughtered; construction projects could collapse and bury the workers (Luke 13:1-4). And yet Jesus could still assure his followers that they ought to place all their trust in God and not to worry: "Of how much more value are you than the birds!" (Luke 12:24).

The existence of moral evil, of course, cannot be blamed on God, except insofar as God created us with freedom. The consequences of disobedience were clearly spelled out by Moses, and thus the simplest way of accounting for suffering was to interpret it as deserved. Tobit prayed, for instance:

> Do not punish me for my sins
>> and for my unwitting offenses
>> and those that my ancestors committed before you.
> They sinned against you,
>> and disobeyed your commandments.
> So you gave them over to plunder, exile, and death,
>> to become the talk, the byword, and an object of reproach
>> among all the nations among whom you have dispersed us
>>> (Tob 3:3-4).

The idea of suffering as the result of either personal or national sinfulness runs through Scripture. Human actions, after all, always carry consequences. But the notion of divine chastisement runs counter to another major element of biblical experience. Sometimes suffering far exceeds both the individual's and the nation's just deserts, and this experience creates some conceptual tension. Does Israel's God behave recklessly? Appealing to the fact that God demands obedience, prophets often threatened the people with punishment if they refused to read the signs of the times and repent. One scholar argues that such threats reached a climax with Jesus:

> Jesus emerged on the scene convinced that within a generation God would act climactically to judge Israel. His whole mission was concerned with delivering God's message to that final generation. Jesus preached impending

doom, and the way to avoid that doom was to repent from sin and to adhere to his covenantal reformation. His whole ministry, then, was tied into and shaped by his insight from God that a judgment was coming on Israel. Jesus' view of God, his breath-taking announcement that the kingdom was drawing near, and his ethical affirmations . . . were all part of his agenda to lead Israel away from a national disaster and toward a redemption that would bring about the glorious kingdom.[2]

But these apocalyptic stresses within the message of Jesus can make it harder for us to relate to what he was doing and saying. Does Jesus' call to repent at the beginning of the story (Mark 1:15) contain a veiled threat that if the people did not repent they would be punished? And would the events of 66–70 C.E. constitute the historical actualization of that threat? No conscientious historian, theologian, or exegete would argue that. National calamities can strike despite the religious fidelity of the people, and not every episode of private or public infidelity is automatically followed by disaster. If Jesus did not subscribe to the Mosaic logic of blessing and curse on the individual level, it is hard to believe that he would have thought in terms of that logic on the national level. If people's personal misfortune was not necessarily a sign they had broken their covenantal faith, then why should the destruction of Jerusalem (which Mark's Jesus foresees) be attributed to divine punishment for *spiritual* failure? Indeed, what might the people have done of a religious or political nature so as to prevent the wholesale destruction of Jerusalem?

Chastisement, at any rate, is a brittle, problematic category for making sense of suffering. What are we saying about God when we claim that suffering has been "deserved"? That evil actions frequently have repercussions in one's own life and in the life of a society goes without saying. That God is the one who punishes us may correspond to the literary character of God in many biblical passages, but God the literary character and God as the holy mystery behind the world are not identical. The wretched conditions under which millions of Third World people today are reduced to living have nothing to do with their moral state, and the catastrophes that have struck struggling economies are often due to circumstances outside the control of those communities. Given the political reality of the imperial world of the first century, the spiritual and moral reform of Israel would not have been enough to bring about the definitive liberation of the Jewish people.

When the moral evil in some human hearts leads to suffering that crushes the breath out of innocent and defenseless people, then the victims

[2] McKnight, *New Vision for Israel,* 12–13.

clamor for justice and summon God to account, as in Psalm 10. The most sustained scriptural consideration of the problem of undeserved suffering occurs in the book of Job, a writing that raises more questions about God than it answers. In the end, the writer reaffirms the sovereignty and transcendence of God, but why exactly bad things are "allowed" to happen to God-fearing, well-to-do-people is never explained. The central concern of the book might even be loosely characterized as middle class (to adopt a present-day perspective). If one prays, observes the commandments, and walks humbly before God, then surely one deserves the blessing that Moses promised would accompany a good life. But if the righteous are repaid not with the blessing but with the curse then perhaps this indicates that Moses got it all wrong. Obedience to the Law does not automatically bring prosperity, while disobedience does not automatically invite punishment. The psalmist acknowledges this point when he complains to God about how the wicked prosper.

Gustavo Gutiérrez has suggested that in the end Job discovered the mysterious reality of the everyday suffering of the innocent ones among God's people. Even though he had led a righteous and exemplary life, Job's understanding of God was woefully immature. The route to Job's redemption, Gutiérrez proposes, was twofold. First, it consisted of achieving a deep solidarity with the vast majority of humankind whose misfortune seldom prompts them to question God or cry "Why me?" For them suffering simply has to be endured as a fact of life. Second, Job had to learn that God's love is absolutely gratuitous. Gutiérrez's points are excellent, although I am not persuaded that the author of the book of Job was thinking along liberationist lines such as these.[3]

More theologically satisfying than the book of Job, however, is Second Isaiah and chapters 2 and 3 of the Wisdom of Solomon. In these writings the problematic is different, for the suffering is not contrived as it was in the case of Job. The causes of the suffering were quite different. In the case of Wisdom 2, fidelity to Jewish belief and practice in the midst of a presumably godless culture had led to persecution.[4] To that group of Jewish expatriates Matthew's eighth beatitude surely would have applied:

[3] See Gutiérrez, *On Job*, 93–97.

[4] According to the introductory note in *The HarperCollins Study Bible* (New York: HarperCollins, 1993) the book of Wisdom "was written in Greek by a learned and profoundly Hellenized Jew of Alexandria after that city's conquest by Rome in 30 B.C.E. The earlier optimism of the Alexandrian Jewish community for a rapprochement with the Greeks and for social and cultural acceptance by them had been replaced by a mounting sense of disillusionment and disappointment" (1497).

"Blessed are those who are persecuted for righteousness' sake, for theirs is the kingdom of heaven" (Matt 5:10). The chapter concludes with an affirmation of "the wages of holiness": "[F]or God created us for incorruption, / and made us in the image of his own eternity" (Wis 2:23).

That the righteous should have to suffer simply for the sake of being faithful to God is practically taken for granted; the author places the blame on "the devil's envy." The explanation does not answer everything, for we still do not know what it is about creatures—whether angels or human beings—that leads them to abuse their God-given freedom. In Wisdom 3 the author proceeds to make some sense of the suffering of God's children: ". . . because God tested them and found them worthy of himself" (Wis 3:5). At least some forms of human suffering can be accounted for in terms of God's testing, refining, or disciplining us. Such a perspective certainly helps people to understand that what is happening in their lives belongs to God's providential care for those he loves. If the faithful find themselves being persecuted, they should not lose heart, for suffering is the route to immortality.

Second Isaiah reflects a very different and much earlier set of historical circumstances. The Jews who had been led captive to Babylon were undergoing the pain of exile, national humiliation, and the near collapse of their confidence in God. The writer faced the twofold task, first, of animating the exiles so they would not abandon hope in the God of their ancestors and, second, interpreting their tragic circumstances. The idea that misfortune is a penalty for sin takes one just so far. There comes a point when the suffering undergone becomes terribly disproportionate to the evil committed. Under these historical pressures, then, the writer develops the notion of a servant—a small group of God's faithful ones—whose suffering mysteriously leads to the salvation of the many. Once again a biblical writer was attempting to make sense of the people's misfortune. The solution was ingenious.

Experientially, all of us can relate to the idea that what we are called upon to endure individually (say, as parents raising a family) in the end bears fruit for the next generation. On the social level we have examples of how the suffering of a minority (say, for racial or ethnic reasons) bears fruit both for the wider group and for society as a whole. Why God should have arranged things this way is, of course, not directly addressed; perhaps the speculative issue does not have to be considered. Nevertheless, to invoke the category of divine Wisdom in order account for unmerited suffering without specifying the logic of that Wisdom (insofar as one can) would be to dodge the issue. From a theological perspective the logic has to be revealed to us, for human reason on its own will never discover it (1 Cor 1:18-25).

Still another instance of an effort to find some meaning in suffering is apocalyptic literature.[5] In this literary genre the conflict and alienation that engulf God's righteous ones are accounted for in terms of cosmic powers battling one another; the disasters that befall God's people are the historical reflection of this combat. Why reality should have been so constructed that the powers of good and evil are forced to slide past one another like tectonic plates, generating enormous heat and causing tidal waves and earthquakes, is once again left unanswered. In other words, the sources of evil are portrayed in mythological categories; evil is not accounted for theologically.

The book of Daniel, with its unswerving confidence in God's sovereignty over historical events, was written to encourage fidelity in the midst of persecution. A cross between prophecy and apocalyptic, the book's response to why such suffering occurs basically takes the form of an assertion:

> The kingship and dominion
> > and the greatness of the kingdoms under the whole heaven
> > shall be given to the people of the holy ones of the Most High;
> > their kingdom shall be an everlasting kingdom,
> > and all dominions shall serve and obey them (Dan 7:27).

For the author of this text, the only durable response to persecution has to be holding fast to one's hope in the ultimate victory of divine justice. Those who suffer now will inherit the earth. The descendants of God's righteous ones will be given *in this world* a kingdom governed by righteousness and justice that will never cease.[6]

---

[5] For background on apocalypticism see Murphy, *Religious World of Jesus*, 163–86. Also, the various entries under "Apocalypses and Apocalypticism" in *The Anchor Bible Dictionary* (New York: Doubleday, 1992) 1:279–92.

[6] Murphy points out that the apocalyptic worldview managed to transcend the problem of the suffering of the innocent by insisting upon reward and punishment *after* death, as in Dan 12:1-3 (*Religious World of Jesus,* 164). However attractive the prospect, the idea of future reward and punishment tends to divorce salvation from history and render the world unredeemable. Prophetic writings such as Ezekiel 37 and Isaiah 24–27 are anticipating national restoration when they speak of overcoming death (see John Collins, "Early Jewish Apocalypticism," 1:284). While Jesus certainly believed in life after death (Mark 12:24-27), his message about the coming kingdom of God did not mean the end of the space-time continuum (see N. T. Wright, *The New Testament and the People of God* [Minneapolis: Augsburg Fortress Press, 1992] 280–338). Thus divine salvation retained its this-worldly face.

Turning to Mark

Mark does not address the problem of theodicy directly, although he does fall under the spell of apocalyptic. The Gospel is certainly aware of how painful the human condition can be, for almost every chapter either mentions or alludes to the reality of human suffering. Throughout the story individuals parade before us with their afflictions: unclean spirits, paralysis, blindness, deafness, fever, ailments of various kinds, hunger, poverty. Lepers and lunatics suffer twice, first because of their disease and second because of their enforced isolation. In addition, just beneath the surface of the Gospel text there lies a host of social and political evils that plague God's people. We become aware of their sinister presence, for example, in the story of the beheading of John the Baptist, the disputes Jesus has with religious leaders, the question about paying the imperial tax, the story of the demon-possessed man of Gerasa, the parable of the wicked vineyard workers, and so on. In short, Mark is fully aware of the wretched conditions under which many human beings are forced to live.[7]

In no way can it be said that God wills human suffering, either in our case or in the case of Jesus. This would be at least one of the messages disclosed in the healing activity of Jesus and in his exorcisms. For if it was God's will that human beings should suffer from disease, unclean spirits, paralysis, and so on, then the miracles of Jesus become impossible to comprehend. Yes, the miracles would confirm the teaching of Jesus; yes, they would testify to the presence of the Spirit in his ministry and to divine authorization. But miracles also imply that it is not God's will that life should be so painful for human beings, however salutary the experience of sickness and limitation might eventually prove to be. Miracles are acts of setting free. In other words, God's kingdom when at last it comes will be marked by physical wholeness and the well-being both of individuals and communities. Thus the healings and exorcisms are first and foremost eschatological markers; they announce and portend the arrival of God's rule.[8] They have nothing to do with medicine and everything to do with faith.

Mark has practically nothing to say about the business of coping with illness and the ordinary burdens of human life. Jesus' words about the need

---

[7] A good description of the narrative world created by the evangelist can be found in Waetjen, *Reordering of Power*, 1–26. Also, Riches, *World of Jesus;* Horsley and Silberman, *Message and the Kingdom*, 1–87.

[8] Adela Yarbro Collins writes: "Jesus' proclamation of the kingdom of God and the miracles attributed to him can and ought to be interpreted in the context suggested by the major features of his life, namely Jewish restoration eschatology" (*Anchor Bible Dictionary*, 1:289).

for his followers to deny themselves and take up their cross (8:34) probably ought not be read as if the cross had at that point of the story suddenly
become a metaphor for all of life's difficulties. Jesus' response to human
misery was to devote himself to teaching and healing, not to providing a
spirituality centered upon resignation or abandonment to the will of God.
The pressing issue that Mark needed to address was the death of Jesus. And
his solution was not to explain how God as good could possibly allow the
death of this innocent man but to situate Jesus' suffering and death within
the framework of the divine will or plan for the human race.

It is important for readers of the Gospel to bear in mind that not all
suffering is the same. Bodily suffering is part and parcel of the human
condition, while mental suffering, emotional distress, and psychological
dysfunction strike countless human beings at one time or another. Grief
over the death of loved ones, physical diminishment, the hardship caused
by nature in the form of drought, flooding, earthquakes, or hurricanes are
likewise inescapable.[9] Betrayal, infidelity, and the general weakness of the
human condition will produce their share of pain, while the maturing of
the human spirit itself is accompanied by a form of suffering sensibly described as purifying.

The death of Jesus, however, is not immediately about any of these
things. While we could argue that much of what happens in our lives is the
hard but understandable result of creation's limitations and human finite-
ness, the cross is not about native human limitations or the caprice and un-
reliability of nature. On a purely historical level, the death of Jesus is easy
to understand. He was a prophet and died a martyr for the kingdom, the
victim (as many prophetic men and women are) of destructive social, political, and cultural forces. Mark was keenly aware of that much. He may
not have been a social analyst, but he knew a demon when he saw one.

On the religious level, however, the death of Jesus is fairly difficult to
understand. It forces us to face the question, Why resist evil at all: not evil
in general, but the particular forms of evil that rob men and women of their
very humanity? Indeed, why even struggle against the evil that roots itself
in one's own heart? The challenge is not one of explaining why Jesus (or
anyone else) dedicates himself to assisting others, even to the point of lay-
ing down his life. After all, why we are who we are, and thus why we do
what we do, is truly a mystery of grace and providence. The challenge, rather,

---

[9] Christian eschatology dares to hope that once the work of reconciliation is complete, however, all these "enemies" will also be overcome. Nature itself will be a sign of the
peace that reigns among human beings and between human beings and God. See Rom
8:19-22; 1 Cor 15:26; Rev 21:1.

is to articulate the vision and the hope that grasp a new and different world in front of this one. There is little point in resisting if there is no hope of making a difference. In other words, the death of Jesus and the circumstances that led to it do not make sense theologically outside the horizon of his hope and trust in God. They do not make sense from a human point of view unless his hope at the same time corresponded to the deep aspirations of all those who had symbolically crossed the Jordan with him. In what he hoped for Jesus scarcely stood alone.

Mark writes that Jesus *began* to teach his disciples that the Son of Man must undergo great suffering. The evangelist, of course, had already begun to set the stage for what was going to happen at the end by incorporating so many conflict scenes into his narrative.[10] He informs us as early as chapter 3 that Jesus' adversaries had determined to destroy him. Conflict and resistance as preludes to suffering are not introduced in chapter 8. But what is new here is, first, Mark's connecting the concept of the Son of Man with suffering (rather than with victory and the definitive uprooting of Israel's enemies) and, second, the idea of historical necessity.[11] If the title "Son of Man" here connotes Israel's messianic king, then it becomes easy to understand why some intensive teaching is required.[12] The title had to be reconceived or redefined to fit Jesus, which is exactly what starts to happen in the Emmaus story of Luke 24. In Mark, Jesus begins halfway through the narrative to instruct his followers about a path to their historical salvation different from what had been popularly anticipated, a path that more closely followed the Suffering Servant of Second Isaiah than the politically triumphant Son of Man of Daniel.

The *necessity* involved here is twofold. At the purely historical level there was an inevitability to Jesus' death, just as there was to John's before him—the one who in dying had strikingly prepared Jesus' way—because Jesus had firmly opposed the powers of this world. Jesus collided, apocalyptically speaking, with the rulers of the present age, that is to say, with the forces of injustice arrayed against poor, voiceless human beings, and he would of necessity lose his life.

At a deeper level, however, the evangelist sensed another sort of contest and another type of necessity. Their dimensions were certainly cosmic, signified by the presence of the devil at the outset of the Gospel and

[10] Some of the conflict can be viewed as temptations. See Garrett, *Temptations of Jesus.*

[11] Ignacio Ellacuría speaks of the "historic necessity of Jesus' death" in his essay "The Crucified People," *Mysterium Liberationis,* Ellacuría and Sobrino, 586–88.

[12] Hartman and DiLella, "Daniel," 416–17.

the regular appearance of demons as the story proceeds. For the modern reader demons need to be "unmasked" or explained. In the long run it would not serve the evangelist's interests if his readers were to attribute their historical misfortunes to evil spirits roaming the countryside.[13] The life and death of Jesus may be interpreted as a battle between the forces of good and evil along the lines of apocalyptic literature, but apocalyptic remains simply a literary instrument used to convey a deeper truth.

One can confidently say, therefore, that Jesus was engaged in a genuine contest with human evil and he knew it. For a religious imagination, all the particular manifestations or instances of pride, resentment, greed, ambition, and cover-up eventually coalesce into a single opponent. The innumerable concretizations of wickedness generate a symbol of humanity's long, virulent opposition to the will and Spirit of God, and any individual who is led by the Spirit is likely to feel the presence of that hostility. Even the smallest skirmish with sin's power can bring one face-to-face with the much broader and thicker darkness that wants to inhabit the human heart. It would be stretching beyond the Gospel text to suggest that Jesus had to confront that darkness personally, in his own soul. There is simply no indication in Mark that Jesus underwent such existential combat.[14] Neither the temptation episode, the dispute with Peter when Jesus called him a satan, the scene in the garden, nor the cry from the cross offer any justification for such a claim. In the narrative framework of Mark's Gospel the salvation of Jesus' soul was never in jeopardy.

It appears, therefore, that what God has ordained is a way or process of salvation that conducts people straight through the world and human suffering. There are no detours or shortcuts. Now if the final destiny of the human person is conceived as *individual* union with God and nothing further, then multiple paths to God open up. There would be countless ways to salvation, all of them private, each human being having his or her individual mode of access. But God does not merely create individuals; God creates the human race. God does not only invite us as individuals to lasting union with the divine mystery, but through the Spirit God creates the community of brothers and sisters we call the Church. The salvation of each and every individual human being is bound up with the salvation of the whole human race. As we make our way through the world, therefore, and

---

[13] A striking analysis of what the demons represent can be found in Myers, *Binding the Strong Man,* 190–94.

[14] However interesting to read, works of fiction such as Jim Crace's *Quarantine* (New York: Farrar, Straus & Giroux, 1997) or Nikos Kazantzakis' *The Last Temptation of Christ* (New York: Simon & Schuster, 1960) are not premised upon anything in the Gospels.

encounter there *anyone* who has been crucified (to adopt Christian symbolism), what else can our response be except to remove the nails that fasten them and lift the crucified ones down from their crosses?[15] This is precisely what Jesus was doing during his ministry, long before he reached the place of his own crucifixion. Finding God, together, among the world's crucified ones is the concrete form of our salvation in Christ.

All this should make eminent sense to those of us who are not hanging from a cross. But what about the vast majority of men and women on our planet who find themselves on or falling toward the bottom of their societies, for whom life has proven anything but gracious? What would be the tangible form of their salvation? The way one conceives the salvation of the poor provides the test case for every understanding of Jesus' life and death that theologians may propose. Our thinking has to start with the conviction that God does not want *any* of his children to live and die on a cross. Whatever the social, cultural, political, economic, or religious forces that render God's people captives, prisoners, exiles, or slaves are unequivocally contrary to the will of God.

The first thing to say, then, is that the integral salvation of the poor, not just in the hereafter but now, requires the conversion of those above them. For this reason the preaching of Jesus extended to those in a position to bring about a reordering of society, a redistribution of goods, and a realignment of power.

Second, for Jesus the salvation of the poor would depend upon their full conversion too. The mere fact that people are on the bottom does not immunize them against the identical sinful tendencies that afflict the elites above them. The poor are capable of the same greed, violence, and thirst for revenge as the rest. Anyone who wavers about conceding this point has only to read accounts such as Philip Gourevitch's report on the Rwandan genocide.[16] The seed sown among the poor is going to encounter the same hostile conditions—birds, weeds, rocky soil, exposure—that beset financially established, educated, and politically secure people.

Third, the salvation of the poor requires their discovering in the process of following Jesus a solidarity of hope. Perhaps the most arresting characteristic of apocalyptic writing is its burning conviction that God will

---

[15] The phrase comes from Ignacio Ellacuría. See "The Crucified People," *Mysterium Liberationis,* Ellacuría and Sobrino, 580–603. See also Sobrino, "The Crucified Peoples: Yahweh's Suffering Servant Today," *Principle of Mercy,* 49–57, and chapter 10 of his *Jesus the Liberator.*

[16] Philip Gourevitch, *We wish to inform you that tomorrow we will be killed with our families: Stories from Rwanda* (New York: Farrar Straus & Giroux, 1998).

be victorious over all the enemies of a suffering people. Most of us do not relate easily to the rhetoric of apocalyptic literature, first because of its exotic imagery, and second because our circumstances rarely approach the severe conditions presupposed by this form of writing. If we should lose a job, suffer the death of a loved one, or contract a lethal disease, we are not likely to turn to Mark 13 or the books of Daniel and Revelation for solace. The utter collapse of hope among history's victims, however, would constitute the ultimate confirmation of their expendability. It becomes easy to understand why apocalyptic writing would find a welcome audience among them.

Each of these elements can be readily found in Mark. Whether or not the original addressees of the Gospel were poor is hard to say. Given the fact that the initial followers of Jesus are remembered as having left everything (10:28), and given Jesus' instruction to the rich man about selling his goods (10:21), we would have to assume that Mark intended for the members of his audience who had some resources to hear Jesus' message directed to them. And in view of the fact that Jesus specified that the man should give the proceeds to the poor and not, say, to his favorite municipal or religious project, we probably should conclude that the poor were regularly on Jesus' mind. The directive about giving to the poor was not merely a pious suggestion but an indication of how Jesus' own soul stood in solidarity with those who barely managed to scrape by. For the poor the generosity of the wealthy could spell the difference between life and death, a matter of elementary salvation.

That the poor themselves stood in need of conversion accounts for why Jesus did so much preaching and teaching among them. Not only were they with great frequency the beneficiaries of Jesus' miracles, but they also responded to his call to deeper faith. Mark does not tell us so explicitly, but there must have been large numbers of poor people among those who followed Jesus. In Mark 8:1, for instance, we hear of "a great crowd without anything to eat." The large number that had earlier run to meet Jesus and his disciples in a deserted place were surely hungry by the day's end. But it is plausible to think that among them there must have been many who had plenty of time on their hands because they had no work. Those with means would most likely have brought along some food; the fact that so many needed to be fed suggests not absentmindedness but a basic lack of necessities. In other words, poverty was almost certainly one of the conditions that brought men and women to listen to Jesus. Jesus' spending time with the poor and instructing them would have constituted another tangible form of their salvation. Those who teach save us from ignorance and its consequences, those who give instruction about the way of the Spirit save us from the crippling effects of our own moral weakness.

Jesus does not expressly discourse on hope in Mark's Gospel, but hope is tightly woven into the fabric of the story; otherwise, why introduce the story as *good* news? The parable of the sower concludes: "Other seed fell into good soil and brought forth grain, *growing up and increasing and yielding* thirty and sixty and a hundredfold" (4:8). The confident climax of the parable expresses Jesus' joyous conviction about the power of the seed to bear great fruit despite formidable odds. There really is good, fertile land in the human world; there truly are hearts and minds ready to receive the word that he preaches.

Now while the response to Jesus' preaching (however humble and small the numbers) provided a solid confirmation for his own hope, the theme of his preaching—the kingdom of God—was itself essentially a hope metaphor. God's rule on earth as the reign of justice and righteousness was at hand. All good things, therefore, were suddenly possible. Not only were the deepest aspirations of Israel's prophets about to be realized, the incessant pleas of the psalmist were also about to be answered. The Gospel story lacks coherence unless we latch on to the intensity of Jesus' faith in the God of his ancestors. If Israel's God had delivered his people from slavery, captivity, and exile in the past, then that God certainly could *and would* do the same again. The fact that Jesus' ministry abruptly ended in a week that commemorated Israel's deliverance from the dominion of a foreign sovereign must alert us to the context of intense longing and heightened awareness of divine possibility in which Jesus spent his final days.

There would have been no miracles during his ministry if Jesus had not believed in their possibility as firmly, say, as the nameless woman whose faith he commended (Mark 5:34). Similarly, there would have been no raising from the dead at the end of the story unless Jesus firmly believed that God could do literally what had been hinted at figuratively in Ezekiel's great vision of the valley of the bones (Ezek 37). The escalating tension between Jesus and his adversaries in Jerusalem in the days leading up to his arrest did not represent an attempt on his part to bring about his own destruction. It is far more plausible to think that Jesus was counting on divine vindication and deliverance after his prophetic denunciation of the Temple and religious elites. As far as Mark is concerned, Jesus was a person of hope, and "kingdom of God" was hope's primary metaphor. And again, as far as Mark is concerned, Jesus believed that he had been called to play an indispensable role in the process of that metaphor's becoming reality.

Why would Mark have characterized the story of Jesus as *good* news, unless its fundamental message was about victory? For Jesus the good news was that God's kingdom was about to be realized; obstacles may delay but they cannot prevent its arrival. For Mark the good news was that in Jesus risen divine mystery was clearly present and active within the human world. And if God is among us through the Spirit of the risen Jesus, then we have every reason to trust that salvation will be realized, however mysteriously and imperceptibly the process unfolds in human history. Mark does not state things quite this way, of course. But Jesus seems to have been Mark's introduction to the reality of God: a God who is eminently real and whose reality can penetrate and structure the human world afresh each day. Thus as Mark narrates the story the reader keeps perceiving and hearing the mystery of God even though the main figure in the Gospel is Jesus.

One often hears it said, particularly among German theologians, that Christian theology could never be the same after the Holocaust. That horrifying episode challenged the Christian theological tradition not only for the way it had contributed to a centuries-long anti-Semitism but also for not taking with sufficient seriousness the historical power-lessness of God.[17]

In all fairness, however, the point about the Holocaust should be extended to include every instance of genocide. Operating under the influence of racial, cultural, and even religious stereotypes, Christian theology has failed other peoples besides the Jews. One thinks of the tragic history of Native Americans, African Americans, and the indigenous peoples of South America. One thinks too of other appalling twentieth-century genocides, such as those in Cambodia and Rwanda, that represent failures not of theology but of humanity itself. Indeed, Christian theology can never be the same after any of these episodes. In fact, perhaps one should say that theology could never be the same after the crucifixion of Jesus! The failure to view that moment in its fullest historical context has cost us dearly. By elevating the death of Jesus to the transcendental level as the once-for-all event of humanity's redemption from sin, Christian theology actually obscured and softened its scandalous nature. Theology loosened the connectedness of Jesus' crucifixion with the historical fortunes of an oppressed people and thereby with victims everywhere.

---

[17] This is particularly notable in the work of Jürgen Moltmann, Dorothee Sölle, and Johann Baptist Metz. See Jürgen Moltmann, ed., *How I Have Changed: Reflections on Thirty Years of Theology* (Harrisburg: Trinity Press International, 1997).

For Mark, however, there was never a theology of God (if we might speak this way) without the cross. He could not have thought about God and the death of Jesus independently of each other. What God ordained and what God had revealed about the divine mystery itself in the dying and rising of Jesus were conceptually related. Or to express the idea a bit differently, the crucifixion of Jesus as one page from the long history of human oppression tells us something important about the "character" of the God we believe in. This will prove critically significant for any person who prays "Not what I want, but what you want" or "Your will be done, on earth as it is in heaven." To encounter the God whose Son has been crucified is to discover *in that God* the powerlessness of poor, oppressed human beings, yet without losing one's hope that death will simply never have the last word in the story of the human race.

In the end, then, the will of God is a matter of hope. The will of God is not an imposition. It is, rather, a way of confessing our belief that we live from day to day in the presence of God and that we want nothing more than to respond to God's presence with every ounce of moral and spiritual energy at our disposal. The logic of what God is doing among us frequently escapes us, however. That the great project of the kingdom of God should begin among the world's rejected ones is a mystery. That those who follow Jesus would consider themselves blessed to be associated with the "stones rejected by the builders" may be even more mysterious. And this is the theme of the next chapter.

5

A Kingdom of Throwaways

Have you not read this scripture:
  "The stone that the builders rejected
    has become the cornerstone;
  this was the Lord's doing,
    and it is amazing in our eyes"? (Mark 12:10-11).

The organizing power of this passage could easily have occurred to anyone who had been living for two years next to a block-long construction site. A forty-foot dumpster fills up twice, sometimes three times, a week with discarded building materials that someone with a bit of ingenuity could have reclaimed, perhaps even enough to build a suitable home. A skilled carpenter can spot usefulness where the rest of us might see only refuse for a landfill. So too for any of the other tradesmen; perhaps too for their children. Jesus was a carpenter, says Mark (6:3); the son of a carpenter, says Matthew (13:55). In any case, people who labor with their hands usually become pretty adept at seeing things with a great deal of resourcefulness.

The text that Jesus quoted from Psalm 118 is a construction metaphor turned into an expression of popular wisdom. The point of the proverb is to make us aware that what appears insignificant and useless in human eyes often contains enormous potential in the eyes of God, the master-builder. While the early Church regarded the rejection of Jesus by the Jerusalem establishment as the supreme exemplification of this proverb, nothing prevents us from detecting here an insight into the way Jesus conceived his mission to Israel and Mark's own grasp of the divine logic at work in the process of human salvation, a logic Paul had forcefully articulated in 1 Cor 1:18-31. As a matter of fact, in order to understand the application of the proverb to Jesus' life one first has to appreciate its connection with Jesus' commitment to his people.

Who Are the Rejected Ones?

Mark makes no express mention of Jesus' instructing his disciples to seek out the "lost sheep of the house of Israel" the way Matthew does (Matt 10:6; 15:24; Luke 19:10), but a clear focus on the "lost" as the object of Jesus' attention is as characteristic of Mark's story as it is of the other Synoptics. The men and women who regularly commanded Jesus' attention call to mind the countless human beings throughout history whose lives would be considered expendable and of no account by those who love to make their authority felt and behave as tyrants (10:42).

Following the lead of Eduard Schweizer, who had described Jesus as someone who "fits no formula,"[1] Hans Küng wrote over twenty years ago:

> Jesus apparently cannot be fitted in anywhere: neither with the rulers nor with the rebels, neither with the moralizers nor with the silent ascetics. He turns out to be provocative, both to right and to left. Backed by no party, challenging on all sides: "The man who fits no formula." He is neither a philosopher nor a politician, neither a priest nor a social reformer. Is he a genius, a hero, a saint? Or a religious reformer? But is he not more radical than someone who tries to re-form, reshape things? Is he a prophet? But is a "last" prophet, who cannot be surpassed, a prophet at all? . . . He is on a different plane: apparently closer than the priests to God, freer than the ascetics in regard to the world, more moral than the moralists, more revolutionary than the revolutionaries.[2]

Over the last few decades theologians seem to have shifted from existentialist to social categories in their efforts to understand Jesus: not Jesus as the unsurpassably authentic individual who has achieved complete liberty of spirit and holiness but Jesus ever in relationship to his people. Writers today are more likely to point out how Jesus could have been perceived as a revolutionary because he was a "boundary breaker."[3]

[1] Schweizer, *Jesus*, 13–51.
[2] Küng, *On Being a Christian*, 212. Küng also used the category of solidarity to highlight an important feature of Jesus' ministry (pp. 265–77), but I think he construed the category along existentialist lines instead of seeing it as a revelation and expression of the divine preferential option for the poor. Solidarity is more than personal virtue; it is being human in such a way that the people of God dwell within us. Thus solidarity always entails justice and a "politics of relationality" (see Sturm, *Solidarity and Suffering*, 1–16).
[3] Dunn, *Jesus' Call to Discipleship*, 62–91. Along similar lines, Borg explains Jesus' challenge to the purity system of his day. See his *Jesus in Contemporary Scholarship*, 107–12.

The intention behind this phrase is not to suggest that Jesus was by disposition or on principle opposed to laws and customs; Jesus, after all, did direct the leper to make the offering Moses had required (1:44); he faithfully attended synagogue services; and presumably not just once, he celebrated Passover and the festival of Unleavened Bread in Jerusalem (14:1). The description of boundary breaker means, rather, that for Jesus human beings in need of salvation always take precedence over artificial lines created by etiquette, social class, religious authority (even the highest human expression of religious authority in the person of Moses), family ties, tradition, culture, or national identity and being descended from Abraham. When Jesus declared "so the Son of Man is lord *even* of the sabbath" (2:28), he was referring not only to the regulations governing Sabbath observance but indirectly to all human conventions.[4] And his use of the title "Son of Man" was certainly not meant to exclude everyone else. If that had been the case, then his disciples then and now would have had less freedom of movement than Jesus himself; they would have been imprisoned by the letter of the Law.[5] In short, whether under the title Son of Man or Son of God, Jesus' inner "achievement" (if one may speak this way) was his complete solidarity with others. Out of that solidarity he knew that if human misery did not pause on the Sabbath then neither could he, and neither could his followers.

Disputes over the proper way to observe the Sabbath are probably the most identifiable examples of boundary breaking in the Gospel, but for most readers the reason for those disputes ("Look, why are they doing what is not lawful on the sabbath?" [2:24]) hardly sounds all that consequential. "So what," we ask, "if someone plucks grain—or heals—on a holy day?" Far more disconcerting to his adversaries (and comprehensible for us) is the fact that Jesus touched the "unclean," that is, he consorted with those who had incurred ritual defilement because of their physical

---

[4] J. A. Soggin notes that according to rabbinic teaching danger to life allowed for suspending Sabbath regulations but that rabbinic teaching did not consider illness and physical impairment sufficient justification for healing. See *Oxford Companion to the Bible,* 665. But from the perspective of the individual in need of healing, life was constantly being jeopardized by hunger, alienation, and even despair—a perspective Jesus readily understood. That may explain Jesus' words in Mark 3:4 about saving life or killing on the Sabbath. In peasant society a withered hand could turn into a matter of life and death. Regarding the Sabbath controversies see Borg, *Conflict, Holiness, and Politics,* 156–73.

[5] Regarding the title "Son of Man," see Hooker, *Gospel According to Saint Mark,* 88–93. Caird writes: "The Son of Man is an open-ended term which includes all who are prepared to respond to the preaching of the Gospel of the Kingdom, who share with Jesus the demands the Kingdom is making on the Israel of the new age" (*New Testament Theology,* 380).

condition, their occupation, their moral state, their inability or unwilling-ness to follow the Law's requirements as conscientiously as the Pharisees. Mark nowhere hints that Jesus touched these "unclean" people purely in order to annoy the Pharisees; that would have amounted to using the poor for the sake of a religious debate. Lying beneath the surface of the two con-troversies over Sabbath observance at the beginning of the Gospel story was Jesus' firm rejection of the view that national identity could be estab-lished and the nation's survival could be guaranteed through exacting ob-servance of the Mosaic Law. By the end of the Gospel story this rejection would turn into outright condemnation of the Temple itself, the religious establishment that had created and maintained its institutional form, and all that the Temple had come to represent in terms of Israel's place in God's plan. Jesus critiqued and utterly rejected the "politics of holiness" practiced by the religious elites.[6] As N. T. Wright points out:

> All the evidence suggests that at least the majority of Pharisees . . . had as their main aim that which purity symbolized: the political struggle to main-tain Jewish identity and to realize the dream of national liberation. . . . Purity (in its very different manifestations such as food laws, handwashing, and so on) was not . . . an end in itself, if indeed it was ever really that. It was the symbol, all the more important for a people who perceived them-selves under threat, of national identity and national liberation.[7]

But what merits our attention most are the particular circumstances from which human beings needed to be delivered, because these account for why Jesus went about crossing social and religious boundaries and challenging the religious establishment in the first place. Most of the fig-ures who populate the narrative world of the Gospel would not have had to think twice about what they wanted to be saved from. As we have seen, the woman with the flow of blood whose story is told in chapter 5 and the father with the epileptic child in chapter 9 knew exactly what they wanted *from God*. Their coming to Jesus was not a blind, desperate im-pulse but a vivid expression of what they had been constantly begging from God. Isolation or separation from community, the inability to work because of disease or physical impairment, the hunger that was conse-quent to being landless or unemployed, the oppressive nature of scribal teaching and the burden of an ideal of holiness that effectively disenfran-chised the majority of people, demons (and all they represented), crip-

---

[6] For more discussion of this expression see Marcus J. Borg, *Jesus: A New Vision*, 86–93; and also Borg, *Conflict, Holiness, and Politics*, 66–155.

[7] Wright, *Jesus and the Victory of God*, 378–79.

pling taxation and tithing: these were the things that sentenced men and women to lifelong suffering.[8]

And what about the men and women themselves? Their distinctiveness and individuality became invisible, concealed behind the economic and political conditions that robbed them of any memorable identity and enclosed them in the mass graves of the socially dead. Indeed, the peasants were needed to supply the labor that generated the products that fed the empire. Nevertheless, many of the characters who appear in the Gospel would have been adjudged by the elites as *desechados,* the expendable ones, those with no legal or social standing. That what the builders have rejected should become the cornerstone of God's own dwelling place was an idea that had relevance to Jesus' mission long before he arrived in Jerusalem. As a Jewish prophet he would have known that the kingdom could only be a work of God, not of human hands. What more astonishing way to highlight that truth for all time than to form the people of God anew, calling to discipleship the faceless ones, healing their broken lives, and erecting a lasting temple on the basis of sinners?

That Jesus, following a pattern set by John the Baptist, called the people of Galilee to repentance is quite certain. To claim further that, morally speaking, the Galileans were indeed sinners might be simply stating the obvious and missing the real point, however. All are sinners; all need to keep turning toward God, even the righteous. Thus in calling sinners to repentance Jesus was hardly engaging in anything revolutionary; repentance was central to Jewish religious practice and the essence of every prophetic summons. The novelty consisted in Jesus' message that the kingdom of God was *of* and *for* sinners, and that anyone who thought otherwise had gotten Israel's history and calling all wrong. That repentance was a condition for entering the kingdom goes without saying. But to suggest that the kingdom could be built with the sort of men and women with whom Jesus associated must have been tantamount to blasphemy if not downright lunacy (Mark 3:21-22).

---

[8] Anthony J. Saldarini writes: "Jesus' popularity with the crowds, their eagerness to hear him and experience his power, and the opposition of the authorities all fit within the context of Galilean Jews who had been conquered by Rome, were sternly ruled by a Jewish proxy of Rome, and suffered heavy taxes with no avenue of appeal or control over their own society." See Howard Clark Kee and others, *The Cambridge Companion to the Bible,* 399. To grasp the enormous pressure under which the people of the land lived, therefore, some knowledge of the tax system in the time of Jesus is indispensable. See Horsley, *Galilee: History, Politics, People,* 137–44, 216–21. On the double taxation from temple and empire, see Borg, *Conflict, Holiness, and Politics,* 44–49.

The Story Is Not (Directly) About Us

Given our own cultural, economic, and social situation within a wealthy democracy at the close of the twentieth century, it may be nearly impossible for us to imagine ourselves realistically in the position of first-century Galilean peasants. For sound reasons none of us wants to be poor and oppressed, and we are far too removed from the narrative world of the evangelist to relate meaningfully to the desperation and aspirations of its people. If God in Jesus, then, was building a new Israel with the stones rejected by the official planners and craftsmen, where does that leave us? We are educated, financially secure, politically free men and women. One could, of course, allegorize the physical conditions of the Gospel's poor and declare that all human beings are poor and oppressed in some way or other; but such maneuvering proves expensive. Identifying ourselves in this literal way with the nameless and faceless human beings who gathered around Jesus prevents us from grasping an important message in the Gospel story, and that misstep in interpretation could mortgage our salvation.

We are *not* the man with a withered arm, the demon-possessed wretch of Gerasa, the kneeling leper, the hemorrhaging woman, or the paralytic; we are not even the disciples whose hunger led them to pluck grain on the Sabbath. Indeed, we need to relate to all these texts; but we can never do so fruitfully by pretending to be something other than we are. As we use our imaginations to create the harsh everyday world in which those figures lived, their brief appearances evoke an awareness in the reader of whole groups and classes of people and their bleak histories. But they are not us, and we shall never be them. There are, of course, many impoverished Christians in the world; and they could legitimately and effortlessly substitute themselves for any one of the Gospel characters we were just recalling. Once again, however, that is not something we can do.

Several cautions may be in order here. First, Mark does not romanticize the physical or spiritual conditions of the poor, and neither should we. The paralytic of chapter 2 is hardly depicted as the classic sinner type. He is not a repentant David. Nothing suggests that he has the disposition of the woman whose tears bathed Jesus' feet. He is not a tax collector grown fat and rich off his countrymen, like Zacchaeus. Nevertheless, Mark allows that the paralytic is really a sinner (otherwise the story falls apart). The poor, even the sick poor, are susceptible to the same resentment, selfishness, quarrelsomeness, and so forth, as everybody else. In some ways, in fact, poverty exacerbates human sinfulness because sometimes it seems to give people permission to do evil things out of a perverse sense of justice. Life, one rationalizes, has been unfair, and thus one's evil deeds are simply repaying life in the same coin. We know nothing, of course, of the paralytic's inner state except that he and his companions had enough faith in Jesus to approach him for a cure. We are guessing, however, that the picture was more complex both because paralysis and poverty are never things of beauty and because in no life is the journey to holiness straight and smooth.

Second, that the poor are genuinely capable of dramatic conversions is central to Jesus' purpose and the presupposition of his preaching. They, far more often than members of the social and religious elites, were able to respond to the message of the kingdom as Jesus preached it.[9] The episode of the nameless rich man in chapter 10 stands out because that individual was both wealthy and devout and had apparently been watching and observing Jesus for some time. In the end, however, the seed sown in his heart had fallen among thorns. He was unable to respond to Jesus' invitation with the spontaneity of a blind beggar like Bartimaeus, whose name the tradition could not forget. The rich man was a good person, and Jesus loved him; but he was incapable of that solidarity—of selling off the privilege that his family name had bestowed on him and crossing over into the world of the throwaways—which would have given him the one thing he lacked.[10] What exactly it was that rendered the poor open to Jesus' message might have been, for Mark, fairly easy to figure out. What they needed from God was so obvious and what they could do for themselves was so limited that they were the perfect audience for a message about salvation.

Third, as far as Mark was concerned the poor had in large measure responded with enthusiasm to Jesus' message; or to be more precise, of those who had followed Jesus the vast majority were probably poor. Hence the large, favorably disposed crowds that keep appearing practically to the end of the story (2:2, 13; 3:7, 20, 32; 4:1, 36; 5:21, 24; 6:34; 7:14; 8:1, 34; 10:1, 46; 11:18; 12:12, 37). When Mark informs us from time to time that Jesus explained everything privately to his disciples, he does

---

[9] For our purposes it is sufficient to differentiate just two social classes, the ruling elites and the poor, since the majority of Jesus' followers were drawn from those on the bottom of the social pyramid. The actual situation, however, was a bit more complex. See Waetjen, *Reordering of Power*, 5–16.

[10] "The demand to sell what one possesses, if taken literally, is the demand to part with what was the dearest of all possible possessions to a Mediterranean: the family home and land." See Malina and Rohrbaugh, *Social-Science Commentary*, 244. The rich man found the cost of solidarity too high.

not intend to exclude the crowds so much as to *include* the listeners (which would be us).[11]

Thus if Jesus' preaching had failed to move the poor to open themselves to the kingdom of God, if there had been no enduring faith among them, then it would have been extremely difficult for those to whom Mark addressed his Gospel to relate to the story. The Gospel story "works" only to the degree that those who hear or read it locate their own stories within it. Mark's sense of the kind of people who historically had followed Jesus and to whom Jesus felt himself sent was surely affected by the composition of the Christian communities Mark knew some forty or fifty years later.[12] The only group of peasants to reject Jesus outright, it seems, were the villagers of Nazareth. The people of Gerasa did not reject Jesus; they just feared the consequences of his presence. The hostile crowd that arrived in the garden to arrest Jesus was composed of people loyal to Jesus' enemies; but that was a different case.

We ought to add that the idea of Jesus' positive reception by the poor exists in some tension with Mark's conviction that Jesus' mission to Israel had actually failed. Israel did not convert as Jesus had envisioned. The evangelist never attempts to resolve this tension in his narrative, and so it appears that both details are true: the poor followed Jesus; *and* Israel, at least at the corporate level, rejected its Messiah. Perhaps the best way to clarify matters is to suggest another explanation for the mission's failure. It is possible that Jesus had expected God to intervene *and God failed to*

[11] For instance: "When he was alone, *those who were around him* along with the twelve asked him about the parables" (4:10). When Mark has Jesus say, "To you has been given the secret . . . but for those outside, everything comes in parables" (4:11), Mark is not suggesting that the crowds who eagerly followed Jesus had been excluded from the kingdom of God. The expression "those outside" is a technical phrase to designate men and women without faith in his words. Later, in 4:33-34, the idea may be slightly different. If Jesus was an effective teacher, then people must have learned from him; if he had spoken to peasants in riddles, however, he could have been received as a popular entertainer but not as a teacher or a prophet. Thus Mark's point in 4:33-34 must be to stress the instruction that Jesus gave to his followers (and continues to impart to us) rather than to imply that the crowds who sought him were not equally worthy of such close attention.

[12] In his article "Windows and Mirrors," 1-26, Donahue suggests a Roman setting: "Through Mark's Gospel, we may see, as through a glass darkly, the trials and hopes of the Roman church in the early seventies of our era" (p. 26). Arguing for Roman-occupied Syria, Waetjen writes: "[It] seems probable that the original addressees of the Gospel were village folk residing in a rural territory that, as the Latinisms suggest, was occupied by Roman legions and exploited by Roman business entrepreneurs and traders . . . an area in which Greeks and Jews lived side by side" (*Reordering of Power,* 13–14). For our purposes, however, the more pressing issue is how the Gospel addresses us.

do so. We touched on this in the last chapter and shall come back to it later. There remains, however, one other possibility. Israel's failure to listen to Jesus might have been part of the divine mystery or logic through which the God of Israel would be revealed to be the God of the nations. Rejection by Israel thus led to the creation of the Church. While it looks as if Mark (along with many others) inclined to this last possibility, his narrative certainly invites serious consideration of the idea that perhaps God had failed. If Jesus had actually been counting on God, the fact is that there was going to be no burning bush, no parting of the seas, no thunder and fire from the sky. The throwaways followed him, but in the end what could he offer them that would make a profound difference in their lives? There was no guarantee that the multiplication of loaves would be repeated every day.

Going Beyond Jesus

How then does Mark engage us when he presents Jesus as assembling the throwaways of society for the new Israel? The most obvious way is that we have to ask ourselves whether we are inside or outside Jesus' circle. Next we have to reflect on whether or not we want to live in the company of those whom societies around the world disesteem and reject. And finally we have to ask whether a project so important as the kingdom of God (which is, after all, only a biblical metaphor for prompting us to imagine a world re-created along the lines of justice and peace) could in fact be ushered in without our energy, faith, zeal, and compassion. That the kingdom can only be God's gift goes without saying. To urge that it will come in spite of us would be both irresponsible and contrary to long historical experience. Mark knew that the historical Israel had refused Jesus' message. But the vineyard would not be abandoned; it would be given to others (12:9). The divine plan may be resisted, but it cannot be frustrated.

Inside or outside? The most honest answer is that we are inside, certainly by baptismal commitment and through a lifelong ambition to be in every respect faithfully Christian. That we fail in our discipleship, frequently and sometimes even seriously, should never lead us to distrust the integrity of our desire to do all that God asks of us. In this regard Mark has provided us a singular help in portraying Peter as the one who denied Jesus, not to mention his showcasing the other disciples in all their human deficiencies. The truth is that we are already inside Jesus' circle, every bit as much as the men and women who filled the room in Mark 2:2, and even more poignantly in Mark 3:32, where the biological family was left standing outside.

Alongside the throwaways? This question may be harder to answer because it is asking us to gauge the breadth and depth of our solidarity with the world's poor. And that calls for an examination not of one's conscience (since all of us seek to do what is right) but of one's loyalties, affections, and politics. I do not believe that God calls any of us to material poverty and its effects, but God does call those who have been materially blessed to walk alongside those who are deprived, exploited, neglected, and impoverished.[13] Accompanying the throwaways, however, is going to spell a profound change in the way we live, whether the poor dwell next door, across the city, or in another part of the world. To feel the press of the crowds around Jesus is to feel in oneself the weight of their tortured, burdened, and anxious lives together with their intense longing for deliverance. To feel the press of the world's poor is to feel the weight of the one who, though rich, became poor for our sake (2 Cor 8:9). Mark does not state this in so many words, but how could his readers avoid reaching such a conclusion, given the fact that Jesus is constantly surrounded by crowds? When Mark's readers imaginatively insert themselves into a Gospel scene, who realistically are the other people standing or sitting around?

With us or without us? Jesus was undoubtedly counting on a divine response to human need. The miracles seemed to confirm that not only was God on Jesus' side but that God was about to do even greater things for the salvation of his people. Still, the very fact that Jesus proclaimed a message indicates that he was anticipating a human response and that nothing could happen in Israel unless the nation as a whole responded. It appears that for Jesus the failure of the leadership would lead to a disastrous outcome for the nation as a whole: "Do you see these great buildings? Not one stone will be left here upon another; all will be thrown down" (13:2). Whether or not Jesus actually foresaw the events of the years 66–70 does not really matter here. What is important is that for Jesus the fate of the nation had been determined by the misbehavior of its central institution. This implies that the poor, however converted they are and however much loved by God, are powerless, politically speaking, to change the course of history. One can also draw three conclusions. First, a peasant revolt against

[13] The poverty of vowed religious is no exception to this general rule but its exemplification. The poverty of religious life is a poverty arising from solidarity, not a world-denying asceticism. Its Gospel foundation is the example of Jesus as the one who became poor in order to accompany human beings (following the insight of Paul in 2 Cor 8:9). See William Reiser, *Religious Life Today: Re-Thinking a Promise* (Los Angeles: Rogate Publications, 1994) 56–57; also, "Reformulating the Religious Vows," *Review for Religious* 54:4 (1995) 594–99.

the economic and political power structures of the day would have been doomed from the start. Second, Jesus was aware of that fact. The parable of the wicked tenants concludes with the crushing of the workers' revolt: "He will come and destroy the tenants and give the vineyard to others" (12:9). Jesus was a realist. And finally, while the conversion of the individual is absolutely essential to the arrival of the kingdom, so long as conversion does not spread to many others and reach a critical mass the structures of the social world that form and define us will remain unaffected.[14]

In purely human terms, therefore, there is no escaping the dynamics of historical process, with its attendant social, political, economic, and cultural components. The coming of the kingdom is not going to happen apart from historical process. Mighty interventions from heaven have no place on the horizons of our imagination. In this regard we have to go beyond Jesus and the apocalyptic beliefs that shaped his worldview.

But historical process means that, because of the great privilege and resources entrusted to us, we have roles to play in bringing about the redeemed world and the truly humanizing society for which we pray whenever we earnestly say, "Thy kingdom come, thy will be done." Thus we need to go beyond Jesus in a second regard. The kingdom of throwaways requires the goodwill and cooperation of disciples of privilege, like us. To be sure, Mark has supplied us, particularly in chapters 8 through 10, with a criterion for critiquing ourselves, namely, the values Jesus tried to impress upon his followers: service, humility, renunciation, compassion. How, the Gospel queries us, was our position of privilege reached? How is it maintained? Does the power and security enjoyed by some necessitate the virtual enslaving and impoverishing of countless others?

At any rate, the throwaways are not going to escape their situation unless our hearts are moved so that we want to accompany them in a lasting, effective solidarity. It would not be off the mark to suggest that if there had been a middle class at the time of Jesus on the scale of what has

---

[14] An illustration might help. Whenever a single individual in our society realizes the damaging nature of the consumerist ethos that surrounds us and determines to live counterculturally for the spirit, there is real conversion. Unless many share that experience, however, one's children will have to face a very conflictual world. In other words, we cannot live gospel values in a vacuum. It is not enough for one person to change; all must do so. And when a sufficiently large number of men and women come to share the same viewpoint, then they will have to face the global structures and forces that reinforce materialism, individualism, and so forth. Thus in the Gospel story Jesus had great success with individuals, but those conversions did not immediately coalesce into a spiritual force that could take on the false values of the empire.

emerged in modern industrial states, then the Gospel story would have been shaped very differently. Jesus would have been addressing us directly.

The fact that Jesus belonged to the rural poor is both historically and theologically significant. We ought not assume, however, that the Gospel's preference for the poor creates such a rigid pattern that unless we become exactly like those on the bottom we shall not be saved. The reality may be much more subtle. The poor will not be saved in any meaningful way without us, and we will not be saved in any lasting way without them. I am not referring to eternal reward and punishment but to the perfection and liberation of our common humanity here and now. Indeed, sometimes camels slip through the eye of a needle; sometimes the harvest yields thirty, sixty, even a hundredfold. Sometimes, Mark has assured us, extraordinary reversals take place. We need the reminder, lest the categories from which we judge others become rigid.

Jesus—The Quintessential Throwaway

For Mark, Jesus was the stone rejected by the builders first and foremost. Our mind's ability to perceive other human beings as throwaways is nurtured and stretched by our familiarity with the story of Jesus. The Gospel text continues, "This was the Lord's doing, and it is amazing in our eyes," following Psalm 118:23. The verses of the psalm appear to commemorate an actual instance of deliverance from distress, but their meaning can be extended to include Israel itself, least among the nations yet chosen by God to be the foundation stone or capstone of a living temple. It is important to reflect on the image. A stone does not become the cornerstone until it is cemented in place; its "identity" or function is relational. If Jesus, therefore, is the stone that has been rejected because his politics did not conform to those of the religious leadership, then the rejection of Jesus amounted to the rejection of the poor themselves as the principal bearers of the divine promise and the principal historical markers of divine election. That the new community should still be built in spite of the incompetence of the original builders is nothing short of miraculous. Hence the cry of the faithful: "By the LORD has this been done; / it is wonderful in our eyes."[15]

Applied to Jesus, this text acquires an altogether new meaning in light of the resurrection, as Luke will make clear (Acts 4:10-11). Mark certainly understood the deeper application, too. But if the resurrection revealed how God had inserted Jesus into the central position within the new temple—

---

[15] Translation of the Psalms from The New American Bible (1991).

the new Israel—it had also revealed that the poor—the throwaways—were themselves the cornerstone of the new people of God. Jesus and the people with whom he lived and died in solidarity could not be pulled apart. Being capstone or foundation stone is equally their position, and it will never be taken away from them, since God in Jesus had "embodied" them. Perhaps this revelation provides the key for understanding one of the charges against Jesus: "We heard him say, 'I will destroy this temple that is made with hands, and in three days I will build another, not made with hands'" (14:58).

In the Markan text, Jesus could not have meant an overnight construction project, he was not referring symbolically to his own body (as in John 2:19-21), and he would not have been thinking of his resurrection as a temple. If there was any basis to the accusation, it appears likely that Jesus had scandalized the leadership by suggesting that the throwaways were holy enough to house the presence of God. The living temple would be a work of the Spirit, and it would be "wonderful in our eyes."

Jesus, of course, was not rejected by the builders—by the religious and political leadership—without reason. While there are numerous controversies related throughout the Gospel, perhaps none illustrates better why Jesus was so bitterly disliked (and thereby viewed as expendable) than the story about paying Caesar's tax. This is the scene we shall next consider.

6

Paying the Emperor's Tax

Then the scribe said to him, "You are right, Teacher; you have truly said that 'he is one, and besides him there is no other'" (Mark 12:32).

Some commentators regard Jesus' prophetic, symbolic cleansing action in the Temple as the proximate and compelling reason for his arrest and execution. The scene serves as a parable in action. In a gesture worthy of Jeremiah or Hosea, Jesus was announcing the end of the Temple and what it had come to represent, and his was not the first prophetic voice to have done so. Jesus was not merely delivering a negative message about the Temple's failure, however. We have just seen that Jesus had a clear vision of the living temple that would replace the old.[1]

In terms of its ramifications for the Gospel's readers and hearers through the ages, however, the story of the imperial tax seems much more subversive than the dramatic cleansing scene. The Temple disappeared from history, but the legacy of the empire did not.[2] The story of the imperial coin forces upon its viewers and listeners the matter of absolute trust in a very unsettling way.

Morna Hooker explains why this particular tax was so neuralgic:

The story centres on the payment of . . . a tax imposed on the population of Judea, Samaria and Idumaea in A.D. 6, when these districts became a Roman province under the rule of a procurator. The imposition of the tax,

[1] For a discussion of the significance of the cleansing scene, see Wright, *Jesus and the Victory of God*, 413–28.

[2] It would be incorrect to counter that the church took the place of the Temple. Temple refers to a building; church does not. While both terms are loaded with symbolism, temple featured prominently in Israel's identity and consciousness as a nation. Church is neither ethnic nor national but, by definition, universal.

like the arbitrary parcelling out of Jewish territory to suit the convenience of Rome, was regarded by the Jews as an outrageous act of interference on the part of their foreign rulers. It caused the simmering hatred of Rome to boil over in the revolt under Judas referred to in Acts 5:37, and according to Josephus . . . it gave rise to the Zealot movement, and so led to the revolt of A.D. 70. The issue of whether or not the poll-tax should be paid was therefore a burning one, and the question put to Jesus was a direct challenge to him to declare on which side of the fence he stood.[3]

There are three important issues embedded in this episode: (1) the political problem created by Roman occupation, (2) the conscience difficulty caused by paying this tax, and (3) what Jesus' response reveals about his own political holiness. As we shall see, perhaps there was some justification after all for the accusation brought against Jesus during his trial before Pilate in Luke's passion narrative that Jesus was at least implicitly forbidding the payment of taxes to Caesar.[4] Although Mark's story is framed by the historical circumstances of first-century Palestine, in the comments that follow I am more concerned with the logic of the story as Mark tells it: not as a "window" onto the world of Jesus, and not as a "mirror" of the evangelist's own world, but as a story whose logic forces us to look closely at the depth of our own trust in God.

Setting the Scene

The Gospel text reads:

[13]Then they sent to him some Pharisees and some Herodians to trap him in what he said. [14]And they came and said to him, "Teacher, we know that you are sincere, and show deference to no one; for you do not regard people with partiality, but teach the way of God in accordance with truth. Is it lawful to pay taxes to the emperor, or not? [15]Should we pay them, or should we not?" But knowing their hypocrisy, he said to them, "Why are you putting me to the test? Bring me a denarius and let me see it." [16]And they brought one. Then he said to them, "Whose head [literally, image] is this, and whose title [literally, inscription]?" They answered, "The emperor's [literally, Caesar's]."

---

[3] Hooker, *Gospel According to Saint Mark,* 279–80.

[4] Regarding this episode Ignacio Ellacuría writes: "It is clear that Jesus did not make a clear-cut reply in favor of paying such taxes, for when he comes before Pilate he is accused of inciting the people, opposing tax payments to Caesar, and claiming to be the Messiah king. That such accusations may be false is of little consequence here. The point is that if Jesus' preaching and way of life had given the opposite impression, then there would have been no basis for accusations of this sort" (see *Freedom Made Flesh,* 70).

[17]Jesus said to them, "Give to the emperor [Caesar] the things that are the emperor's [Caesar's], and to God the things that are God's." And they were utterly amazed at him (Mark 12:13-17).

However dishonest their motives, Jesus' adversaries have described him accurately. He is sincere, he is *not* intimidated by high social station or wealth,[5] and he earnestly teaches others about the will of God without any thought of personal gain, offending his audience, public embarrassment, and so on. These very qualities are important to the narrative tension, because Jesus' enemies are counting on his speaking and behaving true to form. If their designs against Jesus are to be realized, they need him to incriminate himself with the Romans by replying, "No, it is *not* lawful to pay the tax." The suggestion that an affirmative answer would have cost him popular support does not strike me as likely, given the fact that Jesus is acknowledged to show deference to no one, presumably not even to the poor.

Readers have to approach this passage with some suspicion, for Jesus' response in verse 17 sounds much too clever. Contemporary biblical scholarship has fortunately abandoned the Reformation way of interpreting this text, which claimed that Christians are citizens of two commonwealths or worlds, with obligations to both. That position is understandable, given the fact that the early Gentile Christian communities did not consider themselves unpatriotic and enemies of the state (neither did Paul, for that matter), but it totally misses the radical point behind the present controversy.[6]

The word "image" in verse 16 puts us in mind of the passage from the book of Exodus where the Israelites were forbidden to make or possess images of any created thing:

> [Y]ou shall have no other gods before me.
> You shall not make for yourself an idol, whether in the form of anything that is in heaven above, or that is on the earth beneath, or that is in the water under the earth. You shall not bow down to them or worship them (Exod 20:3-5a).

[5] Commenting on this scene as it appears in Matthew's Gospel in *The New Jerome Biblical Commentary* Viviano notes: "This odd idiom *[you do not regard the position of men]* expresses a basic aspect of the biblical idea of justice, an impartiality that refuses to take a bribe and tilts in favor of the poor litigant" (665). What he says about Matthew's text should apply equally to Mark's. His adversaries recognize, in other words, Jesus' partiality toward the poor. They would thus expect Jesus to say nothing about the poll tax that would betray the interests of the poor.

[6] Patristic reflections on this text are interesting though thoroughly dehistoricized. See *Mark,* Ancient Christian Commentary on Scripture Series, 167–68. On the other hand, Revelation 17–18 proves that not all Christian communities were eager to demonstrate their civic virtue to the Romans.

The word "inscription" alerts us to recall the great confessional text from Deuteronomy:

> Hear, O Israel: The LORD is our God, the LORD alone. You shall love the LORD your God with all your heart, and with all your soul, and with all your might. Keep these words that I am commanding you today in your heart. Recite them to your children and talk about them when you are at home and when you are away, when you lie down and when you rise. Bind them as a sign on your hand, fix them as an emblem on your forehead, and write them on the doorposts of your house and on your gates (Deut 6:4-9).

The only inscription a son or daughter of Israel is allowed to have in their hand is the words of the great commandment itself about the oneness ("there is no other" [Deut 4:35]) of Israel's God. Even though we are following this passage in terms of Mark, we should not forget the warning Jesus gave about not attempting to serve two masters (Luke 16:13) when we come to verse 17. Mark may not have included that saying, but as a Christian he certainly would have subscribed to the sentiment. It seems to me that Ched Myers brings out the prophetic sharpness of this episode more effectively than Morna Hooker does.[7]

The Narrative Tensions

It is hard to imagine that Jesus' view on the tax question would not have been already known by his adversaries. Indeed it would be inconceivable that first-century Jews, whether rich or poor, whether they lived in Galilee or Judea, should not have preoccupied themselves continually with political and social realities, especially with something so vexing as taxation, and doubly inconceivable that Jesus, precisely as a prophet of Israel, would have had nothing to say about the major economic issues, social questions, and political troubles facing his people.

But it is also essential to point out that in the narrative framework of the story it would have been singularly poor judgment on the part of the Herodians and Pharisees to spring such a delicate political question while unsure of how Jesus (we have known for some time that they were determined to eliminate him) might respond. Unless they were already reasonably

---

[7] See Myers, *Binding the Strong Man,* 310–14. Compare with Hooker, *Mark,* 278–81. She writes: "Jesus' answer accepts the legitimate demands of the Roman government, but immediately switches our attention to the far more important demands of God" (280). And again, "However much the inhabitants of Judea dislike it, they cannot escape the authority of Caesar and the obligations that entails" (281).

certain of Jesus' position, if not on the tax issue directly then at least his view of the imperial character, then his adversaries risked being made to look foolish in front of the people. The Pharisees must have either known or surmised, therefore, what Jesus' position was. They could have inferred it on the basis of Jesus' public teaching on the absolute requirement of placing one's confidence unequivocally and exclusively in God. They had no intention of being caught off-guard.

Equally important to the story's logic is that the theoretical position *and the practice* of the Pharisees must also have been known. The Pharisees, after all, had not spearheaded a tax revolt. They had accommodated themselves to the prevailing political reality and must have been paying the imperial tax as required. Otherwise in short order they would have found themselves confined to a Roman prison. In brief, on this matter the Pharisees were pragmatists; they had embraced a "politics of compromise."[8] But their consciences could not have been at ease, especially in light of their highly visible ethical perfectionism. Paying the imperial tax amounted to collaboration and collusion, to moral and spiritual acquiescence in the face of Roman pretensions and idolatry. Did the Pharisees in particular sincerely believe they had not been rendered both morally and ritually unclean by what they were carrying in their purses and were now holding in their hands?

Central to the story has to be our realization that no Jewish person with any trace of national pride would have paid the imperial tax willingly. The Pharisees and Herodians obviously do pay the tax, but both groups surely do so reluctantly. I think it reasonable to suggest a Markan irony here. Jesus' enemies are guilty of sedition in their hearts, yet now they are scheming to have Jesus receive the punishment for civil disobedience that all of them richly deserve. I think it is also reasonable to argue that Jesus' response should not be interpreted as a brilliant tactical maneuver in order to dodge the consequences of his position. For if Jesus feared arrest and execution, he had no business traveling to Jerusalem and exposing himself to so many heated encounters in the first place. Yet his enemies have already conceded that he is sincere and unafraid of how others might react to his teaching *the way of God.*[9] His response ought not be read, then, as a way of slipping through the imperial noose. "Give to Caesar

---

[8] See Horsley, *Jesus and the Spiral of Violence,* 307–17.

[9] The phrase has the resonance of a refrain that pervades the psalms. For example: "He leads the humble in what is right, / and teaches the humble his way" (Ps 25:9). Mark may be telling us that not only was Jesus a sincere teacher, he was also a person of prayer.

the things that are Caesar's" may tease our interpretative skills, but it could hardly have been an evasive answer for the initial audience.

Myers draws our attention to what he calls "the discourse of the coin."[10] The silver coin contained an image of the head of the emperor together with the inscription "Tiberius Caesar, son of the divine Augustus, Augustus."[11] We are thus sensitized to just how offensive the denarius coin must have been to orthodox Jewish sensibilities about the sovereignty of God, and we are reminded of the national humiliation of being forced to use the currency of an occupying power. Mark does not tell us in so many words that the imperial tax had to be paid with imperial currency, but that seems to be the sense of the passage. If the poll tax could have been paid in non-Roman coin, then the denarius as an offensive symbol of Roman domination would not really figure in here. And Jesus' questions about its image and inscription would not have been charged with any sense of urgency. Likewise, Mark seems to presume that his audience understands the coin's monetary value (a day's wage for an ordinary laborer).[12] Since the poll tax probably amounted to one denarius a year, Mark may be suggesting that to Caesar belongs the fruits of one day's work, but the fruits of the work done on all the remaining days belong to God.[13] Given the enormous contrast in what is due to each, such an answer could hardly have been intended to court favor with the emperor.

"Bring me a denarius and let me see it" informs us that Jesus does not have the coin in his possession. We do not immediately know, however, what the reason for this was in Mark's mind. Was Jesus poor, or had he as a matter of religious principle been keeping his distance from the coin? Even if one of the disciples was tending the common purse, the logic of the story requires the adversaries to produce this particular coin, because if the coin had offended Jesus' sensibilities, it certainly would have bothered the disciples as well.

---

[10] Myers, *Binding the Strong Man,* 311.

[11] See the note on Mark 12:16 in *The HarperCollins Study Bible,* 1941. Viviano, in "The Gospel According to Matthew," translates the inscription: "Tiberius Caesar son of the divine Augustus, great high priest" (665).

[12] *HarperCollins Study Bible,* 1929.

[13] "The census meant the assessment of the population for land and head tax *(tributum soli* and *tributum capitis),* that is, entry on lists for future taxation. All male members of a household *(familia* or *oikos)* who were fourteen or older and all female members at least twelve years old were obligated to pay tribute, which probably meant one denarius per head annually (cf. Mark 12:13-17)." See Stegemann and Stegemann, *The Jesus Movement,* 117. I am grateful to Daniel Harrington for this reference.

Finally, we cannot be sure whether most of Jesus' opponents routinely carried a denarius or two, or whether the words "and they brought one" implied that many of his adversaries did *not* regularly carry the imperial coin either. In fact, the story makes better sense if his adversaries themselves (who were hardly admirers of Rome) were reluctant to carry the coin precisely because it so offended Jewish sensibilities. The entrapment thus affords Jesus the chance to expose the Pharisees as compromised men. They want to do what is right but they cannot, for they fear (and understandably so) the consequence of resisting Roman power. If that was the case, then Jesus does not carry the coin, not because he is poor (although I think in Mark's mind Jesus undoubtedly was poor) but (perhaps like many Pharisees) out of religious reasons.

At any rate, Mark gives no indication that Jesus ever paid the tax. And why should he pay? To pay the poll tax, or any tax, implies an acknowledgment of the claims of some earthly authority. But it strikes me as improbable that Mark could have entertained the possibility that in some areas the Son of God had to recognize the claims of an earthly power. The one who possessed the freedom to go beyond the authority of Moses would surely not have felt constrained by the authority of Caesar. Myers comments: "no Jew could have allowed for a valid *analogy* between the debt Israel owed to Yahweh and any other human claim."[14] Above all, this would have been true of Jesus.

One difficulty is that Mark does not explain what exactly the trap consisted of. Jesus' enemies do not think out loud the way they do in Mark 11:31-35, when Jesus countered an unfriendly question with one of his own about the origin of John's baptism. One could conjecture that at least some Pharisees, loath as they were to pay the tax, were inclined to support resistance movements. Historically, the Pharisees clearly had political interests.[15] The trap then would have been to lure Jesus into joining a nationalist movement, or at least declaring his support for one. If Jesus answers no to paying the tax, then he must be for the resistance. And if he answers yes, he becomes a collaborator. But they are not counting on a yes and Jesus does not give one. If such a conjecture has any merit, then the underlying reason for the hostility between Jesus and the Pharisees could have had something to do with very different strategies for bringing about Israel's deliverance. It would almost be as if Jesus had answered, "No, do not pay the tax" and "No, do not take up arms against the Romans when they come to punish you."

[14] Myers, *Binding the Strong Man,* 312.
[15] For background on the Pharisees see Murphy, *Religious World of Jesus,* 221–39.

Some Conclusions

Let us summarize our observations thus far:

1. The underlying *political* issue involved a reluctant compromise with the imperial government and some degree of collusion with all that Caesar symbolized. Not to have collaborated would have resulted in the destruction of the nation. But the imperial tax was also economically burdensome, and its weight would have fallen most severely on the shoulders of people already poor. The Pharisees appear to have chosen the lesser of two evils, namely, the politics of compromise. In Jerusalem, the site of the income-producing Temple, such compromise would also have worked to the economic and social advantage of the religious elites.

2. The underlying *religious* issue was that such compromise required finding justification for disregarding the precepts of the Mosaic Law, which forbade graven images, inscriptions, and idolatry. The Pharisees, with the unclean coin in their hands, might actually have chosen the greater rather than the lesser of two evils. For they had determined that political and economic security warranted their accommodation with the powers that be, and they must have instructed the people that this course was permissible. The questions we have to ask, then, are these: Was Jesus a political realist? Or was he adamant about defending the things of God—zealous for his Father's house (see John 2:17)? In other words, was he a prophet in the line of Jeremiah, Amos, and Ezekiel, or was he being as politically pragmatic as his adversaries? It is further possible, of course, that some of the Pharisees favored a course of active resistance against the Romans. If that were the case, and if Jesus had advocated the payment of the imperial tax, then those Pharisees would have appeared in the eyes of the people more reliably Jewish than Jesus. But Mark gives no hint that he was thinking along these lines.

3. We ought to exclude any reading of this passage that would propose that Jesus was being deliberately evasive in his answer. There is no indication in the various confrontation scenes that Jesus was attempting to duck the consequences of his prophetic challenge to the status quo. The idea that he would craft a subtle answer in order not to give his enemies grounds for charging him with civil disobedience does not add up. In the end, that was precisely the charge that led to his execution. If Jesus wanted to avoid risking his life, he should never have gone to Jerusalem. His actions and speech in the Temple precincts were bold and deliberately provocative.

4. If Jesus' answer had been a clear acknowledgment of the imperial claims to obedience in civil matters, then it is difficult to imagine how anyone could have seriously alleged that he was subversive in the matter

of paying taxes, or indeed how Jesus could have posed any threat to political stability. The charge "King of the Jews" (15:2, 9, 18, 26) would have been utterly groundless. To argue that Jesus saw himself as a spiritual king but that his followers and others mistakenly understood him to be talking about political sovereignty in this world implies that he was not an effective teacher and that his message was far too subtle for the ordinary person. Jesus did not distance himself from the world in this way; that is not what his words "Give to Caesar what is due to Caesar" meant.

On the other hand, if Jesus had actually answered in such a way as to expose the complicity of the religious elites and if he had revealed that the pragmatists were fundamentally faithless because they had chosen the things of Caesar over the things of God, then we have a very different possibility. Rather than expressly calling for a taxpayers' revolt, Jesus had called for a referendum on the sorry state of national confidence in God and for a recommitment on the people's part to belief in the power of the God of Israel to liberate from all oppression, no matter how demonic that oppression was. Jesus had bypassed the tax question by shifting the ground on which the Pharisees were challenging him. He had moved the legal question to the more basic issue of their failed allegiance to God, a failure made all the more grievous because they belonged to Israel's religious leadership.

In short, the allegation about forbidding his countrymen to pay the imperial tax probably had some justification. Since Jesus does not appear to carry the Roman coin on religious grounds and not because he was too poor, it is probable that he would not have paid the imperial tax. The Pharisees had correctly inferred from Jesus' teaching and behavior that having anything to do with Caesar's coin was contrary to the obedience Israel owed God alone. What they had not counted on was being openly exposed as men who put more confidence in their own wits than in God's power when it came to the matter of cultural, political, and economic survival. Jesus, as they said, shows no deference, is not beguiled by high social station, and teaches the way of God in accordance with truth, fearlessly. The irony of the Pharisees' policy of accommodation is that about forty years later, in the years 66–70, the Roman forces did arrive and destroyed both the Temple and the city of Jerusalem. The institutions of temple and priesthood went out of existence.

5. This passage contributes to a portrait of Jesus who is more a prophet than a serene, prayerful ascetic or an earnest, sensitive teacher. Clearly, the exchange here is meant to sound adversarial and confrontational; Mark speaks of a trap. Jesus does not come across as a clever lawyer more skillful at resolving moral questions than the Pharisees. Rather, he is outspoken, firm, and more "righteous" (or more zealous for the Law and for Israel's

covenant with God) than the religious establishment, who built their repu-
tation on strict observance of law and custom (see Mark 7:1-13). Jesus
trusts the God of Israel absolutely. He does not place his trust in anything
else, such as wealth, treaties and alliances, family ties, the princes and politically powerful ones of this world, military might, or his own intelligence;
nor in angels, the ability to work miracles, or the power to expel demons.
There should be no doubt that Jesus would have been as unafraid or unim-
pressed by Tiberius and the power of his empire as John the Baptist with respect to Herod, or Moses with respect to the Pharaoh. The Son of God was
no superhero, but neither was he a friend to the Caesars of this world.

6. Finally, shortly after the tax issue in chapter 12 we read about a
scribe who, after listening to the dispute between Jesus and his adversaries, asked Jesus which commandment was the first and greatest of all
(Mark 12:28). Jesus responded by quoting Deut 6:4-5, to which he joined
Lev 19:18.[16] It is possible that this exceptional scribe had caught the
underlying flaw in the strategy of the Pharisees as Jesus had just exposed
it. The scribe's recalling the great commandment at that moment signaled
that he had understood Jesus' prophetic response with respect to the imperial tax. Thus Jesus states that the scribe is not far from the kingdom of
God (12:34). Jesus knows immediately and without any philosophical
fuss what his (and our) primary obligation and loyalty require. "And besides him *there is no other*" is very important here. We have to hear this
scribal affirmation as the background of Mark 12:17. For in verse 17, to
follow Myers' insight, Mark has not set up a parallelism but an antithesis.

7. Jesus would hardly have intended his audience to walk away
thinking they should be *both* faithful to God *and* obedient to the emperor, for God shares moral and spiritual authority with no one. There is
only one Lord, one sovereign of history who raises up and pulls down
royal houses, to whom *all* obedience is due. God and emperor are not par-
allels here. In the end, Jesus answered with the directness of a prophet
(which is to be expected, given the way the adversaries addressed him in
verse 14). He has uncovered the uncleanness of the religious elite, he has
done so in Jerusalem itself, and he makes it clear that the emperor's values and God's are worlds apart. The people of Israel should have nothing
to do with the godless ones of the present age, even if somebody happens
to be "a great one" (Latin, *augustus*) in secular terms.[17]

---

[16] "You shall not take vengeance or bear a grudge against any of your people, but you
shall love your neighbor as yourself: I am the LORD."

[17] On the nature of the imperial cult see Price, "Rituals and Power"; Zanker, "Power
of Images," 47–86.

8. Jesus' answer should be heard in terms of his conviction about the imminent arrival of God's rule. The reason why he does not take a long-range view about what will best insure national survival has nothing to do with the madness of taking on the Roman legions and everything to do with God's coming judgment and power to save. The story is not about civic responsibility, obedience to civil authorities, fair or unfair tax burdens, and so on. The Pharisees are not political scientists or moral philosophers debating taxation in general; they do, after all, observe the practice of tithing religiously. The presence of the Herodians adds to the sleaziness of the entrapment, but the story works just as well without them. Jesus' adversaries had posed a genuine conscience problem when they asked, "Is it *lawful?*" That is, "Are we violating the Law of Moses?" Their question is not about a government's right to levy taxes but about paying a tax with a coin that compromised their loyalty to God. They chose prudence over a strict observance of the first commandment, and Jesus correctly saw that their choice amounted to a tacit rejection of covenant faith. Even if the consequence of full obedience to the Law should be destruction of the nation, as Israel's religious elite they were expected to be as obedient to God as Abraham, who was prepared even to lose his son, or the Maccabean brothers, who elected martyrdom over infidelity.

While the story contains no message for us regarding civic responsibility, it does offer a powerful prophetic example of Jesus' refusal to bargain for his life; he had to have known the price of being so forthright and unyielding on a matter of elementary trust. In the end, therefore, Mark demonstrates just how sincere, truthful, and unthreatened Jesus actually is.

The Theological Matters

The story about whether the imperial tax ought to be paid is almost aggressively evangelical. Faced with a choice between obedience to a religious precept and national survival, many of us would probably feel compelled to choose the latter. Fortunately, our choices come in smaller bites, in the small day-by-day decisions we have to make and with whose consequences we have to live. Although we continually use language about Jesus' return to us in glory, none of us realistically believes that God is about to intervene in human affairs to bring about the reign of justice, love, and peace. There have been too many centuries of misfortune, poverty, and war for us to believe that at long last the hour of redemption might be at hand. Nevertheless, the tax story—indeed, the entire Gospel narrative—forces us to consider whether we believe enough in God's providence to hope for real salvation.

Can God be trusted, or not? Given the track record of false messiahs, the Pharisees probably ought not be faulted for failing to take the step that Jesus called for. This Gospel scene is not so much about hypocrisy as about pragmatism versus trust. In fact, the tax question itself might actually be a distraction. The real question was, Will Israel survive its current crisis on the basis of its wits and alliances or on the basis of its absolute trust in the power of God? For Jesus, and for the evangelist, the Pharisees had blundered.

Was the imperial situation all that bad? I think that if one were caught under the empire's heel, it certainly was. Would there be a miraculous intervention to rescue God's elect? Mark believed that salvation had come, but in a form that was totally unexpected and rich in mystery. While the Roman Empire might have exercised too strong a hold on his imagination for him to conceive of a totally different sort of cultural and social world, the impulse of the gospel eventually moves one to think beyond the historical form that was the Roman Empire. For Mark, the gospel was less about Jesus than about the power of God at work in the world through the life, death, and resurrection of Jesus. The story of the coin is about God's claim upon us: relentless, uncompromising, yet liberating. Mark would never have thought of Jesus as advocating insurrection, but he was also firmly convinced that the gospel was strong enough to unseat any demon that pretended to call itself divine.

Like all the other episodes in Mark, this one testifies to Jesus' immersion in the everyday concerns of his people. What would have been more everyday, after all, than financial worry, resentments and resistance, occupation by a foreign power, taxation, abuse of privilege, and so forth? There is no way Jesus could have avoided being pulled into the messy political arena if he lived in solidarity with his people. For ultimately the greater evils that beset the land were political in nature. Sin does not exist and it does not consume in the abstract; it resides in the everyday, in the structural timbers of a society, its power relationships, and so on. Not only from the perspective of Jewish nationalism but also from the perspective of God's holiness the Roman Empire was a sinful force in the world. Jesus could not consistently have uncovered the moral and spiritual weakness of his people without at least noticing the destructive hold of a latter-day Egypt upon his people. To think he could have done something about the first but nothing about the second would seriously underestimate his prophetic vision. If the Temple had fallen under judgment, then so had the empire. The one who predicts the destruction of the Temple and Jerusalem in Mark 13 would have harbored no illusions about prospects for the empire. The apocalypticism of that chapter could certainly embrace a Caesar or two.

Just as Jesus' enemies had correctly discerned in his teaching about power, greatness, justice, and inclusiveness—as well as on the basis of his actions and example—a grave challenge to their thinking about divorce (Mark 10:1-12); so too had they figured out how uncompromising he would be on matters touching upon the first commandment. And they may have known, too, his view about the craving for power and influence so evident among the rulers and "great ones" among the Gentiles (10:42). We shall turn now from the tax question and Jesus' "politics of holiness" to Jesus' parables and the wonderfully hopeful imagination that stands behind them. [18]

[18] I am borrowing the phrase from Walter Brueggemann's book *Hopeful Imagination: Prophetic Voices in Exile* (Philadelphia: Fortress Press, 1986).

7

A World of Parables

With many such parables he spoke the word to them, as they were able to hear it; he did not speak to them except in parables, but he explained everything in private to his disciples (Mark 4:33-34).

The parables Mark relates in chapter 4 must be representative of a much larger store, some of which Mark may have known, most of which he probably had no record. While Mark later presents a number of instances where Jesus teaches in a straightforward manner (for example, when Jesus instructs his disciples in chapters 8, 9, and 10 about being "on the way" with him), it appears that, at least for Mark, Jesus typically spoke in analogies and comparisons drawn from daily life. These would have been woven into his stories and synagogue instruction, his table conversation, and his outdoor preaching. Jesus even spoke to his adversaries in parables, the message of which was clear and pointed (3:23; 12:1ff.). In and of themselves, Jesus' metaphors would probably not have sounded all that remarkable. Yet if readers centuries later are to make sense of them, then they have to situate those ancient metaphors in terms of what weighed most on the mind of Jesus and his contemporaries, namely, the fulfillment of Israel's hope for the reign of justice, for vindication before those nations of the world that had contributed to its suffering and disgrace, and for a lasting victory over the power of death.

Christologically the parables are of interest because they so obviously underscore Jesus' humanness, the immersion of his imagination in the everyday life of his people, a solidarity of culture and perception. The things people saw everyday in the villages and countryside of Galilee are what he saw. The parables are of interest, too, because of the light they shed on Jesus' understanding of the kingdom of God and, perhaps even more importantly, on his experience of God.

It is unlikely that Jesus employed parables merely as pedagogical instruments; it is more likely that he consistently thought parabolically. His imagination may have run in the same vein as that of the author(s) of the book of Proverbs. The world was not exactly a giant metaphor, but it was full of lessons. This idea is hardly novel, although not everyone is contemplative enough to notice what the everyday world has to say. The fact that Mark does not furnish us in chapter 4 with further examples of Jesus' parables would suggest, first, that he figured his listeners would get the point very quickly about what parables are and, second, that then they might even set about creating their own.[1]

It might be stretching Mark's narrative plan to consider the healings and exorcisms as enacted parables, but the reader is certainly tempted to imagine Mark saying to himself, "The kingdom of God may be compared to a leper who suddenly found himself cleansed . . ." Or, "The kingdom of God is like a woman whose little daughter had an unclean spirit; and the woman was a Gentile. . . ." And there is something wildly parabolic about a rich man who cannot separate himself from his wealth in order to follow Jesus, while a blind beggar tosses aside his tattered cloak.

The allegorizing or explanation of the parable of the sower gives us a glimpse, again through Markan eyes, of Jesus' regular practice of decoding everyday experience, demonstrating for his listeners how every aspect of daily life has something to report about the mysterious presence of the kingdom of God. Reality has a message—indeed many messages—for those with ears trained to hear them. Jesus would hardly have used parables in order to conceal his teaching from those who had not been divinely chosen to understand and thus to be saved; no teacher aims to be obscure. Tertullian's comment relating to the second half of Mark 4:34 reveals the insight and the concern of someone with ecclesiological questions on his mind, but it fails to grasp the evangelist's perspective:

> Christ Jesus our Lord clearly declared himself as to who he was while he
> lived on earth. . . . Who then of sound mind can possibly suppose that
> those whom the Lord ordained to be leaders and teachers were ignorant of
> anything essential to salvation? Who could suppose that he who kept them,
> as he did, so close to himself in their daily attentiveness, in their discipline,

---

[1] In 7:17 Mark refers to Jesus' homey illustration about true cleanliness as a parable; so also the tale about the wicked tenants in chapter 12. And two short parables appear in chapter 13 with clear eschatological overtones. See Donahue, *Gospel in Parable*, 57–62. If we view Jesus' actions as enacted metaphors demonstrating what the kingdom of God means in terms of the possibility of a new Israel, the demand for renewed practice, and divine judgment, then the Gospel becomes a parable from beginning to end.

in their companionship, to whom, when they were alone, he used to ex-
pound all things which were obscure, telling them that "to them it was
given to know those mysteries," which it was not permitted the people to
understand—now would he leave them ignorant?[2]

As we have already seen, for Mark the term "disciples" did not exclude
everybody except the Twelve; he tells us so explicitly in 4:10 when he writes
of those who were around Jesus in addition to the Twelve. From a narrative
standpoint "disciples" was meant to convey to Mark's audience that they too
had been privileged to belong to the insiders. Existentially speaking, they
were every bit as much Jesus' disciples and companions as Peter, Andrew,
and the others. As John Donahue notes: "'Inside' and 'outside' are existential, religious categories, determined by the kind of response one makes to
the demands of Jesus."[3]

Nevertheless, whatever the theological explanation may have been,
the fact remains that not everyone who listened to Jesus either grasped his
message or responded to it in the same way. The idea of different kinds of
soil or ecological conditions that the seed encountered sheds some light on
the diversity of human reactions; the explanation of the parable is thus important if the reader is going to appreciate the correspondence Jesus observed between inner and outer realities.

But what further reason might there be for the fact that some have
failed to understand unless it was that they never quite mastered the knack
of looking at the world parabolically? Students unable to keep up with what
is being presented in class soon find themselves completely adrift; the longer
they remain in the classroom, the greater their confusion and frustration.
This may be what Mark has in mind when he recalls Jesus' saying: "For to
those who have, more will be given; and from those who have nothing, even
what they have will be taken away" (4:25). Some learn, others do not. This
saying of Jesus may be nothing more than a description, not an evaluation,
of student performance.

"To you has been given the secret of the kingdom of God, but for
those outside, everything comes in parables" (4:11) is Mark's way of con-
veying the effect of Jesus' mission both in Jesus' day and in Mark's own
time. In other words, the key to grasping the parables is not a secret code
imparted only to those closest to Jesus, but closeness to Jesus does bring the
world to light in terms of his apparently endless supply of stories and metaphors about the kingdom of God. When preachers or evangelists attempt

[2] *Mark,* Ancient Christian Commentary on Scripture Series, 62.
[3] Donahue, *Gospel in Parable,* 43–44. This sentence is italicized in the original.

to assess the success of their mission, the effort to account for the negative or lukewarm responses ultimately points them to God. Hence Mark's quotation of Isaiah 6, which reads more fully:

> Then I heard the voice of the Lord saying, "Whom shall I send, and who will go for us?" And I said, "Here am I; send me!" And he said, "Go and say to this people:
> 'Keep listening, but do not comprehend;
> keep looking, but do not understand.'
> Make the mind of this people dull,
>   and stop their ears,
>   and shut their eyes,
> so that they may not look with their eyes,
>   and listen with their ears,
> and comprehend with their minds,
>   and turn and be healed (Isa 6:8-10).

The response to a prophet's message is not invariably one of repentance; God's word often provokes fierce resistance and denial. God does not in any way cause our hardness of heart, for God's will is precisely that human beings should see, hear, comprehend, repent, and be healed. Resistance, however, belongs to the dynamics of the spiritual life, and where sin is systemic, resistance to God's word can be nearly pathological. There are people who do not want to hear the truth about themselves or their society.[4] Not everyone necessarily desires wholeness.

To propose, therefore, that the reason why some human beings listen and bear fruit while others turn away ultimately rests with God (which is exactly what Mark suggests by drawing upon Isaiah) is simply to respect the mysterious dynamics of grace and freedom. Why one per-

---

[4] Exodus 4:21, 7:3, etc., narrate the best-known instance of a divinely caused hardness of heart, the motive for which was that the Egyptians should know "that I am the LORD" (7:5). Still, the Pharaoh oscillates between resistance and repentance, for after giving permission for the Israelites to withdraw and offer sacrifice he implores Moses, "Pray to the LORD to take away the frogs from me and my people" (8:8) and "Pray for me" (8:28). According to the third-century exegesis of Origen (himself an Egyptian!) God's saving will extended even to the Pharaoh; God desired the king's repentance. Needless to say, the story of God's dealing with the Pharaoh cannot, on theological grounds, be interpreted literally. Origen's exposition of this point was brilliant: "And indeed Pharaoh was necessary to God, in order that for the salvation of the many God might display his power in him during his long resistance and struggle against God's will." And again: "[God] knows how by means of the great plagues and the drowning in the sea he is leading even Pharaoh; and his superintending care for him does not stop at this point." See his *On First Principles*, 170, 185.

son is inside while another remains outside the community of salvation was a question Mark and other New Testament writers had to think about. Sociological and psychological explanations of why one human being becomes a Christian while another does not can take us just so far. Mark's solution is reasonable enough, although the problem was not that the meaning of Jesus' parables was by design mysterious or opaque. The problem was that not every imagination was ready to accept the idea that the kingdom of God was about to break into human history along the lines Jesus was proposing. And from Mark's vantage point, every parable that Jesus ever spoke would have to be reinterpreted in light of his death and resurrection. Even though the parables themselves were about the kingdom of God, how could Mark's readers listen to the parable about the sower, the lamp, the growing grain, or the mustard seed and not think of Jesus? Jesus' story becomes the word that is sown, the light that shatters darkness, the missionary seed that slowly but certainly grows, and (perhaps most startling of all) the best illustration of the miraculous turn from poverty and insignificance to greatness and beauty. The inability to grasp *that* parable destines one to remain forever an outsider.

The Parable of the Lamp

The brief saying about the purpose of lighting a lamp may be particularly instructive about both the sheer ordinariness of Jesus' illustrations and the religious insight that stood beneath them. The text reads: "He said to them, 'Is a lamp brought in to be put under the bushel basket, or under the bed, and not on the lampstand?'" (Mark 4:21).

The action of bringing in a lamp implies that it has already been lit, that the family's dwelling is dark either because night has fallen or the house has no windows, and that the proper place for a lighted lamp is the lampstand. Nothing could have been more ordinary or routine. Figuratively speaking, Jesus has been lighting a lamp through his teaching, preaching, and healing; his message is hardly secretive. Moreover, its truth illumines the whole of God's saving design for the world. The connection could not have been more automatic.

But the real actor in the Gospel story was not the historical figure Jesus of Nazareth but God. God was the one who called and missioned Jesus, who had prepared his way, and who poured upon him the power of the Spirit. The mighty deeds, the authoritative teaching, and the stunning expulsion of Satan from human lives and communities altogether point toward the unseen yet ever-present reality of the God of Israel. Thus God could be at the same time the one lighting the lamp, the spark, the light, and the security this light brings. Moreover, the divine intention behind lighting the lamp was obviously and naturally that human beings should "see," that they should live and walk in the light, or that they should be saved. God sends Jesus, therefore, in order that men and women should find their way toward God. For Mark, the meaning of Jesus' life—his teaching and healing, his suffering and death, his resurrection—is in and of itself transparent, clear, unambiguous. Jesus' question "Is a lamp brought in to be put under the bushel basket, or under the bed?" applies to God as much as it applies to us. The hearer absolutely has to be able to draw that connection for the parable to work.

This means that for Mark the parable's interpretation should take into account the entire Gospel story. Thus one could reasonably argue that Jesus' further words "For there is nothing hidden, except to be disclosed; nor is anything secret, except to come to light" (Mark 4:22) anticipate the manner in which Jesus would uncover the political machinations and religious corruption of the Holy City in chapters 11 and 12, and perhaps the signs of the end-time in chapter 13. Figuratively speaking, that was why the prophetic lamp was lit. But in Mark's imagination the overarching parable that takes into account the whole story might sound like this: The kingdom of God may be compared to a carpenter from a small village who was killed by religious and civil authorities but was raised from the dead to be the Messiah for all God's people. This wider parable, together with all its implications for humanity present and future, is what has been placed on the lampstand.[5]

Mark's operating definition of a parable is not all that tight. Sometimes parables are illustrative comparisons based on scenes people see everyday, and sometimes they are stories with a message. While Jesus' own use of parables confirms how deeply his imagination was rooted in the world of Galilean peasants, Mark's sense of the parabolic was undoubtedly shaped in some measure by his understanding of the cross. That is, the everydayness so characteristic of Jesus' parables would have to incorporate the everydayness of human suffering. If one has suffered, then one will be able to understand the cross. After all, the reason for speaking in parables is to show the connectedness between the ordinary and the kingdom of God, a sensibility that ought to be as easy to pick up as learning to walk or to speak.

The daily frustrations, diminishment, persecution, exploitation and oppression, infirmities, and so on, which were endemic both to the people

---

[5] See Donahue, "Jesus as the Parable of God," 148–67.

of Jesus' day and to Mark's, could be linked effortlessly to what had happened to Jesus. His existence became the parable that encoded the meaning of their lives, and the suffering they endured was related to what he underwent. His suffering and death brought their suffering and their deaths into bold relief; Jesus' cross had become a mirror that reflected back their own reality. Not only had Jesus shared their historical, social, and political lot as a member of a subjugated people (for this was part of the image that they saw); he also shared with them an intense desire for the liberation of the nation. That desire had crystalized on the cross, and what got reflected back was the price for the fulfillment of their own deepest aspirations. The cross of Jesus, in other words, had become a unique metaphor summing up human life.

The Parable of the Fig Tree

> From the fig tree learn its lesson: as soon as its branch becomes tender and puts forth its leaves, you know that summer is near (Mark 13:28).[6]

Mark has connected this saying with Jesus' apocalyptic words about the events that would signal the coming of the victorious Son of Man. *Look* at the fig tree and *think* of the arrival of God's justice, for the things of nature are perennial reminders of the things of God, at least for those who know how to read the signs. And since fig trees were such a common sight, this particular reminder would have been constant. The coming of the Son of Man would bring justice and blessedness to those who had been faithful but judgment and punishment to those who had not.[7] The disciple's response ought then to be to stand ready and vigilant: "Therefore, keep awake . . . . And what I say to you I say to all: Keep awake" (Mark 13:35, 37). Just as the parables of chapter 4 envision Mark's audience as the insiders, so too does chapter 13. It begins as a private instruction to four disciples, but its final admonition is to everyone.

The parable of the fig tree and several others like it (12:1-9; 13:34-36) highlight an element of Jesus' awareness that had been present since the beginning of the Gospel. However hopeful he was at the outset of the

---

[6] Donahue notes (*Gospel in Parable,* 58) that the Greek text reads: "From the fig tree learn the parable." Morna Hooker explains: "the fig tree is one of the commonest trees in Palestine. It is the most obvious harbinger of summer, since so many of the other trees are evergreen. Moreover, the fig tree was commonly used in Jewish literature to symbolize the joys of the messianic age" (*Gospel According to Saint Mark,* 320).

[7] On Mark 13 see Wright, *Jesus and the Victory of God,* 339–68.

story that people would welcome his liberating message and respond enthusiastically, Jesus could not have been unaware from the start that rejection of a prophet's message invites condemnation. The note of resistance and rejection was evident from the moment he taught for the first time in the synagogue at Capernaum and a demon attempted to bring his instruction to an abrupt end. God's news was indeed good for those who listened, but it would bring judgment upon those who refused.[8]

The issue that surfaces in the parable is one of eschatology. Jesus' preaching was framed by an expectation of disaster if the nation did not pay attention. Jesus taught that God's reign was finally at hand, that the only thing standing between promise and actualization was a wholesale turning toward God and a firm rejection of idolatry in all its forms, that the messenger and the message were intimately linked, and that the price of refusal would be national destruction. By the time Mark's reader comes to chapter 13, it is clear that both the message and the messenger have been rejected by the people who count. Judging from the accusation brought against him about destroying and rebuilding the Temple (14:58; 15:29), it seems quite likely that Jesus envisioned the total collapse of the Temple, perhaps even the destruction of Jerusalem, so deep was his prophetic disgust for the nation's religious, social, and economic establishment.

Nevertheless, the disastrous events of 66–70 C.E. should not be read as the result of Jesus' apocalyptic forecast. Jerusalem and the Temple were destroyed, but the words of Jesus were neither the theological nor the historical cause of that misfortune. As prophet, Jesus could judge the nation, but he could not punish it. The Roman army that laid siege to the city, scattered or killed its inhabitants, and tore down its magnificent buildings was not a divine instrument. For a prophet's threats are intended to produce reform. It is highly tempting but theologically dangerous to conclude after the fact that God has acted to punish and destroy individuals or nations for their infidelity, no matter how terrible the sin was. Historical and theological categories ought not be confused. The historical reasons for the collapse of Jerusalem had little to do with the religious message of Jesus, unless he had been advocating complete submission to imperial rule and his political advice went unheeded.

Consider the book of Revelation by way of comparison. Writing toward the end of the first century, the author knew, perhaps even firsthand, about the fate of the Holy City and its Temple. He detested Rome both as a city and as a symbol of godless imperialism; he regarded its emperors

---

[8] See Marius Reiser, *Jesus and Judgment,* 197–301.

as allies of Satan; and he forecast the most violent end to its pride, its exploitation, its cult of the emperor, its power and wealth. Hebrew that he was, the author understandably harbored only the most bitter hatred of Rome for what the empire had done to Jerusalem. Whatever the complicity of Jewish and imperial leaders in the death of Jesus, Jerusalem does not seem to have merited the awful events the seer of Revelation may have witnessed or about which he certainly knew.

Despite his extensive visions concerning Rome's sudden and richly deserved dissolution, however, his book's central prophecy never materialized, any more than did Jonah's prediction about the ruin of Nineveh. The people of Nineveh, nobles and peasants alike, had at least repented in sackcloth and ashes, but in spite of the various opportunities in terms of partial punishments that God had offered them the Romans did not. Of course, within two centuries Rome would have a Christian emperor, a prospect not only not foreseen by the author of Revelation but an outcome that would probably have struck him as a divine betrayal. That failure has to affect how readers approach Revelation today. A fate unrealized, despite the certitude of the prophet's forecast, implies that God is not bound by a prophet's visionary experiences, no matter how vivid the images or vehement his denunciations. Neither the catastrophe nor the promise imagined by the seer ever materialized.[9]

In Mark 13, therefore, Jesus could not have been announcing a divinely determined fate for Jerusalem and its religious establishment. Mark, of course, may well have known what had just happened or what was still going on in Palestine when he wrote verse 2: "Do you see these great buildings? Not one stone will be left here upon another; all will be thrown down." The reader, of course, has a historical advantage. But the point bears repeating that the prophetic warnings about impending disaster that we find, for instance, in Mark 3:28-29, 9:42-48, 12:9, or throughout Mark 13 are essentially a summons to repentance. Marius Reiser writes:

> The depictions of judgments in early Jewish writings are quite often dictated by an unconcealed hatred and thirst for revenge: the hatred of the pious against the godless, of the righteous against the wicked, of the tortured against their torturers. In these texts, the eschatological judgment brings not only righteous punishment for sinners, but also serves for the final satisfaction of those who, against all obstacles, remained true to God and God's law. . . . The "prophets" who speak in texts of that kind reveal

---

[9] My comments on Revelation are based on Murphy, *Fallen Is Babylon*. See pp. 442–444.

such a desire for revenge that they entirely forget the call to repentance; in fact, one has the impression that they are not at all interested in the repentance of sinners.

Nothing of that can be found in the preaching of Jesus. His words about judgment are not inspired by hatred of sinners, but solely by love for them. . . . Jesus proclaims judgment to "this generation," because he wants to preserve them from it.[10]

Nevertheless, the fortunes and destinies of nations are governed by social, economic, and political forces, some of which they can control and some of which they cannot. A theological reading or interpretation of historical process can be far too tempting and often much too shallow. The Temple may well have degenerated into a den of robbers (Mark 11:17), but its disappearance ought not be viewed as divine retribution. Likewise, the Roman *imperium* eventually went into decline, but for reasons far more complex than that Roman society had succumbed to moral chaos.

As Mark writes, the coming of the Son of Man is still awaited, and the best answer he can give to those who are wondering about the delay is that they should be patient and ever alert. We find similar responses, for instance, in 1 Thess 5:1-11 and 2 Pet 3:8-13. The "not yet" of Christian experience appears destined to perdure for a very long time, and as a result believers run the perennial risk of becoming unsteady and losing focus. They might even remain dedicated to their Christian practice, but unless their moral sensibilities are fused with a sense of Jesus risen, then their discipleship risks turning into a practice without hope, a sense of duty without vision. The waiting of those who have no hope is the worst sort of resignation.

The end of the world prophesied by the seer of the book of Revelation did not mean that he believed in the utter disappearance of the universe; he believed, rather, in the creation of a new heavens and a new earth. The end would be like the beginning, but infinitely better. God would once more take up his dwelling with human beings (Rev 21:3), doing for all of his daughters and sons what God had once done with and for our first parents. If we did not believe that Jesus shared this profoundly hopeful sensibility, then it would be hard to avoid the impression that the Gospel story as a record of the activity and fate of Jesus is in the final analysis depressing. The fig tree's parable would be a constant signal of the ultimate reckoning, not a reminder that a new heavens and new earth were on the way to being realized.

---

[10] Marius Reiser, *Jesus and Judgment*, 321–22.

Mark presents a Jesus who is confident that a new beginning is on the horizon. After citing the apocalyptic signs of wars, earthquakes, and famines, Jesus says, "This is but the beginning of the *birthpangs*" (13:8). Between the beginning and the end lay persecution, the giving of testimony, and a world-wide proclamation of the gospel. Thus Jesus' words "and you will be hated by all because of my name" (13:13) refer preeminently to his followers in the future—to Mark's audience and beyond. Mark obviously believed that giving testimony about Jesus would be central to the Church's historical mission, and that this testimony would include both faith's narrative about Jesus and the pattern of prophetic practice that Jesus had set. Jesus was crucified because of the bold things he did and not simply because of his teaching or his claims. Mark does not spell out what the grounds of Jesus' confidence in God were, but the ground of Mark's confidence was the resurrection.

Contemporary christology has been at pains to elucidate the connection between Jesus' death and the prophetic ministry of Jesus that led up to it. No reputable theologian today would treat the death and resurrection of Jesus as if these moments could be dissociated from the rest of Jesus' life and the history of his people. Their transcendent meaningfulness arises from within human history, not outside of it. There were specific reasons of a social, political, economic, and religious nature for the death of Jesus. Consequently, we need chapters 1 through 12 of Mark to help us understand why Jesus died on a cross.

But what would happen to the narrative if we excised chapter 13 and skipped from the ending of the story of the exploited widow in Mark 12:44, "For all of them have contributed out of their abundance; but she out of her poverty has put in everything she had, all she had to live on," to chapter 14: "It was two days before the Passover and the festival of Unleavened Bread. The chief priests and the scribes were looking for a way to arrest Jesus by stealth and kill him" (14:1)? Having followed the tense course of Jesus' ministry through chapters 11 and 12, the decision of the Jerusalem authorities comes as no surprise to the reader. Although Jesus' Galilean adversaries are no longer in the picture, the evangelist could hardly have thought that the conflicts he had recounted in the first ten chapters were unrelated to what was about to take place in Jerusalem. For if Jesus' sole concern was with the sorry state of the Temple, then it becomes difficult to figure out why Mark devotes so much of his story to Jesus' travels through Galilee. Besides, Mark must have been aware that Jesus' dramatic entry into Jerusalem in chapter 11 could not plausibly have been his first time there. At any rate, if we were to bracket or remove Mark 13 because of the difficulty of making sense of its annoying apocalypticism, we would miss a major insight into the abiding relevance of Jesus' death. Before engaging us with the passion narrative Mark apparently wanted to frame the death of Jesus in cosmic terms.

And so Mark has tied the suffering and death of Jesus into the much wider passion story of Jesus' faithful witnesses, hauled off before the governors and vassal kings of Roman imperialism, and hated by all because they bear his name. The worldwide disasters into which disciples of the future will be pulled seem to be the sufferings associated with the end of the world as we have known it and the dramatic re-creation of humanity and civilization in terms of the reign of God. For Mark, then, the cross of Jesus has its historical explanation in the conflicts of Jesus' life.[11] Then there was the broader context of the conflictual social reality that God's people were forced to endure as a result of Roman imperialism. And just as Jesus uncovered, denounced, and resisted the injustice and idolatry of his time, so too would all those who followed him later.[12] Finally, there was the cosmic conflict where forces of good and evil contested for the ownership of humanity itself, a struggle to which the powers of nature would testify through famines, earthquakes, falling stars, and a darkened sun and moon. The death of Jesus, Mark appears to be saying, must be interpreted against the broadest possible canvass of historical and cosmic events. The cross of Jesus does not simply have a history; it creates history. By establishing a victim as the axis of divine/human imaging, Mark has made solidarity with all victims a central category of gospel spirituality. The result is that human history is reconstituted in a way that gives primacy to those on the bottom.

The end is not yet, but with the cross and resurrection of Jesus the kingdom of God will have established a beachhead. In Mark 13:26 Jesus speaks of "'the Son of Man coming in clouds' with great power and glory,"

---

[11] Donald Senior writes: "The passion story should not be disconnected from its moorings in the rest of the Gospel. . . . Jesus is not a mere victim with death imposed. Jesus chose the way that led to the cross and, as Mark repeatedly states, the cross as a sign of life given on behalf of others is inseparable from the heart of Jesus' teaching" (*Passion of Jesus,* 140).

[12] Once again the book of Revelation is instructive. The letters to the seven churches encourage active resistance to anything connected with the empire or that served its commercial and civic interests. There is nothing accommodating about the author's attitude toward Rome. The imperial cult, for instance, was an abomination. The author was equally uncompromising in the matter of buying meat in the marketplace that had been sacrificed to idols or marriage with anyone outside the Christian community. One has to surmise that the seer would never have tolerated a Christian serving in the imperial legions either. For a Christian, therefore, waiting was never considered to be a passive affair. In the meantime, one acts prophetically, as Jesus did, no matter what the consequence. Again, see Murphy, *Fallen Is Babylon,* 105–66.

and during the trial before the religious leadership Jesus tells his adversaries, drawing upon Dan 7:13,

> "You will see the Son of Man
> seated at the right hand of the Power,"
> and "coming with the clouds of heaven" (Mark 14:62).

If Mark has Jesus saying these words to his enemies, then clearly as far as Mark is concerned the events heralding the arrival of God's rule are imminent. For Jesus, his own vindication is near, and God's judgment against those who have resisted God's rule is about to be rendered. For Mark, the course of history is now in the balance.

Listen to the parable that fig trees teach. Recognizing that the end-time is at hand ought to be no more difficult than watching a fig tree as it blossoms, matures, and yields its fruit. Indeed, one's realization that summer is near does not depend upon the leafing of a fig tree, but the leafing of the tree means that all the natural processes that have been silently working together have reached their purpose or fulfillment. As in the earlier parable about growing seed (Mark 4:26-29) the mystery here is to be found in the interval, the period of waiting, when numerous forces imperceptibly, tortuously, but irresistibly conspire to bring history to its fruit-bearing moment. Needless to say, Mark is not advocating that we all become farmers and spend our time studying stalks of wheat, mustard plants, and fig trees as if they were nature's allegories. What we need to do, rather, is to observe closely our historical moment in order to perceive there the signs that indicate that more is going on than meets the eye. For the Christian the victory of God is assured; that much is central to Easter faith. But imagination has to be enabled to harvest the signals that confirm this faith. And for this enabling the parables the world provides can be of singular assistance.

If the story of Jesus is the great Christian parable about struggle and protest, justice and victory, then we might find ourselves wondering whether suffering is an absolute requirement for Christian discipleship. And if suffering is not only inescapable but also somehow necessary, does Mark mean to tell us that we ought to be on the lookout for occasions to suffer and even to welcome as many crosses as our shoulders can possibly bear? This is the question we shall consider next.

8

Does Mark Encourage
a Cult of Suffering?

He called the crowd with his disciples, and said to them, "If any want to become my followers, let them deny themselves and take up their cross and follow me" (Mark 8:34).

Given the prominence of the cross in Mark's account of Jesus' life and the central role it plays in our discipleship, an outsider could get the impression that the Christian religion encourages suffering, viewing it as meritorious and even to be sought after for the perfect imitation of Jesus. But such an impression would not represent an accurate reading of Mark. To be sure, Paul welcomed the sufferings that constantly attended his ministry because they confirmed his apostleship and the integrity of his call and, thereby, his authority. He also rejoiced in the suffering he incurred as a result of coming to know the crucified and risen Jesus. Paul thought of himself as personally sharing in Jesus' sufferings, and thus he saw himself becoming increasingly like the one he loved. Many saints have followed this Pauline slant on discipleship, even in some cases to the point of receiving the stigmata. Yet I do not find any evidence that Mark, however much he loved and worshiped Jesus, shared this spiritual inclination.

Not All Suffering Is Alike

We have already seen that not every form of suffering is the same. Sickness and diminishment, for example, are intrinsic to the human condition, while other suffering is the consequence of events in nature. Some suffering results from our own foolishness or sinfulness. Another class of suffering is made up of the struggles of daily existence, perhaps more appropriately described as schooling. Through these we learn about humility, wisdom, self-control, and patience. There is also the suffering that we may be forced to endure as a result of the sinfulness and stupidity of other men and women, and finally there is the suffering that comes as a result of our standing by our convictions and living out our faith. The suffering that Mark normally has in mind is the suffering of the prophet who testifies to God's word and the suffering that accompanies the following of Jesus; this is prophetic living. A non-Markan expression of this idea would be Jesus' words: "Blessed are you when people revile you and persecute you and utter all kinds of evil against you falsely *on my account.* . . . [F]or *in the same way they persecuted the prophets* who were before you" (Matt 5:11-12).

The inescapability of suffering within the life of discipleship is apparent from the three passion predictions in chapters 8, 9, and 10. What Jesus predicts for himself the evangelist is forecasting for the community of his own day. For obvious reasons the disciple's suffering will seldom take the form of death by crucifixion. Mark is no literalist about the cross. But suffering will entail self-denial (8:34), humility and service (9:35), and becoming the least of all and the slave of all (10:43-44). Mark takes advantage of the three predictions to instruct us about the condition of continuing on the way with Jesus. "*If* any want to become my followers, *let them* deny themselves and take up their cross and follow me" might well be the major text about Christian spirituality within the Gospel as a whole. In one form or another the cross is going to be a consequence of discipleship. If the cross does not surface in a person's life, then the integrity of one's following of Jesus needs to be examined.

After the transfiguration scene Jesus says, "How then *is it written* about the Son of Man, that he is to go through many sufferings and be treated with contempt?" (Mark 9:12). This saying implies that Jesus' suffering was foreseen in the Old Testament. It would be more accurate to say, however, that the mistreatment and rejection of the Son of Man is to be understood as the fate that awaits every prophet and even Israel itself as God's righteous servant. The Hebrew Scriptures, in other words, testify to the likely fate of those who proclaim God's word in a sinful world. In Mark 9:13 Jesus states that Elijah has come "and they did to him whatever they pleased." The allusion is to John the Baptist. If John, the messenger who had prepared Jesus' way (1:3), suffered imprisonment and death, then Jesus would scarcely be able to escape a similar destiny. The detailed story of John's death, sandwiched between the going forth and return of the disciples, not only anticipates Jesus' death, it also points to the possibilities awaiting anyone associated with Jesus in his mission.

It is understandable, then, why someone might conclude that either consciously or unconsciously Mark is fostering a cult of suffering. A suggestion often given to account for Mark's stress upon the cross is the historical situation of the community for which he was writing. It could have been a community of Christians in a pagan society that had to face suspicion, social marginalization, political danger, or religious persecution, a point that may be intimated in such passages as the stilling of the storm in Mark 4:35-41 and the prediction of persecution in Mark 13:9-13. Mark's purpose in writing, then, would have been to urge the community to remain steadfast by contemplating the example of Jesus.

But while the painful surroundings in which the community may have found itself could certainly have prompted an apostolic letter, would they call forth a gospel? Might it not be just as plausible that the Gospel's stress upon the cross reflects the catechesis Mark himself had received, or even the evangelist's own experience of conversion and subsequent effort to live as a Christian?

Jesus himself was drawn into conflict as a result of his bold proclamation of the kingdom of God and, like a flesh-and-blood parable, his enacting of that reality through his meals with sinners, his healings and exorcisms, and countless interactions with the people of Galilee. What was his entry into Jerusalem, seated upon a donkey, if not a parabolic enacting of the sort of kingdom he represented (and which, presumably, his adversaries did not)? The actual reason for suffering in Jesus' life was not illness, accidental misfortune, anxiety over the welfare of his family, or destitution. It was fidelity to God's word, to his mission, and to the people of Israel. As we have seen, the *necessity* of suffering in God's plan has to do with the conflict provoked by prophetic living.

The point bears repeating that God takes no delight in human suffering. It would be inconsistent of Mark to tell the story of Jesus as one who relieves men and women of their burdens while at the same time urging his readers to welcome suffering, unless we know what sort of suffering he is talking about. "Let them deny themselves and take up their cross and follow me" is not an invitation to a wooden or unthinking imitation of Jesus or to a literalist interpretation of the word "cross."

The text about how the Son of Man "*must* undergo suffering" (Mark 8:31) connotes prophetic necessity, not divine decree. The reason why the early Christians spoke that way was their conviction that Jesus' death was no accident and that whatever happened in the world could only have happened according to God's plan. But Jesus' dying on a cross was a contingent event. It did not have to happen, and maybe his crucifixion would not have occurred had people responded favorably to his message. Edward Schillebeeckx writes:

> Suffering is not redemptive in itself. But it is redemptive when it is suffering through and for others, for man's cause as the cause of the one who says that he is "in solidarity with my people," who has "conquered the world" (John 16:33b). The New Testament does not praise suffering but only suffering in and with resistance against injustice and suffering. It praises suffering "for the sake of the kingdom of God" or "for the sake of the Gospel" (Mark 8:35; 10:29), for the sake of righteousness (1 Pet 3:14), "unmerited suffering" (1 Pet 3:17), "for the good" (1 Pet 3:17), "suffering although you do right" (1 Pet 2:20f.), in solidarity with one's brothers (Heb 2:17f.). Suffering itself goes with the crooked lines which men draw. "The hour is coming when whoever kills you will think that he is offering service to God" (John 16:2b). . . . Therefore instead of a "divine must" or an apocalyptic necessity, Hebrews says in a more restrained way, more on a human than a divine plane, "It was fitting that he for whom and by whom all things exist, in bringing many sons to glory, should make the pioneer of their salvation perfect through suffering" (Heb 2:10). For the name of God is "the one who shows solidarity with his people," and this people suffers.[1]

The type of suffering Jesus has in mind when he speaks of people taking up their cross is, I would argue, the suffering of prophetic living. Undoing injustice, defending those whose rights have been trampled, assisting those who have been robbed of human dignity to recover it, keeping a vigilant eye for the most vulnerable members of society: these are prophetic works. Prophetic suffering arises from a solidarity that is both real and effective. To the degree that one lives with and for others, one is naturally going to share in whatever happens to them. For some solidarity will translate into accompanying the poor physically. For all it will require accompanying them politically. And from the poor themselves Jesus demands the same readiness to take up "their cross" as he expects from those who are financially and socially advantaged. Poverty and deprivation do not automatically induce solidarity with the wider human experience of suffering. If they want to follow Jesus, even poor people have to learn to deny themselves and to live for others.

Commenting on Mark 8:34, Morna Hooker notes a difficulty with the translation "deny themselves." She explains:

> The traditional translation, "deny himself," has been warped through being interpreted in terms of asceticism. The attitude called for is one in which self-interest and personal desires are no longer central.[2]

[1] Schillebeeckx, *Christ*, 640.
[2] Hooker, *Gospel According to Saint Mark*, 208.

Her point is well taken. Mark's verb, she notes, actually means "to disown" or "to renounce a claim to." The idea would seem to be, then, that one cedes ownership of his or her life to another (and not merely puts the ownership up for grabs). The other person could be Jesus, of course, but that invites a further question: in whose favor did Jesus "disown" his life? To answer "God" would be correct but perhaps too abstract. Earlier in the narrative Jesus exposed the hollow devotion of the Pharisees when he quoted them as saying to their parents, "'Whatever support you might have had from me is Corban' (that is, an offering to God)" (Mark 7:11). In that case, dedicating something for sacred use was a way of dodging the responsibility to one's parents enjoined by Moses. Thus to cede ownership of oneself to God could be a way of sidestepping other obligations. Moreover, as Creator, God already lays claim to us. Perhaps the more challenging way to interpret the text is to suggest that one is expected to yield ownership of oneself to the people.

Hooker continues with Jesus' instruction about taking up one's cross:

> This vivid image, in which the disciple of Jesus is likened to a condemned criminal carrying the transverse beam of his own cross to the place of execution . . . is an obvious one to use of Christian discipleship after the crucifixion of Jesus himself. It is not so clear whether it would have been meaningful before the event. Certainly crucifixions were sufficiently common for the comparison to be used, but some have questioned whether Jesus was likely—unless he foresaw the manner of his own death—to have used this particular image, *since crucifixion was associated in men's minds with the activity of criminals: the words might even have seemed to be a call to rebel against Rome, and risk the consequences.* If the image does go back to Jesus, then presumably he used it to convey—in a way which would certainly shock his hearers—the shame and disgrace which discipleship might mean.[3]

In this case the distinction between what a cross would have signified in the popular mind before the death of Jesus and what it signified for the Christian community after his death is important. It is unlikely that any of Jesus' followers would have warmed to the idea of being branded as criminals for their identifying mark and considerably less likely that Jesus advocated armed resistance against Roman imperialism. After Easter, of course, the cross was fused with resurrection faith. Thus taking up the cross in a paschal context would have to involve taking on oneself the whole project or mission of Jesus. The "shame and disgrace" that follows is ultimately the shame and disgrace of being associated not with the risen Jesus but with people who have been disowned, disesteemed, and disenfranchised by their

---

[3] Ibid. 208–209. Emphasis added.

societies. Standing alongside the lowest and least among God's people is precisely what taking up the cross amounts to.

Actually, Mark uses the word "cross" only four times in his narrative: once in 8:34 and three times as he narrates chapter 15 (vv. 21, 30, 32). The verb forms "crucify" and "crucified" appear eight times in chapter 15 and once in 16:6, and in each instance they merely indicate historical action, not theological reflection. Mark 8:34 stands alone as an expression of the cross as religious symbol. Two conclusions may follow from this usage. First, that the cross was the physical instrument of Jesus' execution was so deeply woven into Christian memory that there was no need to say more about it earlier in the Gospel narrative. When Jesus three times predicted that he would be killed, Mark's audience already knew the historical details.

Second, the community's abiding interest was less the cross as an instrument of torture and death than as the symbolic expression of Jesus' life, teaching, and service. Although Mark does not develop the point, the significance of the words "Then they led him out to crucify him" (15:20) would not have been lost on him. The fact that it was in Jerusalem that Jesus was arrested, tried, and sentenced to death might account for why the risen Jesus returns to Galilee; Jerusalem had proven to be a treacherous city and its Temple an insidious place. The cursing of the fig tree, the graphic parable about the vineyard and its murderous tenants, and the prediction of the Temple's destruction leave little doubt as to where Mark stood on the matter of Jerusalem. Thus the symbolism of the cross also included Jesus' rejection by the religious establishment of Israel, perhaps even his being killed as a rebellious son. Despite its rather straightforward tone, every last detail of the passion narrative carried another message beyond the literal one for those with ears to hear. Mark knew that. He was not simply reporting or mindlessly transmitting the record of Jesus' final hours; his ear was not deaf to the rich scriptural resonances of the tradition he had received. "Then they led him out" would easily have suggested to Mark that the Son of God had been definitively disowned by the Jerusalem elites. The disowning of oneself thereby takes on the additional meaning of joining Jesus in disgrace because one has sided with those whom the political and cultural establishment regards as the throwaways who live permanently "outside the camp" (Heb 13:13).

Furthermore, in its ongoing remembrance of the cross the community would have never isolated Jesus' humiliating death from his resurrection; indeed, how could it do so? Cross without resurrection would cast only another long, tragic shadow across human history. The resurrection, on the other hand, was not the invention of zealous imagination. The notion of an individual (and not the nation as a whole) *being raised from the dead* would have struck a Jewish audience as terribly peculiar, and it would have spelled complete nonsense among cultured people in the Hellenistic world.[4]

The raising of the dead was an apocalyptic image for the ultimate triumph of God over all the enemies of God's people and for the definitive restoration of Israel as God's chosen and beloved child. Ezekiel's vision in the valley of the bones, where the prophet "sees" the marvelous restoration of a defeated people, bears eloquent testimony to the burning hope that resided in many Jewish hearts (see Ezekiel 37). Joining that notion of divine victory to Jesus involved far more than an artful pairing of ideas, however. By employing an apocalyptic image to express the significance of what happened after the crucifixion, the early Church was pointing to an action of God, an action that had penetrated and gradually transformed the religious sensibilities of Jesus' first followers. It left them with no doubt that Jesus and everything he represented had not been defeated by Roman imperialism and the hostility of the Jewish religious leadership after all. Mark did not engineer that fusion of image and concept; he would have inherited it from communities steeped in the Hebrew Bible. In raising Jesus from the dead, at least as far as the evangelist was concerned, God had turned Israel's great image into reality.

Mark's summing up of Jesus' life in terms of the cross, then, supposes a fairly rapid emergence of a distinctively Christian spirituality. Its starting point was the resurrection. The horizon of its experience was primarily the history of unjust suffering, rendered vividly real and unforgettable in the crucifixion of Jesus. Its narrative world was everyday life among

---

[4] The resurrection of the dead and the personal immortality of the righteous are not equivalent notions. The former is an apocalyptic expression that confidently announces the future restoration of Israel, while the latter looks to the reward God "owes" to those whose obedience and fidelity to the truth were never compromised even in the face of excruciating torture. The belief in personal immortality can be found, for instance, in the Wisdom of Solomon 2:22-24 and 3:1-7. Yet even here the belief in national vindication can be found (see v. 7). Christians sometimes blur the difference when they think of the resurrection. Yes, we believe that we shall live forever with God; but is this the message that God was revealing in raising Jesus from the dead? Did belief in the afterlife require divine confirmation? Or was the primary message of the resurrection about the inauguration of the reign of God's justice and the certitude that justice will prevail against all enemies? Again, our preaching about the resurrection combines both elements, but the more challenging element is the second. At first glance, it is easier to believe in personal immortality than in the complete victory of God's justice and the transformation of human history. Yet if God can guarantee life after death but not the vindication of crucified people in this world, what sort of power over death would that be?

first-century Galilean peasants. Its magnetism lay in its intense confidence that God would establish justice upon the earth and vindicate all those who had suffered at the hands of wicked, faithless men. Its religious energy sprang from an experience of being in the company of the risen Jesus.

Life as Ransom

There is a companion text to Mark 8:34 that is relevant here. The verse "For the Son of Man came not to be served but to serve, and to give his life a ransom for many" (10:45) not only abbreviates the life of Jesus, it also furnishes the basic formula for joyful Christian living. The disciple verifies experientially that fulfillment and happiness come in living for others; following Jesus may be demanding, but it is never oppressive. If the gospel that one lives and puts into practice each day is supposed to be God's good news, then the freedom and peace which that news brings ought to be visible in some measure in the disciple himself or herself. The linguistic ambiguity in the Gospel's opening verse—the good news that Jesus himself is, or the good news of which Jesus was the messenger— could apply equally to Jesus' followers. Not only do they announce the gospel by their lives; they enflesh that gospel through their actions, their prayerfulness and freedom, and their solidarity with all God's people.

The second half of Mark 10:45 contains a metaphor that needs explanation. Jesus' life was not literally a ransom, of course. Any suggestion that Jesus' life was the "price" that had to be paid to Satan in order to buy back the human race twists the metaphor and substitutes mythology for history. Sometimes humanity passes through moments so bleak and destructive that one might be tempted to conclude that God had yielded sovereignty to the powers of evil. But God never vacates the heavens or the earth, never delegates dominion, can never be robbed of power. Besides, even in mythological terms, the death of Jesus would have been of absolutely no use to Satan: a compromised Jesus, yes, but not a crucified one. Ransom, like the word "redemption," has to do with purchasing. The closest analogy we have in our society might be redemption centers: not churches but places where bottles and aluminum cans are "redeemed" and sent off for recycling! The basic metaphor in the words "to give his life a ransom for many" is constructed around the fact that individuals taken captive in war sometimes regained their freedom if their families could raise sufficient cash; so too with slaves and indentured servants.[5]

---

[5] Exodus speaks of ransom in the sense of damages to be paid by a person who failed to restrain a dangerous ox as a way of saving his own life (21:28-32). Obviously Jesus did

What then would Jesus have seen himself buying back? As far as Mark was concerned, Jesus viewed his death as the price of Israel's freedom. If Jesus did view the meaning of his death in those terms, however, what positive, tangible effect did his dying have on the subsequent history of Israel? I think the answer would have to be, firmly, that there was no positive effect. Indeed, in time the Jewish people would suffer severely at the hands of Christians: so much so that the death of Jesus not only did not ransom them, it might even be said to have plagued and imprisoned them for centuries. If the saying in Mark 8:34 was intended to anticipate the cross and interpret its meaning, then we need to point out that Jesus' death would have accomplished nothing unless God had constituted it an instrument of revelation. In other words, Jesus could not have made his own death a means of salvation. Only God could do that.

The metaphor of ransom, then, is about freedom. It is about living in such a way that men and women recover the freedom that is properly theirs as sons and daughters of God. And the recovery of that freedom was not restricted to the household of Israel, as Mark well knew. Throughout the Gospel story Jesus set many people free: from diseases, from physical impairment, from demons, from the threat of hunger, from religious exploitation, from their fears, and from sin. In fact, immediately after declaring that the Son of Man had come to serve, Jesus encountered the blind Bartimaeus, and he asked him (perhaps in the deferential manner and tone of a servant), "What do you want me to do for you?" (Mark 10:51). Jesus set the poor man free from his blindness, and once free, he joined the procession to Jerusalem.

A reader looking for the theme of love in Mark should pay close attention to Jesus' saying about his life as ransom. There is a tenderness in

---

not have that sense in mind. The word "redeem" may be far richer than "ransom." "Redeem" normally refers to regaining ownership of one's land or one's farm animals, things absolutely essential to a family's survival, which may have been lost because of indebtedness; but "redeem" can also refer to unfortunate Israelites who had to sell themselves into servitude or virtual slavery (see Lev 25), and the noun "redemption" also embraces the action of God in delivering his people. The idea seems to be that God does not want alienation of any sort: alienation of familial property, one's means of support, or even of one's own person. God does not want Israel to exist in a permanent state of exile, servitude, or religious estrangement. See Unterman, "Redemption (OT)," 5:654–57. In the companion entry "Redemption (NT)," Shrogen notes: "While moderns may speak of redemption as a metaphor for the entire saving act, the NT writers used it precisely in the context of well-known social customs" (5:655). In other words, in Mark 10:45 manumission is the metaphor for what Jesus does for his people.

the words "If any want to become my followers, let them deny themselves and take up their cross and follow me" (8:34), which could easily be missed in view of the harsh exchange with Peter that precedes it. For the verse does not simply lay down a theoretical condition of *if* and *then;* the saying is an appeal for fidelity, not a shakedown of the weak-kneed among his followers. So too in Mark 9:36-37. Following the second passion prediction Jesus takes a child in his arms. The warmth of the scene flows backwards and contributes to how we should hear his words about betrayal and death in 9:31. But Mark 10:45 (especially when linked with Jesus' readiness to serve Bartimaeus: "What do you want me to do for you?") is particularly tender. Ransom becomes the metaphor for love. Mark, we ought to conclude, has not been advocating a cult of suffering. Whatever suffering arises results from the solidarity created by love.

Lest the passion predictions make his message about the cross seem unrelenting, maybe Mark felt that his audience would appreciate a word of divine assurance at this stage of the narrative. The story of the transfiguration relieves some of the tension the reader or listener may be experiencing by the time we reach chapter 9, but it introduces more than an intimation of glory. Why does the evangelist situate Jesus alongside the figures of Elijah and Moses, and what bearing does this scene have on the way we view our own lives? Such is the question that will occupy us in the following chapter.

9

In the Company of Prophets

"Who do people say that I am?" And they answered him, "John the Baptist; and others, Elijah; and still others, one of the prophets" (Mark 8:27-28).

Consistency is not necessarily a virtue even for inspired writers. Unwilling to discard stray sayings or duplicate traditions, a biblical writer or editor may incorporate everything at his disposal that seems consonant with the faith he has received. Scripture's first example is the inclusion of two creation stories in Genesis, while at the end of the Bible the book of Revelation betrays several distinct compositional strands. The lack of smoothness that appears in Mark, at any rate, is not an indication of literary inattentiveness but of pastoral, liturgical, or catechetical function.

In chapter 13 the evangelist presents a Jesus who knows the future, but in Mark 5:30 we find him asking, "Who touched my clothes?" On the one hand, crowds are pressing around Jesus so they might be healed (3:10); on the other hand, Jesus wonders who touched him. How come one who reads human hearts (2:8) has to ask the blind Bartimaeus, "What do you want me to do for you?" (10:51). In Mark 1:43-44 and 5:43 Jesus, somewhat unrealistically, enjoins strict silence after performing miracles that are bound to be noticed, but in 5:19 he commands just the opposite. Why would the disciples ever have entertained the least hesitation in following Jesus after witnessing the calming of the wind and the waves (4:39), or the walking over the water (6:48-49), or the multiplication of loaves not once but twice? Or how is it that Mark 6:5-6 reports that Jesus was unable to work any deeds of power in his hometown because the villagers of Nazareth lacked faith, although he had shortly before calmed the sea for his fearful disciples while chastising them for their unbelief (4:40)? What led Jesus spontaneously to drive out a multitude of unclean spirits from a demon-infested Gentile in Mark 5:1-20, while he resisted the request of a Gentile woman to drive an unclean spirit from her daughter in 7:24-30? Above all, how could it be that the three disciples privileged to share the theophany on the Mount of Transfiguration failed to distinguish themselves during the hours of Jesus' passion?

Add to these instances sayings that appear to be inserted into the text without much regard for their setting, and the reader is tempted to wonder about the literary astuteness of the author. Jesus' words in Mark 11:23, "Truly I tell you, if you say to this mountain, 'Be taken up and thrown into the sea,' and if you do not doubt in your heart, but believe that what you say will come to pass, it will be done for you," are followed by these of verse 24: "So I tell you, whatever you ask for in prayer, believe that you have received it, and it will be yours." Mark seems to be implying that God will grant even the most preposterous requests! Verse 25 is beautiful, but it stands unconnected from the two preceding verses: "Whenever you stand praying, forgive, if you have anything against anyone; so that your Father in heaven may also forgive you your trespasses."[1]

Making literary sense of the Gospel is surely a challenge, although it is not impossible. The fragmentary character of the narrative, its inconsistencies, and its protruding sayings suggest that the Gospel reflects not so much a manner of writing as a manner of teaching. It does not matter to Mark, for instance, that in one scene Jesus could ask, "Who touched my clothes?" and that in another scene sick people were reaching to finger the fringe of his cloak (Mark 6:56). Similarly, it does not matter to Mark that the disciples could both witness Jesus transfigured and later fail to grasp the meaning of his mission, for the lessons are different. One can appreciate how early Christian writers intent upon demonstrating the harmony and coherence of the four Gospels would have found Mark particularly troublesome. Today the note of fragmentation seems curiously contemporary.

"And he was transfigured"

From the point of view of narrative alone, the story of the transfiguration may be one of the most intriguing in Mark's Gospel; clearly, it has no parallel. Its historicity is easily challenged by careful exegesis, yet even

---

[1] If we adopt Wright's point that the mountain in question is Mount Zion, on which the Temple sits (*Jesus and the Victory of God*, 334–35), then the meaning of the prayer would appear to be a request for the Temple's elimination. It would still be difficult, however, to reconcile that sentiment with the instruction that follows about never standing in God's presence without the attitude of forgiveness.

as a story its theological importance is considerable.[2] There is a potentially serious stress line in the story, however. Why Jesus would invite three of his closest followers to witness such a supernatural event in a gospel where everything depends upon faith and where Jesus rejects the craving for signs is puzzling. If the transfiguration is intended to confirm the disciples' faith, then surely such confirmation is not something they need and nobody else. But confirmation of faith through miraculous or supernatural signs does not seem to be Mark's understanding of what belief is all about.

In his homily on Mark 9:1-7, Jerome sets out the basic points of the story this way:

> "Now after six days Jesus took Peter, James and John, and led them up a high mountain off by themselves, and was transfigured before them." This, they say, is Christ ruling; the apostles saw what kind of king Christ was going to be. When they saw Him transfigured upon the mountain, they saw Him in the glory that would be His. This, therefore, is the meaning behind the words: They shall not taste death, until they have seen the kingdom of God—which came to pass six days later. The Gospel according to Matthew has: "Now it came to pass on the eighth day." There seems to be a difference in the chronology, for Matthew says eight days, Mark, six. What we have to understand is that Matthew counted the first day and the last, but Mark reckoned the time in between. The historical facts are that He ascended a mountain; He was transfigured; Moses and Elias were seen speaking with Him; Peter said to him that he was delighted with this glorious vision: "Lord, if thou wilt let us set up three tents here, one for thee, one for Moses, and one for Elias." Immediately, the evangelist adds: "For he did not know what to say, for they were struck with fear." Next, he says that a cloud appeared, that this same bright cloud overshadowed them, and there came a voice from heaven, saying: "This

---

[2] The transfiguration episode serves (1) a *narrative* function, relieving the tension after the first passion prediction and signaling to the reader that glory is on the horizon; (2) a *sociological* function, by strengthening the authority of these prominent figures (see 2 Pet 1:16-18); and (3) an *apologetic* function. (On the use of the story in 2 Peter see Brown, *Introduction to the New Testament,* 763–64). Since there were no eyewitnesses to the raising of Jesus from the dead, at least three of the original apostles could be reported to have seen the glorified Jesus at some time during his earthly life. The episode thus eased a certain awkwardness or embarrassment over the fact that no one was at the tomb site on Easter morning. For background, see John Michael Perry's brief but helpful *Exploring the Transfiguration Story* (Kansas City: Sheed & Ward, 1993). In his 1996 apostolic exhortation *Consecrated Life (Vita consecrata)* John Paul II used the transfiguration as a meditative point of departure for presenting a theology of the religious life. The story's rich symbolism makes it an attractive metaphor of the soul's ascent to union with God.

is my beloved Son; hear him. And suddenly looking around, they no longer saw anyone with them, but Jesus only." That is history.[3]

Jerome understood the transfiguration to be the coming true of Jesus' prediction in Mark 9:1, "Truly I tell you, there are some standing here who will not taste death until they see that the kingdom of God has come with power." Then, having delineated what he took to be the historical details, Jerome proceeded to the more important level of the story. The rest of the homily becomes largely an allegorizing of the individual details; he explains the relevance of the story to the believer's interior life. For example:

> The earthly man cannot whiten his garments; but he who abandons the world and ascends the mountain with Jesus, and meditating mounts to heavenly contemplations, that man is able to make his garments white as no fuller on earth can do.[4]

But Jerome also picked up on what had become a major Christian theme, namely, that Jesus is the key to interpreting the Law and the Prophets and that Jesus surpasses them the way the brightness of the sun makes it impossible to notice the light of a lamp. Peter's mistake, corrected by the heavenly voice, was to regard the three figures in the vision as equal. Jerome concludes:

> If the sun is shining, the light of the lamp is not visible, so when Christ is present, the Law and the prophets, by comparison, are not even visible. I am not detracting from the Law and the prophets, rather I am praising them, for they proclaim Christ; I so read the Law and the prophets that I do not remain in them, but through them arrive at Christ.[5]

Mark does not mention what Elijah and Moses were conversing with Jesus about. To answer that, Jerome had to borrow from Luke. Jerome also glossed over the fact that Mark identified Elijah before Moses (although Peter subsequently reversed the order), and he failed to explain how Peter was able to identify who the two figures were. But Jerome does find a reason for Peter's lack of spiritual insight. In effect, Peter had failed to grasp the unity of the Law, the Prophets, and the Gospel, because the paschal mystery had not yet unfolded: "O Peter, even though you have ascended the

---

[3] *Homily* 80 [On Mark 9:1-7], *Homilies of Saint Jerome,* vol. 2, trans. Marie Liguori Ewald, The Fathers of the Church Series, vol. 57 (Washington: The Catholic Univ. of America Press, 1966) 161.
[4] Ibid., 163.
[5] Ibid., 168.

mountain, even though you see Jesus transfigured, even though His garments are white; nevertheless, because Christ has not yet suffered for you, you are still unable to know the truth."[6] Jerome's comment is interesting; he is arguing that the cross furnishes the proper context for interpreting the transfiguration. Or, more precisely, that Peter's having experienced the depth of Jesus' love is the condition for grasping the truth about him.

That the cross is central to every version of the Christian story goes without saying. Nevertheless, the bold relief into which Mark has set the cross by devoting two chapters to the passion narrative and by evoking the reader's remembrance of it as early as chapter 8 should not dull our awareness of the pervasive presence of Easter. The three passion predictions are also predictions of the resurrection, and if we take into account the words "he ordered them to tell no one about what they had seen, until after the Son of Man had risen from the dead" (Mark 9:9), then we may even have a fourth Easter prediction. It was to the risen Lord that Mark was converted, and it was in the presence of Jesus risen that Mark's audience heard the Gospel. It is unlikely they would have drawn a connection between the transfiguration scene and a resurrection appearance for the simple reason (following Jerome) that the cross and resurrection lay in the future. Likewise, *pace* Jerome, they would probably not have taken the transfiguration to be the fulfillment of Jesus' prediction about not tasting death until the kingdom of God had arrived with power, again for the simple reason that both Mark and his audience realized that the kingdom had not yet arrived, and that in any event a vision was not the reality.

Did Mark believe that underneath his human form Jesus was truly something very different and that the vision was revealing to the disciples Jesus' true but temporarily concealed nature? Although the transfiguration occurs relatively late in the Gospel, Mark does have the disciples question fairly early, "Who then is this, that even the wind and the sea obey him?" (Mark 4:41). And the one who shortly afterwards walks across the water is clearly no ordinary man. Does the heavenly voice, in other words, announce who Jesus already is?

The evangelist, however, does not clearly differentiate a pre-Easter and post-Easter Jesus. The post-Easter Jesus had a human history, but the character of that history has been thoroughly reheard in light of his having been raised from the dead. The heavenly voice, then, is announcing what could only have been known as a result of Easter.[7] The transfiguration cannot be

[6] Ibid., 166.

[7] Regarding the baptism, Raymond Brown notes: "The voice of God at the baptism speaks *for the sake of readers* to tell them at the outset who Jesus is" (*Introduction to New*

described as an Easter apparition, but the genesis of the story would be hard to explain unless Jesus had already been raised from the dead. In other words, it appears to be an Easter-inspired meditation on the significance of Jesus—the glory of God turned toward the world and the one who speaks with God's own voice. The title "Son of God," as we saw earlier, could not have been applied to Jesus until after he had fulfilled his mission. For the early Church, Jesus gave the expression "Son of God" its fullest meaning, but he could not have done so before the cross, as Mark 15:39 implies.[8]

It may be worth noting that Jesus does not bring about the transfiguration. The whitening of his garments and the flaming brilliance of his person are manifestations of his being vested with glory or his sharing in the radiance of God. In other words, God "transfigured" Jesus.[9] If we follow the story too literally, however, it might appear that Jesus was showing off in front of his followers, not helping them to grow as believers.

The visionary experience of Mark 9:2-7, then, anticipates the death and resurrection of Jesus. The three disciples, as historical figures, actually have a benign presence in the story; it is not about them. Elijah and Moses appear (in that order) perhaps because Mark was fascinated by the figure of Elijah, who was in some ways the quintessential prophet. Was

---

Testament Christology, 84). The voice at the transfiguration serves a similar purpose. The reader could mentally supply the words "Listen to him!" as shorthand for "Follow him!" in the baptism scene without interfering with the text. Since the three disciples do not really comprehend Jesus and his mission until after the resurrection, the divine instruction at the transfiguration about listening to Jesus is more likely directing the reader/listener to pay attention to the passion predictions and the teaching that accompanies them.

[8] For Mark the major import of the title is that if Jesus is truly Son of God, then he should be followed. In an essay on the transfiguration Ernest Best writes: "Scholarship today tends to have a Christological fixation; it is doubtful if the early Christians were as much concerned to express the nature of Christ as we are to understand their expression of it. Christianity was for living, not for definition." See his *Disciples and Discipleship*, 221.

[9] By the same token, neither the transfiguration nor the resurrection ought to be thought of as miracles. In the Gospel, Jesus works miracles through the power of the Spirit; but Jesus did not "work" the transfiguration, and he did not raise himself from the dead. To say that God works miracles is a truism. Everything God does, by definition, is "miraculous," even though human beings do not consistently perceive the world as the work of God's hands. One of the things miracles do is to elicit or confirm faith: no faith, no miracle. Creation is not usually classified as a miracle (for there were evidently no witnesses), but we may have to turn to creation to gauge the sort of event the resurrection is. The transfiguration had observers, but the story is essentially didactic. Creation and resurrection provide the coordinates for the Christian understanding of God, but they are essentially saving acts, displays of divine power and love. That does not seem to be the character of the transfiguration episode.

Elijah the mold that gave definition to Mark's sense of John the Baptist? Indeed, what was it about Jesus' behavior that led some to conclude that he could have been Elijah (Mark 6:15; 8:28)? The figure of Moses, on the other hand, makes eminent sense in the scene, for he represents all that had been written in the Hebrew Scriptures. Morna Hooker comments: "[S]ince the term 'Torah' could be loosely used of the whole of Scripture, not just the Pentateuch, Moses would be an obvious symbol for 'what is written' and so may appear here as another 'herald' of Jesus, pointing forward to his coming."[10] Together, the two figures give symbolic expression to the catechetical formula "the Law and the Prophets."

That the tradition should have joined these Old Testament figures, Elijah from the eighth century B.C.E. and Moses from the thirteenth, is not all that surprising. A number of Renaissance painters took similar liberties with the figures of Jesus, Mary, and the saints, thereby giving artistic form (the *Sacra Conversazione,* or "sacred conversation") to a profound religious and cultural sensibility about the timelessness of truth. Raphael's *St. Cecilia,* for instance, includes the figures of Paul, John the Evangelist, Cecilia, Augustine, and Mary Magdalene, while Domenico Veneziano's *Madonna and Child with Saints* shows Mary with Saints John the Baptist, Francis, Lucy, and Zenobius. Not only does the Christian community live within a communion of saints, but the saints of every time and place live in one another's company. On the purely historical level this is manifestly impossible, and whoever had the insight that led to the transfiguration story, like the artists of a much later time, would have realized that fact as much as we do. The contemporaneity, however, is an effort to depict a mystery. For God there is neither past nor future: "He is God not of the dead, but of the living" (Mark 12:27).

The figures of Elijah and Moses are linked further by two mountains, or rather by the manifestations of God that took place on the summits of Mount Horeb and Mount Sinai, which makes the topographical setting of the transfiguration literarily interesting.[11] If Mark sees an analogy here, then maybe the transfiguration is meant to convey something of *Jesus'* experience of God and not to furnish us with a glimpse of a glorified Jesus through the eyes of terrified disciples. Or does Mark intend for us to witness in this scene Jesus' participation in the glory of God as a prelude to what one day will be ours? Inviting as this possibility might be, it seems more likely that, given its location in the text, the scene is meant to confirm that divine

[10] Hooker, *Gospel According to Saint Mark,* 216–17.
[11] See Exodus 24; 33:17-23; 34:29-35; 40:34-38; also 1 Kgs 19:1-14.

mystery overshadows the whole Gospel narrative and that Jesus lives constantly within the immediate presence of God. The transfiguration obviously did little to illumine and strengthen the three disciples, but it might steady the reader. The transfiguration pierces the Markan silence about what happened after the empty tomb not by recounting an Easter apparition but by drawing the listener into the "cloud" of the divine presence. Walking in the company of Jesus, one is also living in the presence of God.

There is an artful though probably unintended ambiguity in verse 7: "Then a cloud overshadowed them, and from the cloud there came a voice." One is left wondering whether Mark imagined the cloud to have overshadowed the disciples, or just the figures of Moses and Elijah, or these two figures together with Jesus, or all six of them. Since he does not specify more carefully, Mark probably thinks of the cloud as coming over the whole summit, just as it had on Mount Sinai: "The glory of the LORD settled on Mount Sinai, and the cloud covered it for six days; on the seventh day he called to Moses out of the cloud." (Exod 24:16).

This would suggest that in contemplating the scene the viewer has momentarily been pulled into the painting and become a contemporary of all these figures. When the cloud lifts, of course, the disciples see "only" Jesus. And so the divine warning addressed to Moses—"you cannot see my face; for no one shall see me and live" (Exod 33:20)—does not apply in the case of Jesus. Jerome was on the right track after all; but so was Origen before him:

> Do you want to see that Moses is always with Jesus, that is, the law with the Gospel? Let the Gospel teach you that when Jesus "was transfigured" into glory, "Moses and Elias" also "appeared" with him in glory, so that you might know that the law and the prophets and the Gospels always come together as one and stay together in one glory.[12]

For Mark, the Law and the Prophets must henceforth be discovered in Jesus.

As we saw above, Origen had likewise appreciated the deeper, spiritual meaning of the transfiguration story. But unlike Jerome, Origen may have sensed that miraculous revelations need to be approached with theological caution. Commenting on Psalm 27, he reasons:

> We do not think that God speaks to us from outside. For those holy thoughts that arise in our heart, they are the way God speaks to us. This is what it means when you hear [in Scripture] that God has spoken to such and such a person.[13]

---

[12] Hans Urs von Balthasar, *Origen: Spirit and Fire,* 118.
[13] Ibid., 234.

Perhaps Origen's belief about how God speaks to individuals through the inner senses has a communal application. Did the three disciples physically hear the heavenly voice, or was the divine message communicated to them inwardly? Might the story have been composed as a result of a community's having inwardly "heard" an inspired message about Jesus and his relationship to the history of Israel? One thing seems clear. Though figures like Origen and Jerome reverenced the biblical texts, they were challenged, not boxed in, by literalness.

Living in the Presence of Prophets

While Mark thinks of Moses as Israel's teacher and then casts Jesus in the role of Moses' true successor (as, for instance, when Jesus revised the Mosaic instruction about divorce), the fact is that Moses was also considered to be a prophet. The book of Deuteronomy concludes with these words:

> Never since has there arisen a prophet in Israel like Moses, whom the LORD knew face to face. He was unequaled for all the signs and wonders that the LORD sent him to perform in the land of Egypt, against Pharaoh and all his servants and his entire land, and for all the mighty deeds and all the terrifying displays of power that Moses performed in the sight of all Israel (Deut 34:10-12).

Never since, that is, until the coming of Jesus. *Mighty deeds* and *displays of power that terrify* are common in the first twelve chapters of Mark. The two feeding stories in Mark, which sound as if they are patterned more after Elisha's feeding of the one hundred men with twenty barley loaves than after the story of the manna,[14] are prophetic actions: not parabolic condemnatory actions like the cleansing of the Temple or the cursing of the fig tree, but parabolic celebratory actions that confirm God's presence here and now and anticipate the time when all will eat and be filled (Mark 6:42). It is not the kind of food but the abundance that matters in the story.

Historical sands have erased forever any possibility of our knowing what moment in the life of Jesus may have provided the impulse for this remembrance, but the story of the loaves proclaims the coming of God's kingdom as assuredly, say, as Daniel's vision of the "one like a son of man" to whom God will give "dominion and glory and kingship" (Dan 7:14).[15]

---

[14] See 2 Kgs 4:42-44 and Exodus 16. It is not impossible that Mark has elided the figures of Elijah and Elisha, not because he did not know the difference between them but for the sake of a less interrupted narrative. Thus Elijah would be both an actual historical figure and a composite.

[15] The note accompanying Isa 55:1-2 in *The HarperCollins Study Bible* explains: "Kings often celebrated the inauguration or establishment of their reign by providing a great

The story of the loaves, therefore, both situates Jesus against two stunning prophetic acts within Israel's history and shows him proclaiming through his action the coming reign of God. The only other point not to be overlooked is the rather obvious fact that in each of the three stories—in the Sinai wilderness with Moses, in the land of Gilgal with Elisha, in the solitary place with Jesus—the people are hungry. "There was a famine in the land," writes the author of 2 Kings. "You have brought us out into this wilderness to kill this whole assembly with hunger," the people complained to Moses (Exod 16:3). And the disciples: "This is a deserted place, and the hour is now very late; send them away so that they may go into the surrounding country and villages and buy something for themselves to eat" (Mark 6:35-36). We can surmise that in the two Old Testament stories, as in Mark's, the problem was not that people had no money, but that money was of no use in the wilderness or when the whole land suffered from famine. But God does not want the people to perish; God wants them to live, *even if God has to feed them himself.*

In the first account of the loaves the disciples quickly figured out the simplest remedy: disband the crowd. In the second account the condition of the multitude seems much more severe; the people cannot be sent away without peril (Mark 8:2-3), and there is no food in the desert (v. 4). Thus the people are not pictured as suffering from chronic hunger. If they had been, then the message of the miracle would have been blurred. Some might have erroneously concluded that Jesus was promising that whenever they were hungry God would leave baskets of food at their doorstep. The key to the story is not that the people were hungry and therefore Jesus fed them, but that people ate to satisfaction and there was an extraordinary amount of leftovers. Nevertheless, these details also force us to notice that the image of such abundance would be particularly attractive in a world where the majority of people seldom or never eat to the point of satisfaction. Abundance of food as a kingdom metaphor supposes hunger as the norm, not the exception. The *action* of Jesus proclaims and anticipates that those who hunger will have their fill, but the blessing and sharing of the loaves must have been preceded by some instruction about the kingdom of God.

In Mark's imagination the miracle illustrated and confirmed what Jesus had been speaking to the crowds about—in the first instance for an entire day, and in the second instance for three days—even though Mark

---

banquet for their people . . . , so God, the divine king, uses the metaphor of such a free banquet (cf. Prov 9:1-5; John 7:37) to invite Israel to accept God's coming restoration of the nation" (1092). That Mark may be portraying Jesus as king in the feeding story is possible, but more likely Jesus is the prophet announcing and enacting the kingdom of God.

does not feel called upon to elaborate. Indeed, the fact that the story is given in two versions not only underscores the importance of the message that would have accompanied the sign, it also suggests that Jesus had preached the same message on numerous occasions. It would be hard to imagine Jesus describing the kingdom in terms of a superabundance of food unless he was talking to people for whom that prospect would have been beyond their wildest dreams. To speak of never again having to worry about where one's bread would come from must also have been to speak to the people about their physical hunger and the concrete reasons for it.

The fact that the people preferred to listen to Jesus rather than go off and procure something to eat testifies not to any passivity on their part but to their eagerness to hear what the prophet had to say about their lives, their times, the moral and political condition of the nation, and so on. The connection Mark saw between the story of the loaves and eucharistic practice (evident in the formulaic description of the actions of Jesus: taking, blessing, breaking, giving) allows us to highlight the parabolic nature of the Eucharist meal. It also forces us to be mindful of why being at table became such a pronounced feature of the Gospel memories about Jesus. Around Jesus one experiences reconciliation with God and one's neighbors but also the joyous abundance that would mark the messianic era. Each time Christians break bread together in remembrance of Jesus they render themselves mindful of those in the world who are chronically hungry, and they reaffirm their commitment to sharing the bread they have with those who have none.

By withdrawing to solitary places Jesus was hardly advocating a cult-like withdrawal from village life and its demands. Indeed, Mark probably envisioned that the miracle had inspired the people to return to their homes with fresh understanding and renewed hope. Once we view the story of the loaves as a parable of the kingdom (five loaves made to satisfy the hunger of thousands comes pretty close to the seed that yields a hundred percent), we see how it is different from the Old Testament feeding stories. The hunger endured by the crowds who followed Jesus was not the result of a flight from Egyptian captivity or the consequence of prolonged drought. The causes of their hunger lay in social, political, and economic conditions largely outside their control. In feeding them Jesus had prophetically defied those conditions, challenging their legitimacy and declaring God to be the enemy of those responsible for the hunger of his people.

Before leaving this section, I would like to reflect on what might have led Mark to include two nearly identical feeding stories. Although it makes sense to argue on literary grounds that Mark has incorporated two versions of the same story into his Gospel, it is hard to figure out what sense Mark made of the two accounts, which he probably thought reflected two distinct events. Morna Hooker believes that the Gospel text really does not support the traditional view that the first story of the loaves involved a Jewish crowd and the second a Gentile one. Mark 7:31 places Jesus "in the region of the Decapolis," that is, in Gentile territory; but Mark 8:1 is too vague, she argues, to make Jesus' continuing presence in non-Jewish land certain.[16]

Mark's previous reference to the Decapolis occurs in chapter 5, at the end of the fascinating tale about the madman of Gerasa. We were told: "And he went away and began to proclaim in the Decapolis how much Jesus had done for him; and everyone was amazed" (5:20). If we take Mark at his word, then the man appears to have gone around spreading his testimony everywhere, convincingly. Mark devotes too much space to this earlier episode for the outcome to trail off inconsequentially. Given the engrossing story the man would relate about his own salvation, could it be that (according to the way Mark imagines what happened subsequently) the testimony of that liberated Gentile sparked such keen interest in the prophet from Galilee that religious and cultural outsiders would eagerly spend three days in his company? And could it be that while those Gentiles spent three days with him, Jesus' adversaries who had asked for a sign (8:11) were loath to spend a single moment? The fact that the transitional verse begins "In those days" and that the Pharisees suddenly appear in verse 11 does not mean that Mark's imagination has yet left the Decapolis.

We may be stretching a long bow here, but there is something wonderfully parabolic about a person whose life had been wrecked by evil forces becoming a messenger of the liberating love of the God of Israel. The throwaway becomes the cornerstone; a Gentile encounters, believes, and wants to follow Jesus. Mark could not have been unconscious of the connectedness. Jesus arrived in the Decapolis after someone had traveled the roads ahead of him, a person who had a lot to say about what life was like after Legion had been expelled. A Gentile crowd would not have grasped the Old Testament resonances of the miraculous feeding, of course, but that limitation would not have troubled Mark. He situated the second account in the region of the Decapolis not because he was recording history but because he was thinking like

---

[16] Hooker, *Mark,* 188. Myers sees the two accounts in terms of a Jewish and then a Gentile audience (*Binding the Strong Man,* 205–10), as do Howard and Peabody, "Mark," 1349. See also Nineham, *Saint Mark,* 205–11; Donahue, "Mark," 993. The vague "in those days" of Mark 8:1 may represent Mark's imagining of a period of time in Gentile territory. Although I agree with Hooker that the *textual* case for a Gentile reading of the second account is not strong, the *contextual* case seems a lot stronger.

a theologian. It would not have been enough for the Prophets and the Law to come together in Jesus; Gentiles and Jews had to find their principle of unity in him as well. What more effective way to teach this than to have him feed them both? The second account of the loaves is prophetic in the same way the book of Jonah reveals a God who is merciful to Gentiles, or in the way Isaiah proclaims a God whose salvation is also for the nations. The Gentiles—the "nations"—are capable of great faith, which was hardly the sort of sign the Pharisees were looking for.[17] The "leaven of the Pharisees" prevented them from recognizing the signs that the kingdom of God had really drawn near. For Mark, even Jesus' disciples run the risk of being contaminated by that myopia. The difficulty of integrating what the first followers had twice witnessed in the wilderness with their everyday needs and concerns tells us something about the Gospel's ongoing challenge. Miracles, mountaintop wonders, the calming of the seas, and the expelling of demons do not automatically translate into a steady, comprehending following of Jesus.

Prophets and Their People

One cannot think of Elijah and Moses without the people to whom they were sent. The people with their historical fortunes, social and economic conditions, remembrance of suffering, and so forth, in large measure create a prophet's soul. The same rule holds for both John the Baptist and Jesus. "A ransom for many" (10:45) and "my blood . . . poured out for many" (14:24) are but two tiny yet significant expressions of this dimension of Jesus' own prophetic consciousness. The line that distinguishes the prophet from the teacher is permeable, because while not all teachers are prophets, all prophets teach. The formula "the Law and the Prophets" is catechetical shorthand for textual division, not biographical profile. Moses was a teacher and a prophet, and Elijah as representative of Israel's prophetic voices cannot be separated from all the words of the Lord that prophets "received" and delivered.

The extent and depth of prophetic solidarity are strikingly evident in the fact, for instance, that Moses too had to endure the Sinai wilderness,

---

[17] Interestingly, Jerome observed that the four thousand men had *greater* faith than the five thousand because there were fewer leftovers! In other words, they ate more of the Lord's word. If the four thousand were Gentiles, then his suggestion means that the nations were more receptive to the gospel than Israel itself. Perhaps the key is not the leftovers but the number of days spent with Jesus: the second group spent three, and such earnestness may have been Mark's way of signaling the readiness of the Gentiles for faith. See *Mark*, Ancient Christian Commentary on Scripture Series, 106.

that the prophet behind Second Isaiah stood among his people during the humiliating exile in Babylon, that the author of the book of Daniel suffered alongside his people in the Seleucid persecution. John the Baptist was hardly the only person to end his life in Herod's dungeon, and Jesus was by no means the only innocent Jew that the Romans crucified. Each of these prophetic figures lived and died in solidarity with Israel. The menacing political and cultural forces that shadowed the lives of the prophets had first hovered over the people: Egypt, Babylon, Syria, Rome.

By situating Jesus in the presence of two great prophets, the transfiguration story sends a vigorous message not only about the kind of company in which Jesus is to be found but also about the nature of discipleship. To be a companion of Jesus is to live in the company of prophets and even perhaps to take on one's own shoulders the prophetic mantle. To live and pray prophetically entails walking with the people of God without attempting to duck the consequence of having joined one's life to men and women who are heavily burdened.

If the transfiguration scene positions Jesus squarely within Israel's prophetic tradition, then it also invites a crucial question. The mere fact that prophets received divine inspiration did not render them immune to moments of doubt and despair. Jonah attempting to flee his vocation, Elijah under the broom tree, and John the Baptist chained up in Herod's cellar (see Luke 7:18-23) are forceful reminders that trusting God is not always easy, even for men of God. And given the fact that the kingdom of God did not arrive in any identifiable form despite Jesus' confident proclamation, the question about whether God can be trusted is one that Mark could not avoid raising. Such is the concern we shall face in the following chapter.

10

Can God Be Trusted?

At three o'clock Jesus cried out with a loud voice, "Eloi, Eloi, lema sabachthani?" which means, "My God, my God, why have you forsaken me?" (Mark 15:34).

Anyone familiar with the psalms has probably wondered what exactly sustained Israel's faith during those moments or periods of its history when God seemed utterly absent and uninterested in the fate of the people. That the individuals who composed and prayed the psalms did not abandon faith in God altogether is remarkable, given the seriousness of their complaint and the desperation of their pleas. The surrounding nations may have questioned the power of Israel's God and ridiculed their religious claims, but the psalms testify to a steadfastness of belief even during Israel's bitterest hours. The voices behind the psalms wrestled with faith without losing it in the awful emptiness of divine silence.

Most of us would be hard pressed to think of any question more penetrating, more challenging to everyday faith than the one that asks whether God can be trusted. As men and women who have weathered their share of social, emotional, economic, and moral storms over a lifetime, we should be able to answer a profound yes, even though the process by which anyone of us reaches that confidence typically is circuitous, mysterious, and costly. Normally we are not conscious of the redemptive action of God in our lives. Thus occasionally we need to step back and try to figure out how we got to the present moment. Paul's wonderfully hopeful declaration "We know that all things work together for good for those who love God" (Rom 8:28) captured an insight of faith that had been years in the making. *We know,* not because parents or teachers or fellow believers have reassured us but because we have been tracing faith's journey and have learned that while the divine mystery may sometimes feel hidden, it has never been absent.

The question "Can God be trusted?" is an appropriate one to consider as we make our way through Mark's Gospel, not because Mark directly addresses it but because his narrative forces us to come to an existential decision. The question is alluded to in the wilderness episode of Mark 1:13 when Jesus, as the new Israel, was "tested"—a scene that evokes the memory of the old Israel's forty-year schooling in the elementary matter of trusting God. Shall we follow the crucified one, or not? I do not think that Mark believed his listeners had thus far been *unable* to commit themselves to the gospel. In all probability they were intently following Jesus along a demanding and potentially dangerous road. Yet Mark also knew that some seed drifts to the wayside and some inevitably gets choked by the weeds of life, which often turn out to be more than "the cares of the world" and "the lure of wealth." The depth and steadiness of one's response are vulnerable to demons of another sort.

In his engaging account of traveling through the Congo, the naturalist Redmond O'Hanlon describes a scene that has continued to haunt my imagination:

> The huts toward the river were larger than the others, with bigger roofs sloping out over foot-high verandas, and resting on wooden pillars. In one of them, on the veranda, to the right of the central door, on a bench facing uphill, sat a thick-set, middle-aged man in a green tee-shirt, unmoving, his hands on his knees, staring at a small red-mud tomb, its mud headstone surmounted by a crucifix and facing downhill, towards the river, towards him.

Redmond then asked his guide for an explanation, who replied:

> "It's sad. He's a Christian. A missionary came here. That man was converted. Nobody liked him. He took the sacraments, and then his daughter died, ten years old. He sits there like that, every day at this time, and he asks God to tell him, please, why his daughter died, why his daughter was taken away. No answer, of course. Never will be. It would be better for him if he were a sorcerer, or still believed in sorcery, or witchcraft, or magic, or animism—or whatever fancy names you white men invent for it. Then at least he could be angry. He could do something. His friends would understand and they'd talk to him. People would know what do to, how to help. But now, Redmond, he just sits there, bewildered . . ."[1]

---

[1] Redmond O'Hanlon, *No Mercy: Journey to the Heart of the Congo* (New York: Alfred A. Knopf, 1997) 225.

"He asks God to tell him why his daughter died." Not only was the poor man left without his child; his new religion had isolated him completely from everyone in the village and robbed him of the popular religiosity through which he might have made sense of her dying. An incomplete catechesis together with the absence of a supportive faith community can be deadly. More to the point, however, the man had not been instructed about how to relate to God in the event of heartbreaking misfortune. The missionary who converted him did him no good turn.

Mark narrates three stories reminiscent of this one, the story of Jairus' little girl, the Syrophoenician woman's daughter, and the father of an epileptic boy. To be sure, in each of these passages Jesus saves the child. Yet Mark was not so naive as to think that merely because Jesus worked miracles his future followers could count on their loved ones being healed, freed of demons, or restored to life any more than they should count on bread from heaven in times of famine or unemployment.

The sad reality that comes across tacitly in each of these stories is deep parental anxiety; the single nightmare that terrifies any mother or father is the possibility of losing a child. In the first story tragedy appears to have struck suddenly. In the second the illness sounds like a steadily advancing childhood disease; Mark offers no details. We infer the severity of the girl's condition from the lengths to which the mother goes in search of a cure. In the third story, however, Mark unfolds a considerable history of desperation and parental suffering. The first two episodes are miracles pure and simple, but the last one turns out to be less about the child than about the distraught father, and while it concludes with a healing, a major part of its message seems to be about prayer. The story of the epileptic boy once again bears some attention.

Of Prayers and Miracles

The reference to prayer is by no means new to the Gospel or to Jesus at this point of the narrative. Yet the explanation that prayer is necessary in order to expel this class of demons is not something we would have expected here. After all, why would prayer not be necessary for expelling *all* demons? For if healings do not take place apart from faith, then neither do exorcisms: not faith, obviously, on the part of the demon-possessed individuals but faith on the part of Jesus—or anyone casting out demons in his name (Mark 9:38-39). Jesus would not have been able to heal the sick or to drive out unclean spirits if he had not been a person of prayer. The point to consider, however, is whether the demon in question is the one that has taken over the boy or one that has assaulted the father.[2]

For Mark, Jesus is a prophet of great power: "He commands even the unclean spirits, and they obey him" (1:27). Deliverance from oppressive forces *of any kind* is a sign that the kingdom of God is at hand. In this story, however, Jesus' power is connected with prayer and thus with faith; yet Mark makes no mention of Jesus having prayed before expelling the evil spirit (unless we are to imagine that Jesus had ascended the mountain in Mark 9:2 precisely in order to pray). One is left to assume, therefore, that Jesus is not speaking about ritual prayers to be recited before attempting an exorcism but an ongoing state of union with God. The power to expel demons is not magic, above all, not in this case.

Central to the narrative tension of this scene is the way Jesus engages the father and listens closely to the painful account of the family's effort to cope with the boy's condition. There is no reproof in Jesus' words "If you are able!" These are words of encouragement, and they are followed by a moving expression of understanding and conviction: "All things can be done for the one who believes" (9:23). Jesus fully comprehends the man's struggle, not because he is a parent but because he has journeyed through the towns and villages of Galilee, he has listened to many such stories, he has stayed in people's homes, just as his disciples would (6:10), sharing their bread and their very lives. In short, Jesus has been living in solidarity with his people. He also knows a thing or two about being tempted. Although Mark does not expressly say so, at the end Jesus has salvaged the father's ragged belief. The healing of the son is important, but not because the miracle moves the father from doubt to conviction about God's love and power (in fact, the miracle almost seems like an afterthought compared to the exchange between Jesus and the father). Rather, the healing furnishes the story with a happy conclusion and confirms once again the imminence of God's reign.

Nevertheless, it would be a mistake to think that the only thing separating desperate believers from a miracle is deep enough faith. The Gospels can mislead us here. Miracles seem to have occurred with such frequency in the Gospel narratives that the reader might understandably wonder why there are not more of them today. To answer that Christians today do not have strong enough faith would be to dismiss the genuine,

---

[2] See chapter 3 above, pages 77–78. In *Talking About Jesus Today,* 97-99, I suggest that the episode could have been fittingly entitled "The Restoration of a Father's Faith." Also see Hooker, *Gospel According to Saint Mark,* 224.

everyday holiness of innumerable men and women of God. To suggest that the age of miracles more or less ended with the death of the last apostle would be to miss what the Gospel miracles are all about. Miracles ought not be thought of in terms of Christian apologetics but in terms of homiletics. Miracles do not authenticate the truth or the divinely revealed character of our faith. Jesus' adversaries were not able to deny what they saw, but what they saw hardly prevented them from detesting Jesus, even accusing him of being in league with Satan. Nevertheless, whatever the feats that may be worked through Satan's agency, they cannot properly be classified as miracles.

Miracles, it must be insisted, proclaim the gospel. They illumine major facets of Jesus' teaching and mission. Inquiring about why miracles are so infrequent today, however, may be a misdirected concern. The miracles wrought by Jesus and his early followers were cultural constructs. If someone from first-century Galilee were to step into our world, nearly everything the time-traveler would run into would cause astonishment. None of us would describe the technological wizardry and medical marvels of our time as *religious* miracles, except perhaps in those cases where we had perceived the hand of God assisting and healing us through the achievements of modern science. As a term in theological discourse "miracle" always connotes faith. Whenever people viewed something Jesus did as a manifestation of the saving power of God, they were in effect identifying it as a miracle. Those who profoundly distrusted Jesus or hated him could in no way have interpreted what he did as a sign of the presence of God. For Jesus' enemies, no matter what Jesus did, the fact was that he did not work miracles.[3]

For Jesus' followers, however, his performing miracles was part of a broader picture of teaching, inspiring, calling to repentance, and even organizing (at least to the extent of establishing the Twelve). The prospect of miraculous healings and other supernatural acts was a lot more real to them than to us because the possibility—indeed the anticipation—of miracles formed part of their worldview. Their readiness to accept the miraculous afforded them the cultural permission to regard whatever Jesus did

---

[3] Relevant here are two non-Markan texts: "Now if I cast out the demons by Beelzebul, by whom do your exorcists cast them out? . . . But if it is by the finger of God that I cast out demons, then the kingdom of God has come to you" (Luke 11:19-20). And: "If they do not listen to Moses and the prophets, neither will they be convinced even if someone rises from the dead" (Luke 16:31). For a fuller discussion of miracles see Meier, *A Marginal Jew,* chapters 17 ("Miracles and Modern Minds") and 18 ("Miracles and Ancient Minds") 509–616. Also, Adela Yarbro Collins, *Beginning of the Gospel,* 41–61.

as coming from the Spirit. I do not believe that God suspends or circumvents the physical laws of creation, the work of God's own hands, then or now. Whatever the mechanisms that worked through Jesus' touch to restore sight to the blind, for example, they are in principle intelligible and belong to the "natural" or created order. Conversely, however skilled the hand of the surgeon who removes cataracts, the person whose eyesight has been saved has every reason to thank God. Physicians and surgeons may have restored them to health, but people of faith see no inconsistency in attributing their being cured to God. Or to take things one step further, the fact that I understand full well how I came to be conceived and what cultural and social forces formed me does not lessen in any way my profound gratitude to God for the miracle of my existence. The accidents of timing that spare me and my family from grave injury are no less miraculous in my eyes because someone else looks at the world in terms of statistics and chance occurrences. And so on.

The healing and saving actions of Jesus, therefore, should not be labeled miracles because they sound like nature-defying feats but because they call attention to God's goodness in its sheer ordinariness. There is no way we can swap places, say, with the paralytic of Mark 2 or the desperate woman of Mark 5. If we were to announce to the maimed, paralytics, and diseased of today that God will heal them if only they have enough faith, we would frustrate them and betray the gospel. But when, on the other hand, we urge them to pray for the men and women who labor and research in the field of medicine, we stand on theologically surer ground.

The question "*Can* we trust God?" is not the same as "*Do* we trust God?" but the two questions are linked. The first question asks whether God is trustworthy; the second wonders whether God has done things in our lives that demonstrate how worthy of trust God is. One thing that is not helpful, however, is asking ourselves whether our faith in God is strong enough to warrant a miracle. The question "Can we trust God?" should not be stretched into a self-administered test: "If I trusted God enough, then God would heal me." That is not exactly what the words "All things can be done for the one who believes" are aiming at. The father had come to Jesus in search of a healing, and he received what he was looking for. Yet the evangelist could be hinting at an even more critical issue. How does a parent live from day to day and year to year with such apprehension and worry *and not lose his or her faith in God?* Such unrelenting, fatiguing assault against one's belief in God's goodness and providential care is impossible to resist without prayer. That is, only in an ongoing relatedness with God in which one, like Jesus, is forced to wrestle with unclean spirits will a person discover the strength and illumination he or she has been seeking. The disciples experienced the healings and exorcisms as deeds of power; they had yet to understand them as the fruits of prayer. Jesus' concluding words "This kind can come out only through prayer" are not an admonition but an invitation.

The Case Test: The Death of Jesus

The section of the Gospel that presses on us the question about trusting God most forcefully is the death of Jesus. Jesus was killed because of his faithfulness, yet he died with the opening verse of Psalm 22 on his lips. Those words sound all the more chilling to Christian ears because we recognize who Jesus is. It strikes me as highly unlikely that Mark believed that at the very end Jesus was experiencing divine abandonment, certainly not in the sense that the mystery of God had suddenly withdrawn from Jesus' soul. While there is a certain existential attractiveness to the idea that Jesus, like many other holy men and women, felt himself forsaken by God in a moment of extreme crisis, the idea does not seem consistent with the Markan profile of Jesus.[4] Jesus knew how John the Baptist had ended his days in Herod's dungeon and that "they did to him whatever they pleased" (Mark 9:13). Jesus has already predicted his suffering and death three times; he has twice heard a heavenly voice call him "the Beloved"; he has told his closest followers about what lay in store for the Temple and for the world; he appears to have foreseen where his disciples could procure a colt for the dramatic entrance into Jerusalem as well as the guest room where he could eat the Passover meal; he predicts both his betrayal and, of utmost importance, his ultimate vindication by God. Such details alone do not preclude the possibility of Jesus' experiencing himself abandoned by God, particularly in a Gospel untroubled by disjunctions; but how could so insightful a prophet be blindsided to the prospect of such intense desolation? Nothing in Jesus' teaching suggests that feeling oneself forsaken by God was going to be an element of discipleship. Mark would have known about the spiritual low point in Elijah's

---

[4] It would be odd indeed if the first time Jesus experienced the opaque side of faith—those experiences often associated with the dark night of the soul—was his death. Although Mark does not pause over the temptation scene, we should start by looking there for indications that Jesus struggled as a believer long before he arrived at the cross. The heavy resistance he encountered along the way, the painful misunderstanding on the part of Peter and the other disciples, and the prayer in the garden are important pointers. If Jesus' faith had remained untested until the last few days of his life, then Jesus' preaching about the reign of God would have been naive.

career (1 Kgs 19:3-4), but for a Christian there would appear to be more contrast than comparison between Elijah under the broom tree and Jesus hanging on the cross.

Commenting on Mark 15:34, Morna Hooker views things a bit differently:

> It has often been argued that Mark (or Jesus himself) intended to refer not to these words alone, but to the rest of the psalm, in which the psalmist goes on to speak of his hope of deliverance. But the suggestion seems to be an attempt to disguise the horror of the scene as it is portrayed by Mark, and the narrative supplies no evidence to support the contention that Mark had the rest of the psalm in mind. Earlier commentators . . . often found it impossible to believe that Jesus could have died with words of despair on his lips, and since Luke and John both omit the cry of dereliction they may have experienced the same difficulty.[5]

She is absolutely correct to warn against abridging in any way the horror of that moment. But given some of the details in chapter 15 that appear to mirror the psalm, it is hard to see how Mark could *not* have had the whole of Psalm 22 in mind.[6] It would seem to me, however, that the words "My God, my God, why have you forsaken me?" should not be interpreted automatically as an expression of despair for two reasons. First, the psalmist complains but gives no indication of having despaired; despair is not what the prayer is about. And second, what reason would Jesus have had for despair? The only reason for losing all hope that I can think of is that Jesus had concluded at the very last moment that his mission, from beginning to end, had been founded upon a deception. Yet there is no evidence in the rest of the narrative to support this possibility. One might argue from an empirical point of view that Jesus had failed, or

---

[5] Hooker, *Mark,* 376.

[6] Raymond Brown points out that in order to avoid any christological irreverence many commentators have been reluctant to accept the idea that Jesus truly felt himself abandoned and they appeal to the confident note on which Psalm 22 ends to support their position. See *Death of the Messiah,* vol. 2, 1044–51. But the obverse concern, namely, to safeguard the full humanness of Jesus by emphasizing his real isolation and forsakenness, may push too far in the other direction. I do not think it can be proven that Mark was all that concerned about establishing Jesus' humanness. He took that for granted, along with the fact that Jesus could walk on water and calm the wind and the waves. Brown may have stepped too far when he argued that in calling upon God as "My God" and not "Abba, Father" the Markan Jesus has become so isolated and estranged that "he no longer uses 'Father' language but speaks as the humblest servant" (1051). Mark does not appear to be all that interested in Jesus' inner life for its own sake but only insofar as it bears on us.

rather, that Israel had failed to respond to his mission. But Mark as a Christian sees beyond the rejection and disgrace. He does not believe that Jesus' mission failed, nor does he believe that Jesus himself thought he had failed. On the contrary, Jesus had accomplished what God called him for and the rest was in God's hands.

The truth is that we simply do not know what passed through Jesus' mind and heart as he hung on the cross. Whatever dispositions the reader conjectures Jesus to have manifested in his dying should be consistent with what could be observed in his living.

What then are the theological implications of putting the opening verse of Psalm 22 on Jesus' lips as his final prayer? To answer this we first need to think about the nature of the abandonment voiced by the psalm and then the understanding Mark may have had of Jesus' cry. Can God be trusted *to do what?* If Jesus actually prayed those words from the cross, then we have to presume that it was not the first time they crossed his lips. He had to have been intimately familiar with that prayer. If an early community placed those words in Jesus' mouth, then their motive must have been that the psalm richly expressed many of the sentiments of the passion account as it had been transmitted to them.

The psalm speaks in the first person, and no doubt many individuals have prayed it that way over the centuries, identifying with the voice and sentiment of the psalmist. Yet verse 4 reads, "In you *our* [not "my"] ancestors trusted," while verse 22 announces an intention to testify to God's saving action in the midst of the believing assembly in order that *all* of Jacob's children should praise God. Verses 27 and 28 envision "all the families of the nations" worshiping before Israel's God, since the God of Israel is truly God of (and for) the nations. Verse 29 pictures the dead bowing in adoration, and verses 30 and 31 look to the future and to "a people yet unborn." The one praying, then, does not stand in isolation from the rest of the people; in fact, the voice praying could logically be Israel itself, since the psalms are Israel's prayers first and foremost.

The psalm verbalizes a request that is most urgent. God appears to have been absent for a period of time, long enough for adversaries to have mounted a brutal campaign of abuse and humiliation. The enemies do not appear to be an invading military but primarily people who do not share the psalmist's confidence in God. There is intense hostility on all sides, but the fiercest challenge is directed against belief itself:

> All who see me mock at me;
>> they make mouths at me, they shake their heads;

"Commit your cause to the LORD;
let him deliver—
let him rescue the one in whom he delights!" (Ps 22:7-8).

The situation out of which the psalmist is praying is not some vague sense of disappointment, general discouragement, or unfocused depression. The images of disjointed bones, hands and feet wasted (from hunger?), physical powerlessness, nakedness, sword, snarling dogs, and lion's mouth possess a graphic immediacy. The figure here is not merely infirm or even someone struck with a catastrophic disease. The kind of salvation the psalmist is begging for must be understood along the scale of what God had done for Israel's ancestors, and the prime analogate of that would have been their deliverance from oppression in Egypt. "Let him rescue the one in whom he delights" is a bold affront to the person's confidence in God, all the more biting when heard against the background of the heavenly voice of Mark 1:11 and 9:7.

In brief, then, God had been counted upon for deliverance and nothing happened. Mark did not imagine Jesus praying for God to deliver him from death because the destiny of Jesus had been clear practically from the beginning of his ministry. Thus the abandonment does not concern Jesus' dying. God did not let Jesus down by failing to take him from the cross through the hand of Elijah (15:35) any more than God had forsaken John by not rescuing him from Herod's swordsman. If the question is "Can God be trusted to keep us from dying?" then the answer is no both for us and sometimes for our children. No one skirts death and the pain that often accompanies it. If the question is "Can God be trusted to deliver us from our enemies?" then the answer becomes more complicated. Sometimes enemies are converted; our deliverance and their salvation thereby become two sides of a single redemptive coin.

But when the question becomes "Can God be trusted to bring justice upon the earth? Does God hear and answer the cry of the poor?" we are then moving into the theological problematic of Mark's Gospel. The abandonment Jesus experiences is not the personal disappointment of a prophet whose proclamation about the kingdom of God did not come true but the corporate frustration of all God's righteous ones. "My God, my God, why have you forsaken *us?*" is the psalm's presupposition. Whoever prays Psalm 22 is rehearsing both the historical experience of Israel and that of oppressed people everywhere, from all the families of the world. It is their experience that resides in the psalm. They form the body of interpreters who supply the meaningfulness behind those anguished words. As we remarked earlier, Jesus was hardly the first person to pray this psalm, and he has not been the last. The horror of the crucifixion scene, therefore, embraces millions of God's daughters and sons. It is their abandonment by God, the scandalous slowness of divine justice, that brings us to Jesus' dying words in Mark. Dwelling on the torment and isolation that Jesus as the Son of God endured, however pious the motivation, eventually skews our understanding of the cross. Jesus' was no private passion story; history itself had come to expression on the cross.

The cautionary point made earlier bears repeating. Mark did not believe that Jesus had failed; he did not believe that God had literally or even metaphorically abandoned Jesus; and he did not believe that Jesus' followers should prepare themselves for the prospect of never seeing their hope realized. Psalm 22—not just its opening line but the whole prayer— enabled Mark to cast the death of Jesus onto a world stage. One thing we can be reasonably certain of. Mark did not believe in a God who would abandon his Son at the most critical hour of his life. What sort of spiritual legacy would that have left? Theologically speaking, if there was ever a time God (whom Jesus addressed as *Abba* in the garden prayer) had to be present in Jesus' life, it would not have been at the mount of transfiguration but at Gologtha.

"My God, my God, why have you forsaken me?" does crystallize, however, the fearsome isolation Jesus endured and the utter powerlessness of the human being who has been stripped of every shred of dignity. Powerlessness, disgrace, marginalization, and ridicule are not just features of Jesus' dying; at least potentially they await everyone who chooses to stand with him. Moses did not cross into the Promised Land; Elijah did not witness the death of Jezebel; John the Baptist died without the satisfaction of knowing about Herod's end or even whether Jesus would prove to be God's anointed; and Jesus had to share the same prophetic destiny.

God's designs within human history always encompass more than the individual prophet can possibly grasp. Thus Jesus died without seeing the kingdom of God arrive with power, although he had confidently announced its coming. Perhaps he even risked the final confrontations with the Jerusalem authorities because he was counting on God's decisive intervention and imminent judgment: "What then will the owner of the vineyard do? *He will come and destroy the tenants* and give the vineyard to others" (Mark 12:9). The voice behind those words sounds pretty convinced.

But what held for Jesus must also be the rule for his followers. God's designs on their lives go beyond anything they can see or adequately imagine. Incomplete, unfinished, not yet ready for harvesting: this is how the kingdom of God shows itself. And it shows itself this way because we do not share Jesus' worldview. Consequently, the Church transposed the idea of the kingdom of God from its apocalyptic setting and let it readjust itself to a different understanding of historical process. "Why have you abandoned us?" turns into "Why does it take so long?"

In the end, the disciples are going to remain with Jesus and be reconfirmed in their faith. But the basic reason why they stay with him despite the likelihood of having to share in the cross is that they cannot abandon the people of God. While Mark does not state things in these terms, I do not believe we are straying far from the intent of the Gospel text here. In the end, it is not solely for Jesus' sake that his followers will embrace the cross but out of compassion for their suffering sisters and brothers, so much like "sheep without a shepherd" (Mark 6:34).

Trusting Jesus Is Trusting God

The question we have been considering is whether God can be trusted, since that is the form the question would have taken in Jesus' own life. In Mark's Gospel, however, the question assumes a slightly different form. The disciples have to learn whether Jesus can be trusted. When Mark recounts Jesus asking his disciples, "Why are you afraid? Have you still no faith?" (4:40), Mark was in reality addressing listeners and readers of a later time. Jesus was Mark's icon for God, which explains why the call to faith in Jesus is so insistent throughout the Gospel. A careful reading of Mark will show that throughout the story Jesus does not summon people to believe in himself, yet Mark is doing so implicitly and repeatedly. The faith that Jesus is calling for in the scene of the stormy sea is trust in God's protective care, but the impact is clearly christological. When we are in the presence of the risen Jesus, we are also in the presence of God. Thus if Jesus is in the boat, the disciples have no reason to be fearful. So long as Jesus is accompanying them, they have no reason to fret about having no bread (8:17)—or anything else.

Nevertheless, the presence of the risen Jesus among us does not guarantee miracles, as I explained above. It is tempting to answer the question about whether God can be trusted by appealing to the resurrection: "Of course God can be trusted! God raised Jesus from the dead!" But this answer sidesteps the issue, *unless,* of course, we have the possibility of verifying the saving presence of Jesus within our own experience. We may *know* that Jesus has been raised on the basis of the Church's proclamation, but unless we *experience* Jesus in the word preached, in the flesh-and-blood holiness of other Christians, in our own prayer and the circumstances of our lives and times, then Mark's assurance will not avail us all that much. Mark may have been an inspired writer, but only the Spirit can breathe life into his text each time it is read and proclaimed.

In Jesus Mark found God. *Why* that should have been the case is not something Mark was at pains to explain. A heavenly voice twice identified Jesus as "Son" and "Beloved." And in calming the wind and waves, then later walking across the water, Jesus did what God does.[7] Jesus does not raise himself from the dead, however. The messenger had declared, "He *has been* raised" (16:6). This means that while Jesus was God's face and voice, Mark did not simply merge the figure of Jesus with the God of Israel. Yet at the same time, to place one's trust completely in Jesus was an indication of one's loving surrender to the mystery of God.

Because they believed that Jesus had been raised, Mark's audience already knew in a general and notional way the answer to the question about whether God could be trusted. Indeed, many of them, like the evangelist himself, could probably have furnished personal testimony to support their answer. But those of a more theological bent may have wanted to press their reflection further and inquire what sort of God the resurrection of Jesus had revealed. Did God really have to raise Jesus? Is it necessary that God raise us too? This is the reflection we shall consider in the next chapter.

---

[7] See Ps 107:28-29; then Isa 43:16 and Job 9:8.

11

What Sort of God Would Raise the Dead?

"[A]nd after three days [he must] rise again" (Mark 8:31).
"[A]nd three days after being killed, he will rise again" (Mark 9:31).
"[A]nd after three days he will rise again" (Mark 10:34).

Theology Comes First

To understand the significance of the raising of Jesus from the dead one needs to know the whole Gospel story—and more. For the Gospel story presupposes the history of Israel, its sacred writings, its faith, worship, and moral practice. The story of Jesus is projected against the wider story of Israel's God. But it is also projected against the still broader background of human history itself.

Mark recounts many of the things that Jesus said and did, but the resurrection was not one of Jesus' deeds. The Gospel story, we noted earlier, obviously features Jesus; but the principal actor in the story is God.[1] Not God as a literary character with his own "history" colorfully disclosed on innumerable pages of the Old Testament but God as absolute mystery. With the resurrection we become aware of the unseen presence that pervades everything in Jesus' life, the history of Israel, and the entire world. God comes before Jesus, however clumsy this sounds. Although Jesus was the

---

[1] Ernest Best writes in *Mark: The Gospel as Story:* "We have implied here that the central character is Jesus. It might be argued that the central character in the story of Mark is God. Jesus acts according to the will of God as the story of Gethsemane shows; Peter is rebuked for being on the side of men and not of God (8.33); both at the beginning and at the end of the story Jesus is described as 'the Son of God.' But perhaps the distinction is a quibble, and that itself may say something about Mark's view of Jesus" (115). The distinction is hardly a quibble, although it might well be the case that as a believer Mark related to Jesus as he would to God.

one raised, Easter is essentially a revelation about the mystery of God. The resurrection enjoins us to shift our thinking from Jesus to God, and back.[2]

For a number of years theologians spoke of christologies "from above" and "from below." The distinction proved valuable because it enabled theologians and biblical scholars to clarify for non-specialists the differing approaches scholars took to the study of Jesus. The distinction was also beneficial because it drew attention to a major hermeneutical insight. By studying and interpreting the Gospels apart from the doctrinal lenses of later centuries, one comes to appreciate how thoroughly the Gospel texts testify to the humanness of Jesus.[3] Now while the history of doctrine could in large measure be viewed as the history of the Church's exegesis or interpretation of biblical texts, the interpretation of biblical texts should not start with catechisms and creeds. Interpreters and commentators must not be doctrinally blind, but there is a difference between explicating a text and asking a text to confirm culturally conditioned expressions of belief from a later time and place. The line can be razor thin, but the distinction carries immense importance.

Christologies were also characterized as "high" or "low," depending upon whether they emphasized the divinity or the humanness of Jesus. Needless to say, such classification is not all that illuminating. Christologies that gravitate to the extreme ends of high and low wind up betraying the Gospels and Christian tradition, which means that any christology that merits a hearing is going to be nuanced. Besides, the terms "divine" and "human" are not transparent; one needs to explain what being divine and being human mean. And here things become sticky, particularly when focusing upon Mark, because Mark's Jesus is Son of God in a human way. Mark was no metaphysician. His understanding of the expression "Son of God" was not ontological but biblical and functional. The understanding of Son of God in the Fourth Gospel, by way of contrast, is likewise scriptural, although it builds upon the Wisdom motifs from the Hebrew Bible. The tradition Mark inherited looked elsewhere for its controlling metaphors.[4]

---

[2] Within the framework of Christian theology resurrection and cosmology are interconnected. A theology of the resurrection presupposes a theology of creation, and our understanding of creation has to be enriched by our understanding of Easter. The resurrection is never simply a dimension of christology. Mark's picture of God is resurrection centered. That is, the evangelist's experience of God is rooted in his encounter with Jesus risen. This may help explain why Jesus does what God properly does in walking over the water. On the connection between creation and resurrection, see William Reiser, *Forever Faithful*, 19–56.

[3] On the expressions "high" and "low," "from above" and "from below" christologies, see O'Collins, *Christology*, 16–21.

[4] On Mark's use of the Old Testament, see Marcus, *Way of the Lord*.

I certainly would not say that Mark's Gospel presents a "low" christology because the human features of Jesus appear to be stronger there than in the other Gospels. And because his Gospel reveals so much about Mark's own religious experience and that of some early communities, I would suggest that his Gospel actually starts "from below," that is, from within the everyday faith of men and women who had experienced the power of the risen Jesus in their lives. I would suggest further than even the idea of the incarnation arises from below, for belief in the incarnation rests upon an experience of God's solidarity with the world in and through Jesus. In that sense, every follower of Jesus reads the Gospel through an incarnational lens. Mark thus shares this basic Christian sensibility with the author of the Fourth Gospel.

Truth has the power to transform, and the truth of the Gospel fashions individuals and communities in the direction of justice, compassion, solidarity, and forgiveness. Liberationist theologians have underlined and elaborated the vital connection between right doctrine and right practice, between orthodoxy and orthopraxis, or between faithful discipleship and Christian truth. The advantage of liberationist terminology is that it houses an important warning against divorcing religious belief from the demands of our historical moment by spiritualizing Jesus and by concentrating so much on the interior life that we overlook the political dimension of Christian holiness. The disadvantage is that one may be tempted to bypass altogether the role doctrine plays in forming the believer's moral and spiritual consciousness in favor of practice alone. The formula of right practice guaranteeing right belief only works when practice is seen as the most reliable measure of an acceptable understanding of what the Church holds about Jesus. There are lots of good people in the world with fine moral sensibilities, but Christian practice is informed and shaped primarily by an experience of God in Jesus. Mark has certainly mapped for us the path of discipleship, but for Mark correlative to the specifics of Christian practice there is a clear belief about the risen Jesus as Son of God.

One thing the language of "from above" and "from below," of "low" and "high" christologies, made clear is that readers always bring some theology—some prior understanding of God—to their contemplation of the Gospels. Theology comes first. Without a theology, in our reading the Bible we would fail to discriminate, for instance, between God as mystery and God as a literary character. We would be prisoners to the letter of biblical texts. Unfortunately, however, not all theologies are equally serviceable. Too much stress on a particular point or insight, for instance, can make a person's overall grasp of Christian faith unbalanced and his or her reflection idiosyncratic.

Much of the Christian understanding of God derives from Scripture and above all from the Gospels, but not the whole of it. History is God's word, too. God further speaks to believers in and through the circumstances of their lives, their personal prayer, and other human beings. For centuries as the human mind contemplated its world, philosophy was regarded as a divinely arranged prelude to Christian reflection about the nature of God. When it comes to doing theology, the Church necessarily draws on more than Scripture.

Take, for example, the matter of salvation for those who are not Christian. When one resides inside a social world that is culturally Christian, it is easy to regard outsiders as beyond the pale of grace or to view their religious practices as incomplete, second-best, or merely provisional. Whenever culture blends too closely with a particular religion, society often loses sight of the fact that religion requires a totally free response to God. But the more we come to inhabit a culturally diverse world, the less presumptuous our attitudes toward other religions. Underneath today's cultural lesson there is frequently to be found an understanding of God that is in some ways quite new. Just as the early Christians soon realized that the God of Israel had been from the beginning of time the God of the nations and that, consequently, salvation was intended for all, so too Jesus' disciples of today are becoming increasingly conscious that the God of Jesus is not God of and for only those who have been baptized. Christianity may have many adherents, but it is not the world's only religion; in numerical terms, it does not embrace the majority of the human race. How then do the others find salvation? Mark does not help us here, but he stood among those who benefited from early Christian reflection on the universality of God's intentions.

In fact, the category of salvation itself is not so clear as we might wish. Salvation is not an abstract universal but something concrete, tangible, and capable of being experienced.[5] Yet the concreteness of salvation can also become its limitation. Saving Israel in the first century is not exactly the same as saving Sierra Leone, Colombia, or urban populations in the United States at the end of the twentieth. The historical contexts and attendant problems are vastly different. Indeed, one is on unassailable ground to insist that all salvation is ultimately salvation from the power of sin and that the power of sin

---

[5] One of the first works to take seriously the role of experience in the New Testament was James D. G. Dunn's important study *Jesus and the Spirit* (Philadelphia: Westminster Press, 1975). See also Luke Timothy Johnson, *Religious Experience in Earliest Christianity;* Schillebeeckx, *Christ.*

crosses every historical and cultural setting. But the divine work of delivering human beings from the clutches of sin began long before Jesus, and it was hardly restricted to the religious history of Israel. In the wake of Easter a particular Jesus became increasingly the universal Savior; but does he as Savior retain any connection to his particularity as Jesus of Nazareth? Does that particularity possess any normative status? I believe the answer has to be yes and that whenever the post-Easter and pre-Easter Jesus are allowed to drift apart, we run into the problem of high versus low christology. The only Jesus Mark knows is Jesus risen, but the Jesus he loves and follows is unknowable without his cultural particularity and history.

In some ways the experience of salvation is different for everyone, since each person's encounter with Jesus risen in the Gospel text, the Church's preaching and worship, the living testimony of disciples today, and personal prayer is unique. The Gospel stories are not about generalized encounters with Jesus but highly specific ones. For Mark Jesus may be frequently surrounded by crowds, but people are not saved as faceless members of a crowd. The detail almost sound like a narrative aside, but when Mark tells us after the miraculous feedings that Jesus "dismissed" the gathering (6:45) and "sent them away" (8:9), we should not imagine an impersonal dismissal or a wave of goodbye. After all, the disciples who had distributed the food could also have been delegated to disband the people. The dismissal, we can suppose, was personal; Jesus himself had to send them off. But then, of course, tale after tale confirms how salvation came through meeting Jesus personally: a healing, a cleansing of evil spirits, a forgiving of sin, an invitation to sit with him at table, and so on.

Something similar can be said with respect to repentance, for what needs repenting can be quite different from one person to another. Thus the call to repentance had to be applied to particular circumstances. Not all were tax collectors, not all were Pharisees, not all were adulterers or thieves or abusive husbands. But again, what was so revolutionary about calling people to repent? John the Baptist and the prophets of old had done the same. I think the answer is that repentance in the sense that Jesus used it was a kerygmatic code word that stood for a national turnaround. Salvation would thereby consist of God's once-and-for-all deliverance of the people of Israel from alienation, exile, or captivity. Mark's Jesus had mounted much more than a moral crusade. He had undertaken a life-and-death mission to re-form Israel from the bottom up, calling each and every Israelite to this renewal of the nation's public, corporate life. The mission was God's doing, and despite the disgrace and defeat of the crucifixion, Mark could see that the mission had not failed. True, Israel did not turn around as Jesus had hoped, but the mission yielded enormous fruit nonetheless. *All* the seed had not been choked. The rending of the Temple veil was another apocalyptic sign that the national destiny had always been to be a harbinger of salvation for all the families of the earth. Mark grasped that historical dynamic extremely well. Those closest to Jesus were not his relatives from Nazareth and not necessarily people with the same ethnic roots; Mark expected his audience to count themselves as members of Jesus' true family.

I do not think Mark concluded that Jesus' mission was less political and more spiritual because the kingdom of God failed to arrive. Herod figures in early with the mention of John's imprisonment, the dramatic entry into Jerusalem has clear political and messianic overtones, and the issue of the imperial tax pivots on the relation between civic and religious loyalties. Mark's story takes an even more sustained political turn when Jesus is standing before the Roman prefect and when Jesus envisions his disciples of the future bearing witness to him before governors and kings (Mark 13:9). Five times in chapter 15 the title "King of the Jews" is mentioned. Yet Jesus was not looking for power over others. He was neither a civil nor a spiritual ruler, and the reign of God was neither invisible nor other-worldly. Human kingship was too limited a category to capture the fresh reality that was emerging, where poverty, powerlessness, service, humility, and solidarity would be the indicators of true greatness.[6]

Sensitivity to demographics and the cultural state of the world at the close of the twentieth century is forcing us to think of God in ever more global and ever less parochial terms. Moreover, as I have been suggesting, we inevitably bring our theology—our understanding of God—to our reading of Scripture. While the Gospel surely educates us to think of God in the way Jesus did, it also presupposes that God is always greater than human reflection about the divine mystery. This makes doing christology challenging, for the divine mystery transcends every particularity in a way that Jesus of Nazareth could not. The resurrection both loosens Jesus from his cultural moorings and highlights the Jewishness of his life and faith.[7]

---

[6] On the use of "kingdom of God" in Mark, see Duling, "Kingdom of God, Kingdom of Heaven," 4:56–57.

[7] To develop the point a bit further we could point out that human spirituality is obviously broader than the Gospels. One looks to the Gospels in vain for methods of prayer, for example, or for an inventory of human religious experience. Mark could never qualify as a first-century Carmelite, although Carmelite spirituality is thoroughly Christian, and certainly not as a precursor of St. Benedict. That our theology—our understanding of the nature of God—is not exhausted by the writings of the New Testament is confirmed by the history of Christian spirituality.

Standing (Again) Among the Living

The necessity—indeed, the historical inevitability—of Jesus' death as intoned by the passion predictions is comprehensible. The one who lives as a prophet will very likely suffer a prophet's death. But the necessity of being raised up is far less obvious. Although Mark understood the life and death of Jesus to be the unfolding of a divine plan, the evangelist does nothing to clarify why *it was necessary* that Jesus should be raised from the dead beyond implying that everything concerning Jesus was somehow contained in the Law, the Psalms, and the Prophets. The first intimation of this comes in Mark 1:2 with the words, "As it is written in the prophet Isaiah." However, to say that Jesus' death and resurrection were necessary because these things had been "written," does not really resolve the issue.

I use the language of "divine plan" with some hesitation. Mark gives no indication that he understood the life of Jesus to have been scripted by God, certainly not in its day-to-day details. Throughout the Gospel Jesus is clearly free, even with respect to going to Jerusalem at the end of his life. From the perspective of faith it can be said that our lives are governed by a providential logic, but in general we grasp this logic best by hindsight. The social, psychological, and cultural factors that determine the sort of person we are likely to become are not all that mysterious. The development of the human being is organic: some of the soil is biological, and much of it is our cultural and social environment. But the divine determination or direction of a human life largely seems to come from the future, not from a blueprint already drawn. In speaking about the divine plan that unfolded in Jesus' life, therefore, we would do well to think of how Jesus was constantly responding to the God who walked ahead of him, as it were, and who was continually drawing Jesus into an ever tighter solidarity with God's people.

The divine plan, in other words, is simultaneously a project. "Plan" tends to connote something static, already conceived and formulated, whereas "project" suggests openness to the future, process, and action. The life and death of Jesus were far more like moments of a work in progress than the execution of a plan. Mark does not state things this way, but he does portray Jesus at prayer. And for Jesus, too, praying would not have been a matter of unearthing what God has ordained but of creating a path to the future God invites us to. The words "Not what I want, but what you want" testify to a lifelong attitude of openness to God; they are not the sentiment of a single night. *Knowing what God wants,* however, is precisely the business of seeking, praying, and discerning. Later, of course, it will be Jesus who walks ahead of his brothers and sisters.

Negatively, one thing seems clear. The resurrection of Jesus was *not* necessary in order to demonstrate convincingly the power of God over everything in a society that deals death. For Jesus, the effectiveness of God's power was never in doubt. No matter how absent God seemed at various times in Israel's history, Israel never revised its faith about God as Creator and Lord of the heavens and the earth. But the resurrection of Jesus *was* necessary if the raising of the dead was supposed to be an apocalyptic sign that a new Israel was about to be born. In other words, the note of necessity appears to have attached itself more to the coming of the reign of God than to the personal destiny of Jesus. The kingdom *must* come, as surely as the seed sown on good soil must yield fruit.

The use of "again" in the *NRSV* translation of the texts that head this chapter almost sounds like "for the second time," which is obviously not the intended sense. The sense is "he will stand up again" or simply "he will rise." That Jesus does not mean simply "brought back to life," as in the case of Jairus' daughter, is hinted at by the phrase "after three days." The phrase cannot be *merely* a temporal designation. While three days may create a symbolic distance between Jesus' death and resurrection, one could plausibly wonder why not a resurrection on the same day, or the day after? Certainly God's saving action does not cease on a Sabbath, even the Sabbath that follows Passover. "After three days" throws a narrative accent on the power of God to direct the course of history. "Three days later" prophetically anticipates the climax of Jesus' ministry, the moment in which God will finally make clear what Jesus' life has been all about. Cardiopulmonary resuscitation, even of a divine sort, would hardly have amounted to much of a climax.

The raising of Jesus from the dead reveals something wildly mysterious about the universe itself. Indeed, the raising of Jesus ranks alongside the narratives of Genesis and Exodus about creation and deliverance, and the passionate words and parabolic actions of the prophets as a profound disclosure of the nature of God. The God of Israel is also the One who raised Jesus from the dead.

Still, the resurrection of the dead is a biblical, apocalyptic notion; it was meant to signal the arrival of the end-time, the definitive establishment of God's justice and peace upon the earth. If they had been living in a culturally Jewish world, those who heard the early community's proclamation that Jesus had been raised from the dead would have interpreted the message against the background of Israel's longing for the messianic era to arrive soon.[8] To the

---

[8] Robert Martin-Richard writes that "the theme of the resurrection asserted itself in the Jewish milieus at the very moment when apocalyptic views were developing in answer

question "Why the man Jesus?" the communities could variously respond that he alone was God's anointed from his baptism, from his birth, and even from the dawn of creation in the heart of God. His being raised from the dead revealed that he truly was the source of salvation. To the question "Why were not all God's servants raised?" they could respond that eventually all would be, but for now the community must labor and pray patiently until Jesus "returns" to finish the redemptive project, when "the Son of Man . . . comes in the glory of his Father with the holy angels" (Mark 8:38).[9]

Human history has been replete with apocalypses, and yet our own understanding of historical process is by no means apocalyptic. As a result, we are more likely to think of the kingdom of God as an eschatological ideal, only partially realized here and now. The Church quickly transposed or adjusted the meaning of the kingdom of God, at least in terms of time frames, in light of its experience. The failure to do so would have amounted to sacrificing its historical experience in order to preserve a literalist reading of Jesus' announcement about the kingdom. In the same way, the expression "resurrection of the dead" needs some transposition. When Herod surmised, "John, whom I beheaded, has been raised" (Mark 6:16), he may have been wondering whether the final age had arrived in the person of the Baptizer as a latter-day Elijah. But when Mark relates the episode about the Sadducees ("who say there is no resurrection"), the question seems to have turned from resurrection as symbol of God's ultimate victory over the power of sin, injustice, and death to resurrection of the body as entrance into immortality and eternal life.

Nevertheless, for Mark the raising of Jesus from the dead is not intended to be divine confirmation of the Pharisees' belief (and disconfirmation of the position of the Sadducees), and it does not vindicate Jesus before

---

to the distress being undergone by faithful Jews." The text of Dan 12:1-3, for example, composed around 167 B.C.E., reflects the severe distress of Seleucid persecution. He continues: "What counted in the eyes of the biblical authors, in the last days of OT times, was not at all the immortality of the soul or even the salvation of the individual, but the possibility that the 'dead of YHWH' (Isa 26:19) or the rabbim, that is, the many . . . would experience, along with those who had been saved in the hour of torment, the triumph of their God and the glory of the age to come." See Martin-Richard, "Resurrection," 5:683.

[9] The raising of Jesus is not the Christian analogue of resurrection motifs in other ancient religions. Its distinctiveness arises, first, from its association with Jewish apocalyptic thought, and second, from what it discloses about divine solidarity with victims. That is why the motif of dying and rising gods or the nature rituals found in many cultures have never been catechetically helpful when it comes to grasping the raising of Jesus from the dead.

his enemies. Neither does the raising of Jesus mean simply that he now enjoys immortality in heaven, although the resurrection certainly announces that Jesus is more than John the Baptist, Elijah, or any of the prophets of old. For Mark, God raised Jesus from the dead for our sake, not for the sake of Jesus himself. The two mentions of Jesus' walking ahead of his followers into Galilee (14:28; 16:7) draw attention to this important perspective. Jesus stays among his own, "buried" in their hearts, risen in their lives, enfleshed in their fragile humanity.

Why does God raise Jesus from the dead? The answer is simple, as far as Mark is concerned. God has determined that the risen Jesus will reside among his followers to animate, guide, and empower them to continue his mission during the interval between Easter and the final consummation. Such is the Gospel's unifying supposition. Jesus warns, for instance, "Those who are ashamed of me and my words in this adulterous and sinful generation, of them the Son of Man will also be ashamed where he comes in the glory of his Father with the holy angels" (8:38).[10] The evangelist plainly envisions some future moment when judgment will have to be rendered, a time for reward or punishment.[11] But the world is not there yet.

The raising of Jesus from the dead, therefore, is about the ongoing creative/redemptive action of God in the world. To proclaim that Jesus has been raised is in effect to state something about God's relation with the world and the abiding offer of salvation. To announce that Jesus has been raised is to summon men and women to repentance and to hold before the world the very real possibility of a new heavens and a new earth. This repentance involves a great deal more than turning away from the particular history of sinfulness that each of us has; it also involves communities, nations, and increasingly the financial and social institutions that surround and shape us.

Jesus' mission eventually brought him to challenge the Temple and the limited understanding on the part of the religious leadership of his day of what it meant to be a child of Abraham. Conversion of Israel's political, religious, and economic establishment and renunciation of the empty expres-

---

[10] "Adulterous" and "sinful" designate infidelity or faithlessness toward the word of God. What might it mean to be "ashamed" of Jesus and his words? It is less likely that we would be ashamed of Jesus himself than of the sort of people with whom he stands and thus identifies himself. The infidelity (which Scripture frequently compares to adultery) would thus consist of a refusal to accept the demands of solidarity.

[11] The note of reward is sounded in Mark 9:41; 10:30, 10:40, and 13:26-27, while punishment appears in 9:47 and 10:31 and is alluded to 8:38 and 14:62, which evokes the vision in Dan 7:13-14.

sions of national self-understanding would be absolutely essential. Otherwise, the things made by human hands (14:58) would be judged and destroyed. But the same rule governs the offer of salvation to peoples of every time and place. The proclamation that God raised Jesus from the dead is a prophetic summons to conversion. It is likewise a revelation about whose side God has taken in humanity's endless struggle for justice and peace, and a promise. The summary description of Jesus' activity in Mark 1:39 in terms of "proclaiming the message" and "casting out demons" suggests that the preached word was a cleansing word; to proclaim the gospel of God (1:14) is simultaneously to "bind the strong man," to neutralize the powers that tie human beings up. So too the Church's preaching about the resurrection. The announcement that God has raised Jesus from the dead is a message that cleanses lives and sets people free.

Mark does not classify the resurrection as a miracle; indeed, how could he? The raising of Jesus was something God worked directly, unseen, on a par with the very first day of creation. And yet of everything about Jesus that had been remembered it was his being raised that must have struck people as singularly worth telling. Given the enormous amount of suffering in the world, that attention should fasten on the cross is easy to understand. It is simpler by far for preachers to evoke a connection between the suffering and death of Jesus and the daily lives of the majority of people than to arouse the intense hope and confident joy associated with the resurrection. The cross has been a far more potent symbol than the empty tomb. Nevertheless, it is Easter that ought to command the more sustained attention, not because it promises an escape from suffering and exile but because it reveals every moment to be a new beginning.

Mark does not have a great deal to say about everlasting life. This does not mean that he did not consider it an important matter, but not everything important automatically got written down or had to be said more than once. At one point of the story Jesus assures the disciples that in the age to come they will enjoy eternal life (10:30), and at another he reproves the Sadducees because they know neither their Scripture nor the power of God (12:24). From one point of view nothing seems more consistent with the nature of God than the raising of the dead. After all, why should death have the final word about our lives? But being granted eternal life is not the same thing as the raising of the dead. In fact, Mark does not say exactly that *all* human beings must be raised from the dead. He says, rather, that the *Son of Man* must suffer and be raised.

By way of reply, I suppose it could be argued that the raising of Jesus from the dead logically has to be viewed against the background of a wider expectation that all God's righteous servants would be raised up. Jesus appears, then, as the first fruits of the eschatological harvest. Paul reasoned this way in 1 Cor 15:13 ("If there is no resurrection of the dead, then Christ has not been raised"). Yet the *must* of the resurrection prediction does not seem to be a reaffirmation of the belief in the raising of the dead in general but something far more specific. Besides, we are told in Mark 9:10 that the three disciples who had just witnessed the transfiguration did not comprehend what rising from the dead meant. They surely must have known about, and probably shared, the view of the Pharisees and of Jesus about resurrection. So perhaps what they could not fathom was why a single individual—the Son of Man—was going to be raised and not all the dead of Israel. What does it mean to apply this apocalyptic idea to one figure rather than to the nation as a whole? In short, why was it necessary that God raise *Jesus of Nazareth* from the dead?

A Scandalous Particularity

Looked at in these terms, the question about Jesus' being raised is identical to the question about the particularity associated with the mystery of the incarnation, except that from a historical point of view the resurrection arrived on the scene first. The answer moves in two directions. On the one hand, the raising of Jesus calls attention to the fact that Jesus is "more" than any other sacred messenger. The title that best captures his distinctiveness was, for Mark, Son of God. Mark does not have the vocabulary to make his faith more precise, nor does he feel the need to do so. Nevertheless, the Gospel does not discern a great deal of difference between being with Jesus and being with God. To say that Jesus was *more* than Moses, Elijah, or any of the other prophets of old could be misleading. In matters of holiness, dedication to God and God's people, and prophetic suffering, comparisons are unseemly. The "more" that Jesus represents might better be understood, to use non-Gospel language, as an intensification of God's solidarity with his people. The point of the comparison, in other words, is once again less to showcase Jesus than to reveal the closeness of God.

That Mark would never separate Jesus from God goes without saying. That Mark would have thought in terms of Jesus and God on the same level has no basis in the text. Mark does not expressly tell us how the disciples were supposed to relate to the post-Easter Jesus in their prayer, their preaching, and their practice. Implicitly, of course, Mark reveals everything. Discipleship consists of following Jesus, but the only conceivable motive for doing so is one's faith in who Jesus is and where the following is going to lead. The narrative world that Mark has created furnishes the symbols, metaphors, lessons, inspiration, and even some of the vocabulary that Christians of his generation (and every one after that) would inhabit. For them, the world of the Gospel was eminently real; everything else was just shadow. The Gospel's strong appeal to religious imagination and its power to transform the everyday into a symbolic reliving of the disciples' time with Jesus cannot be overestimated. For Mark, one loves and serves Jesus just as one loves and serves God. His language does not become more precise than that, but his images say everything that needs stating about the basics of Christian belief.

If the person of Jesus is one direction the answer to our question takes, the other direction is the people of God. What is it about people—especially the victims, the crucified ones—that God should "be" in solidarity with them? Christian thinkers have reflected long and fruitfully on the revelation of God's love that is so evident in the mystery of the incarnation and *a fortiori* in the resurrection. Yet the other side of the divine disclosure is the people. And just as Mark would never separate Jesus from God, neither does he separate Jesus from his people. Scene after scene in the Gospel makes this abundantly clear. The question, What sort of God would raise the dead? can be reformulated: Why *must* God be found alongside his people? Maybe more than anything else, this is the question that excites the deepest wonder and leads to the heart of Christian faith. There is a divine necessity that links the two testaments, that runs from creation to the resurrection and then on to the end-time; it is the necessity of love. The raising of Jesus places him squarely among his people, to "raise" them from their fallenness and disgrace, to raise up their hopes, to lift up their broken spirits, to raise up prophets and guides from their midst, to breathe movement into ancient bones and energy into tired limbs.

The raising of Jesus is the centerfold of Mark's Gospel, as we have noted frequently. Or rather, the conviction that we are really living in the company of Jesus who has called us, made us whole, instructed us, empowered us, and sent us forth to bear witness is what the resurrection means experientially for Mark. The raising of Jesus is salvation for us, and salvation is something we actually experience. As we draw near to concluding our engagement with Mark's Gospel, there are several details still to consider. What theological sense are we to make of the Markan secrecy motif? Why does the kingdom of God have to be thought of differently after Easter? And what might things be like if Mark were the only Gospel to have survived? These are the final questions we shall take up.

12

The Futility of Secrets

He ordered them to tell no one about what they had seen, until after
the Son of Man had risen from the dead (Mark 9:9).

Why Not Tell Everything Plainly?

A puzzling feature of Mark's Gospel is the way Jesus from time to
time instructs people not to broadcast or reveal who he is or what he has
done. Sometimes his motive is easy to guess. After healing the leper, for
instance, and commanding him to silence about his cure, Jesus appears
merely to be trying to prevent himself from being overwhelmed by
human beings in need (Mark 1:45).[1] One might draw the same inference
from Mark 6:31, when Jesus saw the necessity to withdraw with his disciples because "they had no leisure even to eat." When he silences demons
"because they knew him" (Mark 1:24, 34; 3:11-12; 5:7), the likely reason
is again easy to discern. A declaration by demons has nothing to do with
faith, although it might have something to do with spoiling the story's surprise ending: not for the reader, of course, but for the human characters

---

[1] Myers suggests the reason Jesus was unable to enter the cities was one of hostility
"due to the scandal associated with his social intercourse with a leper" (*Binding the Strong*
Man, 151). Such an explanation strikes me as a long shot, akin to attributing some of
Jesus' instructions to silence as a sign of his humility. After all, within a few days Jesus is
back in Capernaum. Malina and Rohrbaugh comment: "Jesus was born to the low social
status of a village artisan, and his claims to be the 'Son of God' would have been viewed
as grasping in the extreme. Mark allows his readers to know that the claim is being asserted right from the beginning. . . . But Jesus shows himself to be an honorable person
by trying to keep such talk out of the public" (*Social-Science Commentary*, 204). But this
explanation pits honor against disclosure on the part of a man who was acknowledged to
be sincere and truthful in all things (Mark 12:14).

within the story. The demons may know who Jesus "really" is, but that knowledge affords them no control over him.

The idea that the demons are aware of Jesus' true identity beneath the figure of a humble carpenter from Nazareth makes little sense theologically, however. His identity, so intricately tied to the cross and resurrection, comes after the mission is completed, not before it.[2] Besides, if the demons had actually known who Jesus was and spilled the beans (assuming that the demons could peer into the future), then presumably some bystanders would have overheard their sensational disclosure. But Mark gives no indication that anyone picked up on what the demons occasionally blurted out, although not because that possibility had escaped him. Mark portrays the demons as aware of who Jesus is (the reader or listener, of course, already knows) as part of his overall narrative strategy. We are dealing less with history in these moments than with special effects.

Nevertheless, there are several other instances where it seems pretty clear that in Mark's theology any announcement of who Jesus is before the paschal events transpire would not only be premature but could also lead to profound misunderstanding. This seems to be the motive behind Jesus' enjoining the disciples to say nothing to anyone about his being the Messiah (8:30; 9:9). Yet for a Gospel that claims that "there is nothing hidden, except to be disclosed" (4:22), the identity of Jesus in the end could hardly have been a secretive matter.

Mark, however, had discerned an ambiguity in the story of Jesus as he had received it. If Jesus is the Son of God, then surely he must have been aware of God's purpose and his own role in bringing that purpose to fulfillment. Hence statements such as "But let the scriptures be fulfilled" (14:49) and "How then is it written about the Son of Man, that he is to go through many sufferings and be treated with contempt?" (9:12).[3] The fact that the disciples had singular difficulty in grasping both who Jesus was and the nature of his mission suggests that the way they understood Jesus before Easter and then afterwards was quite different, and maybe

---

[2] The identity of Jesus and his self-consciousness are two different things. What Christians came to confess about Jesus is fairly easy to see, but what Jesus thought of himself is largely a matter of induction and inspired guessing. Yes, Jesus appears to have used the title "Son of Man"; but how did he understand its meaning? Yes, he tells a parable of a son's rejection and assassination, which is but a thinly disguised allegory (Mark 12:1-12); but how much can we extrapolate about his being God's [own] "son"? If Jesus did accept the designation of Messiah, with whatever qualifications he may have introduced, then clearly he was embracing the Messiah's role, not the Messiah's self-consciousness.

[3] See also Mark 14:21 and 14:27.

Mark's way of handling this disjunction was to surround Jesus' ministry with a sense of secrecy. In the end, however, the strategy fails. A pre-Easter problem cannot be settled with a post-Easter solution without making some parts of the story sound contrived.[4] I do not find the terms "secret" and "secrecy" helpful in accounting for Jesus' commands to silence for the simple reason that there was nothing secret about the person or mission of Jesus either before or after the resurrection. God's designs may be described as mysterious insofar as they transcend human reason, but there is nothing secretive about them. Jesus taught his disciples plainly the central points, demands, and consequences of his mission (8:31-32), but they could not comprehend what he was saying (9:32).

Still, this is not to say that during his ministry Jesus had no reservations about the popular understanding of the Messiah's role. In fact, aspects of Mark's Gospel become more intelligible if one of Jesus' teaching aims was to correct a widespread assumption that God's Messiah would resolve all the nation's political and social troubles. As James Dunn has argued:

> Jesus believed himself to be Messiah, but . . . his conception of the messianic role was an unexpected and unpopular one. Because the title Messiah had such different connotations to Jesus and to those who heard him he never once used it of himself or unequivocally welcomed its application to him by others; and when his actions or words seemed to encourage the to him false conception of messiahship he tried to prevent it by commands to silence. Nevertheless he did not take what might appear the easiest course— that of completely renouncing the title. He did not deny his right to the title, but attempted to reeducate his hearers in the significance of it for him.[5]

Jesus' conviction about the nearness of the kingdom of God could hardly have been naive or romantic given the hostility he encountered almost from the outset and the sober prospect of being rejected and killed. Simply to have rejected the designation of Messiah for the one who would usher in the kingdom would have done nothing to correct what Jesus had probably perceived to be a popular but grave misconception about Israel's expectations of God and thus God's relationship to Israel. The Messiah would have to suffer; there was no way of circumventing that harsh conclusion. And the reason, as we have noted repeatedly, was that the people

---

[4] For a concise explanation of the origin and meaning of the term "messianic secret" see Hooker, *Gospel According to Saint Mark,* 66–69.

[5] See "The Messianic Secret in Mark," *The Christ and the Spirit: Collected Essays of James D. G. Dunn,* vol. 1: *Christology* (Grand Rapids: William B. Eerdmans Publishing Co., 1998) 73. The article first appeared in 1970.

were suffering. Israel's Messiah—God's own anointed—would have been a religious cipher if that individual did not share the historical fortunes of God's people and drink from the "cup [of suffering]" (10:38).[6] I would suggest, therefore, that the central issue was not one of redefining the title "Messiah" but of articulating a new understanding of the role of suffering in the history and everyday life of the people of Israel. The logic of the story is not that the Messiah will suffer *and no one else.* Rather, to follow *this* Messiah—*this* Christ—is to be drawn into his suffering and death, which turn out to be a mirror of the historical fortunes of God's poor in what they are forced to endure and in the way they resist. Mark never says that because Jesus suffered his followers would be spared.

But if messiahship and suffering had to be connected conceptually, then the definition of salvation in terms of deliverance from suffering would have had to be rethought. Mark accounted for the inevitability of the cross in Jesus' life by appealing to God's plan, but the only thing that appears to be inevitable is that if individuals are born into oppression and deprivation they are likely to remain there as victims of forces totally outside their control. Their deliverance by the Messiah would consist not in his engineering a mass exodus out of the world but in his leading people through the world in such a way that the world would be changed because of their walking through and engagement with it. The evangelist does not state things in these terms, but his understanding of salvation involved more than the personal conviction that one was loved and forgiven by God. The unclean spirits testified to the enormous disruption the presence of Jesus brought about in the everyday world of Galilean peasants. And just as the prominence of those spirits was symptomatic of deep disturbances in the social and economic life of the people and not merely of individual affliction, so also their expulsion from the human world points to the eschatological wholeness of communities and society.[7]

---

[6] On the phrase "cup of suffering" see Harrington, *Gospel of Matthew,* 288–89. There may be an apocalyptic motif in the Markan usage. Commenting on Col 1:24, Dunn writes: "Foreshadowed [in this Pauline text] is the apocalyptic thought that there is an appointed sum of suffering that must be endured in order to trigger (as it were) the final events of history . . . ; the thought then is that the death of Christ has (as it were) activated the first trigger, but those sufferings are not yet complete, otherwise the second and final trigger would have been activated too" *(Epistles to the Colossians and to Philemon)* 116. Thus one drinks the "cup" in order to hasten the arrival of the kingdom of God.

[7] See Myers, *Binding the Strong Man,* 141–43, 190–94. But the point is thematic throughout the book.

In any event, Mark's narrative detail of Jesus' disallowing the demons from speaking and his instructing the disciples to reveal nothing about who he is until after the resurrection is not going to help his readers lead a better life. In this sense there is something futile about the so-called "messianic secret." The people who surrounded Jesus *have already experienced* the suffering that came from living under Roman occupation together with the burden brought on by what appears to have been the collusion of the religious authorities in Jerusalem. There must have been grounds for the two allegations that Jesus had said something inflammatory about the Temple (Mark 14:58 and 15:29). The distinctive form of suffering signified by the cross consists of the solidarity to which Jesus has called *everyone,* poor and rich alike, the landless and those with estates, the defenseless and the patrons, the sinners and the righteous. Following Jesus entailed resisting the everyday manifestations of sinfulness that had wounded individual human beings as well as their families and local communities. Jesus had inherited the prophetic mantle of John and the mighty prophets of old. There was no way, then, that by word and by action he could avoid challenging the hostile structures and forces he saw operative in the land. And there was no way, either, that his followers could avoid being drawn into the same prophetic commitments.

The only "secret," therefore, was that suffering was inevitable for *all* those who dare to "enter a strong man's house and plunder his property" (Mark 3:27). The key to historical liberation was not going to be miraculous deliverance by a hero of mythic proportions like Moses, Samson, or David but painful engagement. This engagement would take the form of a relentless countersign, the asceticism of solidarity: not privilege but service; not wealth and being able to boast of powerful patrons but accompanying those without voice or protectors; not exclusionary but humbly inclusive; not armed resistance but non-violence.[8] That, I believe, may

---

[8] While we do not find in Mark explicit non-violence texts such as Matt 5:9 ("Blessed are the peacemakers"); 5:38-39 ("Do not resist an evildoer"); 5:43-45 ("Love your enemies"); or the parallel in Luke 6:27-30, the Markan Jesus behaves non-violently and communicates a message of non-violence through his practice. To work against poverty is to work against violence, since poverty does violence to human lives. Furthermore, Jesus regularly crossed the hurtful boundaries that divide human beings from one another. Consider, for instance, the violence done against men and women who are "sinners" by means of rules designed to safeguard the social purity of the righteous, and Jesus' association with the unclean. Consider, too, that the centurion's declaration "Truly this man was God's Son!" (Mark 15:39) would be incomprehensible if Jesus had not exemplified in his dying what he had consistently practiced and taught. Jesus did not die an angry man, because that was not how he lived.

have been Jesus' "secret," and not always a very welcome one at that. The community Jesus was founding would have a decidedly messianic character. The Spirit would anoint all of them, making "christs" of each and everyone, as John had predicted: "he will baptize you with the Holy Spirit" (1:8). In the end, maybe it makes more sense to think in terms of a messianic people as the historical instrument of salvation than a single individual endowed with supernatural abilities. Forming such a people would have been central to Jesus' mission, especially since at the time of his death so much remained unfinished; the temple not made by human hands was still under construction (14:58). Although Mark does not stretch the term "Messiah" to cover the people, it is clear that he could not imagine Jesus without the disciples who would be vital to the long-range effectiveness of Jesus' mission.

Yet if any single episode in the Gospel does harbor a secret surely that must be the scene at the empty tomb. Or more precisely, it was the tomb that enclosed the great messianic secret, at least for those whose imaginations have strained to picture what took place early on that first day of the week. To speak figuratively, the how and the when of Jesus' being raised from the dead are something only the walls of the tomb witnessed. The absence of any disciples at that moment should scarcely be attributed to poor timing on God's part or to the fear of being apprehended on the part of Jesus' followers. The women disciples were not afraid to venture out, but not until the prescribed Sabbath rest was over. Thus, given the bewildered reaction of the women (and presumably of the rest of Jesus' followers), it would seem that no one was anticipating what happened to Jesus. The only information Mark could relay was that the tomb was empty. The explanatory words of the white-robed young man did nothing to alleviate the puzzlement of the terrified women. "Look, there is the place they laid him" could be inflected so as to sound like words of exasperation, as if the women had either refused to comprehend the message or were simply incapable of hearing it. "So they went out and fled from the tomb," leaving its secret behind them forever, frustrating piety and scholarship alike. While Mark offers pious imaginations little help in the way of picturing Easter morning, neither does he permit scholars to resolve whether the empty tomb was a narrative vehicle for communicating faith in Jesus risen, or whether he had related the apostolic memory exactly.[9]

---

[9] See Adela Yarbro Collins, *Beginning of the Gospel,* 143–48. She writes: "The effect of this understanding of the resurrection of Jesus is to place the accent on the absence of Jesus more than on the presence of Jesus during the time of the readers" (148). Mark does

Mark's own faith did not rest on the empty tomb, of course. As Kenan Osborne observes:

> There is no indication that an empty tomb by itself is a "proof" for the risen Lord. These women saw an empty tomb, but they did not thereby begin to believe in the resurrection of Jesus. Resurrection faith is not fundamentally faith in an empty tomb. It is faith in the action of God.[10]

The words "there you will see him, just as he told you" pry open the possibility of additional memories and stories that might have been shared about experiences of the risen Jesus in Galilee, for we have no guarantee that Mark recorded everything he had learned about Jesus. Whatever the secret about Easter morning may have been, as far as Mark was concerned it would remain forever sealed in the walls of the tomb. Mark furnishes no image of Jesus unwinding his burial cloths and stepping out of the grave, not even an intimation of this. We can infer nothing from the words "there is the place they laid him." Mark betrays no inclination to historicize the resurrection by portraying it as a physical phenomenon. Jesus truly died. He was truly buried. And he was truly raised. The tomb's "secret" does not really matter.

The Kingdom of God After Easter

Mark does not evidence a univocal understanding of the kingdom of God. The enthusiastic crowds that accompanied Jesus into Jerusalem were shouting, "Blessed is the coming kingdom of our ancestor David" (11:10), while shortly afterwards Jesus assured an earnest scribe, "You are not far from the kingdom of God" (12:34). The people were thinking about the arrival of a new social and political reality, and Jesus did nothing to disabuse them of that idea. Riding the donkey appears to have been a confirmatory, parabolic action, perhaps deliberately evoking the memory of Zech 9:9. And yet Jesus' final words to the scribe make it appear that it was not the kingdom that was closing in; rather, the man himself was advancing toward the kingdom, as if the kingdom were a state of mind and heart.

---

mention that the bridegroom will be taken away (2:20), and in several places he speaks of the coming of the victorious Son of Man, which is an apocalyptic expression about divine vindication (8:38; 13:26; 14:62). But I fail to see how the interval between the cross and the definitive establishment of God's justice could be characterized as one of Jesus' "absence." The kingdom might not have arrived, but who or what would animate, instruct, and guide the followers of Jesus in the meantime if not the risen Lord himself?

10   Osborne, *Resurrection of Jesus,* 38.

Mark 10:15 speaks of "receiving" the kingdom the way a child would, while Mark 10:25-26 seems to make entering the kingdom and eternal salvation equivalent. Later, Mark describes Joseph of Arimathea as a person who was "waiting expectantly for the kingdom of God" (15:43). There kingdom of God does not sound like eternal life, a new social order, or an interior state of blessedness and peace but the coming to fruition of a divine promise. Since the phrase is, after all, a metaphor assembled from a number of Old Testament elements, there was nothing to prevent Mark or Jesus from developing it in a variety of ways. But one point that must have been central to Jesus' understanding of the kingdom comes across unequivocally in his actions, namely, his refusal to accept that things in human society are as they should be. In his healings and exorcisms Jesus is setting many of those things right, revealing through these symbolic gestures a profound vision of wholeness and peace.

Just as messiahship meant something different before and after the cross and resurrection, so also did the kingdom of God; and Mark is writing from the vantage point of Easter. The phrase would never be heard the same way again, at least by Christian ears. Initially the kingdom of God was understood in terms of the redemption and restoration of Israel, but after Easter the very concept of Israel became more of an ideal type than a historical reality, as the Church thought of itself as the new Israel or new People of God.[11]

What would have happened if men and women had subscribed unreservedly and energetically to the way of discipleship that Jesus traced? Indeed, what would happen now? This may be the most intriguing question the evangelist poses through his story. To reply that they would inherit eternal life in the age to come (10:30) would be to state the obvious; indeed, it nearly sounds like an aside in the passage where Jesus mentions it. The more daring answer would be that the world itself would be transformed. The prospect of a transformed world may go beyond the evangelist's horizon, although not too far, since Mark 14:9 confidently envisions a worldwide proclamation of the gospel. But the Christian community Mark knew was small by our standards and the culture around him may have seemed almost intractably mired in paganism. No matter; the Gospel he left us would have amounted to harmless piety unless its author believed that following Jesus would make a difference within history.

---

[11] For an accessible and much more extensive treatment of the kingdom of God than I have given, see Fuellenbach, *Kingdom of God.*

The new reality that was reaching for expression through the phrase "kingdom of God" was not the religious property of Israel nor the intellectual property of its sacred texts. Indeed, it could not even be the ideological property of the Church. The longed-for reality of God's rule in the world belongs, at least as a promise, to all the peoples of the world. "You are the hope of all the ends of the earth," the psalmist chanted, "and of the farthest seas" (Ps 65:5). The concrete realization of God's rule can take different forms. It may be likened to a family, to a religious community, even to an entire society where men and women have followed Jesus in the path of solidarity, driving out demons and spreading the Gospel's word of hope. It may also be likened to a person who makes the monumental discovery of God's merciful closeness and rebuilds his or her life from the bottom up. And it might be likened further to a community of believers, gathered in prayerful praise and in remembrance of Jesus and crucified humanity. After Easter, in other words, the kingdom of God is pluriform, embracing the interior reality of a converted heart, the exterior reality of a community of disciples, and the yearning to behold the birth of a new creation.

Finally, there was the matter of the kingship of Jesus. In the kingdom or reign of God, YHWH was supposed to be the king; but what model of kingship would YHWH enact? In Mark's Gospel Jesus is literally God's parable. Whatever preconceptions human beings have fashioned about God are turned upside down in the figure of Jesus. Service, powerlessness, poverty, humility, and solidarity become the chief characteristics of God's anointed; these same features disclose the nature of God. Pilate was apparently satisfied that Jesus posed no serious threat to Roman interests, even if some folks had acknowledged him to be "king of the Jews" (Mark 15:9, 12). Jesus did not in any way fit a royal profile. Consequently, if Jesus through his life and death demonstrated the manner in which God's kingship ought to be conceived, then the very concept of sovereignty had been deconstructed and reassembled. Easter confirmed the radically different shape of YHWH's rule, and in that paradoxical way it made the divine origin of Jesus' mission absolutely clear.

Suppose There Was Only Mark

If Mark's were the only Gospel bequeathed to us by the ancient Church, then what? That Christianity would look and sound profoundly different goes without saying. We would never have known the concentrated christology of the Fourth Gospel or the ecclesial concerns of Matthew. There might never have been a Chalcedon, never a Petrine primacy, and perhaps never a strong theology of sacraments; there would never have been an anti-Jewish polemic, either. Without the other Gospels, early church writers might have made yet more extensive use of the Old Testament, or else they might have turned more than they did to non-biblical texts and writers to engage them theologically. The question is obviously speculative. Not every development over the centuries has been healthy, but in the long run the Church would have been much poorer spiritually and theologically if it only had Mark.

Nevertheless, historically some early communities may have known only Mark. Thus we could ask ourselves, "Were they fully and integrally Christian even though they did not share the insights and narrative details that are to be encountered in the other evangelists?"

While I would never argue that a believer today could live a balanced Christian existence without the rest of the New Testament and subsequent ecclesial developments, I feel reasonably confident that anyone who has fully appropriated Mark would in no way be deficient in the matter of orthodoxy. The presence of the risen Jesus in the community and within believers guaranteed, for Mark, the genuineness of a disciple's practice and the integrity of his or her belief. For Mark faith in Jesus as the bearer of new life meant everything. Mark could never have thought about the kingdom of God apart from the one who preached it; and the more he narrated Jesus' story, the more the kingdom of God and the figure of Jesus fused in Mark's religious sensibility. For this reason the two water stories are particularly illuminating. Just as Scripture depicts God as walking across the sea in order to deliver his people (Ps 77:19) and hushing menacing waves for terrified sailors (Ps 107:29), so Jesus does the equivalent for his followers in the moments of their distress. Mark is not exactly saying that because Jesus can do such things he must be the Son of God, however. For Mark, the title Son of God describes, not explains. Nevertheless, for the Christian community Jesus is the embodiment of God's providential care; that is what his being Son of God means in those two passages.

Mark would have sensed that he was living in the kingdom, even though it had not yet been historically realized in the fullness that every Christian heart longed to see. While he might not have identified the kingdom with the Church, it is hard to imagine that Mark could have thought of the kingdom apart from the community that nurtured and sustained him and to which he felt so deeply bound. He would not have included a story about forgiveness unless he had experienced that mercy himself, and he would not have spoken about Jesus going off to pray unless praying had become an essential part of his life too. When Mark penned the words "For it is from within, from the human heart, that evil intentions come . . . and they defile a person" (7:21, 23), he was probably not speaking in the abstract; he knew from experience, as all of us do, what Jesus was talking about. When he appended the words "with persecutions" to the list of blessings in Mark 10:30, the evangelist was quite likely revealing a dimension of his own experience of discipleship. In short, there was nothing incomplete or inadequate about Mark's appropriation of the mystery of Christ.

Did Mark think there would be no more accounts of Jesus' life after his? Once again, the question is purely speculative. Indeed, there were other details about the actions and teachings of Jesus that Mark may not have been aware of, and three more canonical Gospels germinating in various hearts. The question is not about amplifying or complementing the Markan Gospel, however. We are asking whether Mark ever imagined that others after him might have something to tell about Jesus. If they did, they would not be writing because they had stumbled upon further historical data but because they had something to share about their own experience of the crucified and risen Jesus. In this sense, there would necessarily be numerous future Gospels.

Jesus prophesied about the woman who anointed him in Bethany shortly before he was killed that "wherever the good news is proclaimed in the whole world, what she has done will be told in remembrance of her" (Mark 14:9). But Jesus could have given a similar assurance with respect to countless other disciples, likewise nameless, who did him a good turn—not directly, but through his little ones (9:37). The good news about Jesus is not about him alone; the gospel cannot be proclaimed without simultaneously telling the stories of those who followed him then and those who continue to follow him now. The story of each faithful, holy life is yet another testimony to Jesus himself; and in every age, as we rehearse the events of Jesus' life, we cannot help but recount the lives of our saints. Men and women who have put the gospel into practice will always provide the most effective testimony to the enduring presence of Jesus risen both in the Church and in the world. In the case of this Gospel, that testimony comes not from the first disciples who followed Jesus but from the evangelist himself.

Mark betrays not the slightest sense of regret that he was not among the men and women who knew Jesus of Nazareth personally, witnessed his healings and exorcisms, listened to his parables and captivating instruction, and accompanied him on his final journey to Jerusalem. Mark understood that merely seeing everything Jesus did and hearing all that he said, without faith, avails one nothing. Believing in Jesus, however, and opening oneself to the God who sent him, transcends time and place. Nothing finite remains fixed and unmoved forever, not even the figure of Jesus of Nazareth. The failure to appreciate this fundamental rule of existence leads to the worst sort of fundamentalism. Instead of setting out and proclaiming the gospel, the apostles would have camped at the gravesite until they died merely to be close to the place where Jesus was laid. Mark composed a marvelous account of Jesus' mission, but there is nothing nostalgic about this Easter-driven flashback. The evangelist is eminently realistic and thoroughly confident about the abiding presence of the risen Jesus.

Finally, we noted in the introduction that Mark's narrative is noticeably fragmentary and then added that a sense of fragmented existence also seems to characterize the experience of many men and women today. Not only do the various pieces of our lives seem to pull us in many directions at once, but the uninterrupted flow of tragic events on our television screens and in our newspapers threatens to drown us. How will we survive spiritually without succumbing to cynicism, emotionally retreating from the world, or resigning ourselves to becoming single-issue people, each individual or group focusing on one problem and overlooking everything else?

The theological glue that cements Mark's many narrative pieces together is his unswerving sense of the presence of Jesus risen. Perhaps the glue that can bind the many facets of modern life together is our sensing in the depths of our being that all of history's victims have pitched their tents inside our souls. The experience of solidarity is powerfully cohesive and deeply consoling: not comfortable, but consoling. The experience of being in solidarity with victims—of sharing pain—is an appropriately contemporary expression of what God's salvation in Christ is all about. Indeed, properly understood solidarity *is* salvation. This is what the rich man of Mark 10 would have attained if he had been able to part with his goods, give the proceeds to the poor, and walk with Jesus: solidarity with those on the bottom. Perhaps the best way to surmount the feeling that history has lamentably distanced us from the time and place of Jesus is to discover him among those with whom he identified. In his book *Torture and Eucharist* William Cavanaugh paraphrases the point about Christian solidarity when he says that "pain can be shared, precisely because people can be knitted together into one body." He then elaborates in terms of a renewed sacramental theology:

> The Eucharist, meanwhile, creates martyrs out of victims by calling the church to acts of self-sacrifice and remembrance, honoring in Jesus' sacri-

fice the countless witnesses to the conflict between the powers of life and the powers of death. The true "discipline of the secret" calls Christians to become the true body of Christ, and to bring to light the suffering of others by making that suffering visible in their own bodies.[12]

Yet the experience of solidarity is also thoroughly paschal. In words that aptly sum up the theological message of Mark, Elizabeth Johnson observes:

> What Christians have in the end . . . is a story and the Spirit. The narrative memory of the life, death, resurrection, and outpouring of the Spirit in Jesus the Christ traces the way of divine compassion in the midst of historical sin, death, and defeat. This living *anamnesis* of Jesus shows that instead of being absent, the gracious mystery of God is in the midst of historical suffering enabling resistance, bringing about healing, promising ultimate liberation. Instead of final failure, a future is promised to the defeated of history, who in the end are all of us. Those who believe are thereby galvanized to be a community of praise and thanksgiving, critically free *from* the world for loving engagement *with* the world, in the power of the Spirit.[13]

A Non-Markan Ending

As a way of bringing these pages to a close, it might profit us to reflect for a moment on the so-called "longer ending" an ancient editor supplied in order to round off Mark's text. Whether Mark intended to conclude the Gospel as he did, whether the last page of the scroll was torn off and lost, or whether the evangelist simply ran out of parchment may be interesting textual questions, but they leave unaddressed the theological problem created by the verses that make up the alternative ending.[14]

Mark characterized the women as fearful and amazed when they discovered the tomb empty and heard the messenger's explanation, and we may reasonably conclude from this that they had not been expecting Jesus to be raised from the dead. But Mark does *not* say that the women did not believe what the messenger had told them.

In (non)Mark 16:11, however, we are informed that when the other disciples received the news that Jesus was alive "they would not believe it."

---

[12] See Cavanaugh, *Torture and Eucharist,* 280, 281.

[13] Elizabeth A. Johnson, "Jesus and Salvation," 18.

[14] I share the view that verse 8 was exactly where Mark intended to stop. Morna Hooker sets out the case for this position and reviews the other arguments (*Mark,* 382–94). See also Cox, *History and Critique.*

The same point is repeated in verse 13: "And they [two unnamed disciples] went back and told the rest, but they did not believe them." Verse 14 reports Jesus scolding his disciples because they had refused to listen to the witnesses. What are we to make of the fact that the disciples would not believe the news that Jesus had been raised?

That the disciples throughout the story had difficulty grasping the teaching and practice of Jesus goes without saying; but, of course, all except Judas stayed with him. Emphasizing their continuing lack of faith even after Easter, however, makes little sense, unless someone was concerned to animate Christians of a later generation to embrace the belief in Jesus risen without any question or hesitation, solely on the basis of the Church's proclamation and testimony. Mark himself had already said everything that needed saying about faith's struggle. He had composed an Easter story. The supposition behind his Gospel was that Jesus was alive and present to the community. The non-Markan ending misses that perspective entirely. Whoever composed it must have read the Gospel as if it were primarily a historical record about Jesus and his first followers; their faith is made to appear just as sorry after the resurrection as before. But, as we have seen, throughout his narrative Mark was greatly concerned about his audience and the integrity of their response to Jesus risen, and he showed remarkably little interest in profiling the disciples themselves as historical figures. The Jesus whom they followed so readily and enthusiastically in Mark 1:16-20 was *Mark's* Jesus, that is, the Jesus whom Mark knew to have been raised from the dead and whom he worshiped. Mark was not troubled by the apparent inconsistency of later introducing the misunderstandings and failures of the disciples, since that feature of the story served a different catechetical purpose.

The alternate ending implies that the eleven would not have undertaken the mission without some final, definitive proof from Jesus that he was indeed raised—a not-so-helpful message for those of us born into Christian faith some nineteen centuries later. And the confirming signs— casting out demons, speaking new languages, handling serpents, accidentally ingesting poison, and healing the sick through a touch of their hands—present an equally bothersome and (in the case of snakes and poisons) a potentially harmful message. For the power and truth of the gospel are not ultimately proven by the miraculous accompaniments to the Church's preaching but by the discovery of new life as a result of following Jesus. If we are correct in suggesting that solidarity represents a contemporary experience of being saved, then it is only through experience that confirmation of this claim can be attained. The only way to verify that Jesus' way is of God is to walk with him and all his people right to the end. If Jesus is going to make his presence known to anyone of us, then as far as the real Mark is concerned we ought to be looking for the ones who bear the scars of crucifixion. As Augustine said: "Here he's poor, there he's rich. . . . But still, as a poor man here [or a poor woman, or a poor child], he's hungry, thirsty, in rags."

Finally, the words of (non)Mark 16:16 "but the one who does not believe will be condemned" invite an intolerance on the part of Jesus' followers that the evangelist himself would have found profoundly unevangelical. To be sure, Jesus had his adversaries. But it would be a mistake to suggest that anyone who did not follow Jesus was automatically a person of bad faith. Mark knows about God-fearing Gentiles and unfaithful Jews, and he also knows about Gentile wickedness and Jewish holiness. Mark would not have believed it possible to reject Jesus without rejecting the God who had sent him (12:6), but only on the supposition that wickedness was at work in a person's heart. The rich man who appears in Mark 10:17-27 may have walked away "shocked" and "grieving," but there is no reason to think that he, like the righteous scribe of Mark 12:28-34, would not be the sort of individual who in every time and place manages to slip through the needle's eye. In the matter of salvation, Mark did not suffer from the theological rigidity we seem to find in (non)Mark 16:16. If the closing words of Mark 16:8 make the Gospel sound unfinished to some ears, then maybe the evangelist would not mind if we proposed that each of us supplies an ending and brings the Gospel to completion as we seek to live Mark's text day by day.

Bibliography

Allison, Dale C. *Jesus of Nazareth: Millenarian Prophet.* Minneapolis: Augsburg Fortress Press, 1998.

Balthasar, Hans Urs von. *Origen: Spirit and Fire. A Thematic Anthology of His Writings.* Trans. Robert J. Daly. Washington, D.C.: The Catholic University of America Press, 1984.

Best, Ernest. *Disciples and Discipleship: Studies in the Gospel According to Mark.* Edinburgh: T. & T. Clark, 1986.

_____. *Interpreting Christ.* Edinburgh: T & T Clark, 1993.

_____. *Mark: The Gospel as Story.* Edinburgh: T. & T. Clark, 1983.

Boff, Leonardo. *Jesus Christ Liberator: A Critical Christology for Our Time.* Trans. Patrick Hughes. Maryknoll: Orbis Books, 1978.

_____. *Passion of Christ, Passion of the World: The Facts, Their Interpretation, and Their Meaning Yesterday and Today.* Trans. Robert R. Barr. Maryknoll: Orbis Books, 1987.

Borg, Marcus J. *Conflict, Holiness, and Politics in the Teachings of Jesus.* Harrisburg: Trinity Press International, 1998. First published 1984.

_____. *Jesus: A New Vision.* New York: HarperCollins, 1987.

_____. *Jesus in Contemporary Scholarship.* Valley Forge: Trinity Press International, 1994.

_____. *Meeting Jesus Again for the First Time: The Historical Jesus and the Heart of Contemporary Faith.* New York: HarperCollins, 1994.

Borg, Marcus J., and N. T. Wright. *The Meaning of Jesus: Two Visions.* New York: HarperCollins, 1999.

Bouley, Alan, ed. *Catholic Rites Today: Abridged Texts for Students.* Collegeville: The Liturgical Press, 1992.

Brackley, Dean. *Divine Revolution: Salvation and Liberation in Catholic Thought.* Maryknoll: Orbis Books, 1996.

Brown, Raymond E. *The Death of The Messiah.* 2 vols. New York: Doubleday, 1994.

_____. *An Introduction to New Testament Christology.* New York: Paulist Press, 1994.

_____. *An Introduction to the New Testament*. New York: Doubleday, 1997.

_____, ed. *The New Jerome Biblical Commentary*. Englewood Cliffs: Prentice-Hall, 1990.

Brueggmann, Walter. *A Social Reading of the Old Testament*. Minnneapolis: Augsburg Fortress Press, 1994.

Bryan, Christopher. *A Preface to Mark: Notes on the Gospel in Its Literary and Cultural Settings*. New York: Oxford University Press, 1993.

Caird, G. B., and L. D. Hurst. *New Testament Theology*. New York: Oxford University Press, 1994.

Callan, Terrance. *The Origins of Christian Faith*. New York: Paulist Press, 1994.

Casey, Maurice. *From Jewish Prophet to Gentile God: The Origins and Development of New Testament Christology*. Louisville: Westminter/John Knox Press, 1991.

Cassian, John. *John Cassian: The Conferences*. Trans. Boniface Ramsey. New York: Paulist Press, 1997.

Cavanaugh, William T. *Torture and Eucharist: Theology, Politics, and the Body of Christ*. Oxford: Blackwell Publishers, 1998.

Charlesworth, James H., and Walter P. Weaver, eds. *Images of Jesus Today*. Harrisburg: Trinity Press International, 1994.

Collins, Adela Yarbro. *The Beginning of the Gospel: Probings of Mark in Context*. Minneapolis: Augsburg Fortress Press, 1992.

_____. "Apocalypticism, Early Christian." *The Anchor Bible Dictionary*. Vol. 1. New York: Doubleday, 1992.

Collins, John. "Apocalypticism, Early Jewish." *The Anchor Bible Dictionary*. Vol. 1. New York: Doubleday, 1992.

Cowdell, Scott. *Is Jesus Unique? A Study of Recent Christology*. New York: Paulist Press, 1996.

Cox, Steven Lynn. *A History and Critique of Scholarship Concerning the Markan Endings*. Lewiston: The Edward Mellen Press, 1993.

Cunningham, Philip J. *Mark: The Good News Preached to the Romans*. New York: Paulist Press, 1995.

D'Angelo, Mary Rose. "(Re)Presentations of Women in the Gospels." *Women and Christian Origins*. Ed. Ross Shephard Kraemer and Mary Rose D'Angelo. New York: Oxford University Press, 1999.

Donahue, John R. *Are You the Christ? The Trial Narrative in the Gospel of Mark*. Missoula: Scholars Press, 1973.

_____. *The Gospel in Parable: Metaphor, Narrative, and Theology in the Synoptic Gospels*. Philadelphia: Fortress Press, 1988.

_____. "Jesus as the Parable of God in the Gospel of Mark." *Interpreting the Gospels*. Ed. James Luther Mays. Philadelphia: Fortress Press, 1981.

_____. "Mark." *Harper's Bible Commentary*. Ed. James L. Mays. New York: Harper & Row, 1988.

_____. "Windows and Mirrors: The Setting of Mark's Gospel." *The Catholic Biblical Quarterly* 57:1 (1995) 1–26.

Duling, Dennis C. "Kingdom of God, Kingdom of Heaven." *The Anchor Bible Dictionary*. Vol. 4. New York: Doubleday, 1992.

Dunn, James D. G. *Baptism in the Holy Spirit: a Re-examination of the New Testament Teaching on the Gift of the Spirit in Relation to Pentecostalism Today*. Philadelphia: Westminster Press, 1970.

_____. *The Christ and The Spirit: Collected Essays of James D. G. Dunn*. Vol. 1: *Christology*. Grand Rapids: William B. Eerdmans Publishing Co., 1998.

_____. *The Epistles to the Colossians and to Philemon: A Commentary on the Greek Text*. The New International Greek Testament Commentary. Grand Rapids: William B. Eerdmans Publishing Co., 1996.

_____. *Jesus' Call to Discipleship*. Cambridge: Cambridge University Press, 1992.

Ellacuría, Ignacio. *Freedom Made Flesh: The Mission of Christ and His Church*. Trans. John Drury. Maryknoll: Orbis Books, 1976.

Ellacuría, Ignacio, and Jon Sobrino, eds. *Mysterium Liberationis: Fundamental Concepts of Liberation Theology*. Maryknoll: Orbis Books, 1993.

Evans, C. Stephen. *The Historical Christ and the Jesus of Faith: The Incarnational Narrative as History*. Oxford: Oxford University Press, 1996.

Fox, Everett. *The Five Books of Moses*. The Schocken Bible, vol. 1. New York: Schocken Books, 1995.

Freedman, David Noel, ed. *The Anchor Bible Dictionary*. 6 vols. New York: Doubleday, 1992.

Fuellenbach, John. *The Kingdom of God: The Message of Jesus Today*. Maryknoll: Orbis Books, 1995.

Galvin, John P. "Jesus Christ." *Systematic Theology: Roman Catholic Perspectives*. Vol. 1. Ed. Francis Schüssler Fiorenza and John P. Galvin. Minneapolis: Augsburg Fortress Press, 1991.

_____. "From Humanity of Christ to the Jesus of History: A Paradigm Shift in Catholic Christology." *Theological Studies* 55:2 (1994) 252–73.

Garrett, Susan R. *The Temptations of Jesus in Mark's Gospel*. Grand Rapids: William B. Eerdmans Publishing Co., 1998.

Gnilka, Joachim. *Jesus of Nazareth: Message and History*. Trans. Siegfried S. Schatzmann. Peabody, Mass. : Hendrickson Publishers, 1997.

Gutiérrez, Gustavo. *On Job: God-Talk and the Suffering of the Innocent*. Trans. Matthew J. O'Connell. Maryknoll: Orbis Books, 1987.

Haight, Roger. *Jesus Symbol of God*. Maryknoll: Orbis Books, 1999.

Harrington, Daniel J. "The Gospel According to Mark." *The New Jerome Biblical Commentary*. Englewood Cliffs, N.J.: Prentice Hall, 1990.

_____. *The Gospel of Matthew*. Sacra Pagina. Vol. 1. Collegeville: The Liturgical Press, 1991.

Hartman, Louis F., and Alexander A. DiLella. "Daniel." *The New Jerome Biblical Commentary*. Englewood Cliffs, N.J.: Prentice Hall, 1990.

Hellwig, Monika. "Re-Emergence of the Human, Critical, Public Jesus." *Theological Studies* 50:3 (1989) 466–80.

Herzog, William R., II. *Parables as Subversive Speech: Jesus as Pedagogue of the Oppressed*. Louisville: Westminster/John Knox Press, 1994.

Hooker, Morna. *The Gospel According to Saint Mark*. Black's New Testament Commentary. Peabody, Mass.: Hendrickson Publishers, 1991.

_____. *The Signs of a Prophet: The Prophetic Actions of Jesus*. Harrisburg: Trinity Press International, 1997.

Horsley, Richard A. *Bandits, Prophets, and Messiahs: Popular Movements at the Time of Jesus*. New York: HarperCollins, 1988.

_____. *Galilee: History, Politics, People*. Valley Forge: Trinity Press International, 1995.

_____. *Jesus and the Spiral of Violence: Popular Jewish Resistance in Roman Palestine*. New York: Harper & Row, 1987. Reprinted Augsburg Fortress Press, 1993.

_____, ed. *Paul and Empire: Religion and Power in Roman Imperial Society*. Harrisburg: Trinity Press International, 1997.

Horsley, Richard A., and Neil Asher Silberman. *The Message and the Kingdom: How Jesus and Paul Ignited a Revolution and Transformed the Ancient World*. New York: Penguin Putnam, Inc., 1997.

Howard, Virgil, and David B. Peabody. "Mark." *The International Bible Commentary: A Catholic and Ecumenical Commentary for the Twenty-First Century*. Collegeville: The Liturgical Press, 1998.

Iersel, Bas M. F. van. *Mark: A Reader-Response Commentary*. Journal for the Study of the New Testament Supplement Series. Trans. W. H. Bisscheroux. Sheffield: Sheffield Academic Press, 1998.

Jerome. *The Homilies of Saint Jerome*. 2 vols. Trans. Marie Liguori Ewald. The Fathers of the Church Series. Vol. 57. Washington, D.C.: The Catholic University of America Press, 1966.

Johnson, Elizabeth A. "Jesus and Salvation." *Proceedings of the Forty-Ninth Annual Convention of the Catholic Theological Society of America*. 1994.

Johnson, Luke Timothy. *Living Jesus: Learning the Heart of the Gospel*. New York: HarperCollins, 1999.

_____. *The Real Jesus: The Misguided Quest for the Historical Jesus and the Truth of the Traditional Gospels*. New York: HarperCollins, 1996.

_____. *Religious Experience in Earliest Christianity: A Missing Dimension in New Testament Studies*. Minneapolis: Augsburg Fortress Press, 1998.

Kähler, Martin. *The So-Called Historical Jesus and the Historic, Biblical Christ*. Trans. Carl E. Braaten. Philadelphia: Fortress Press, 1964.

Kazmierski, Carl. *John the Baptist: Prophet and Evangelist*. Collegeville: The Liturgical Press, 1996.

Kee, Howard Clark, and others. *The Cambridge Companion to the Bible*. Cambridge: Cambridge University Press, 1997.

Kee, Howard Clark. *What Can We Know About Jesus?* Cambridge: Cambridge University Press, 1990.

Küng, Hans. *On Being a Christian.* Trans. Edward Quinn. New York: Doubleday, 1976.

Kuschel, Karl-Josef. *Born Before All Time? The Dispute over Christ's Origin.* Trans. John Bowden. New York: Crossroad Publishing Co., 1992.

Lee, Bernard. *The Galilean Jewishness of Jesus.* Vol. 1. New York: Paulist Press, 1988.

Lorenzen, Thorwald. *Resurrection and Discipleship: Interpretive Models, Biblical Reflections, Theological Consequences.* Maryknoll: Orbis Books, 1995.

Malina, Bruce J. *Windows on the World of Jesus: Time Travel to Ancient Judea.* Louisville: Westminster/John Knox Press, 1993.

Malina, Bruce J., and Richard L. Rohrbaugh. *Social-Science Commentary on the Synoptic Gospels.* Minneapolis: Augsburg Fortress Press, 1992.

Marcus, Joel. *The Mystery of the Kingdom of God.* Atlanta: Scholars Press, 1986.

————. *The Way of the Lord: Christological Exegesis of the Old Testament in the Gospel of Mark.* Louisville: Westminster/John Knox Press, 1992.

Martin-Richard, Robert. "Resurrection." *The Anchor Bible Dictionary.* Vol. 5. New York: Doubleday, 1992.

McDermott, Brian C. *Word Become Flesh: Dimensions of Christology.* Collegeville: The Liturgical Press, 1993.

McDonnell, Kilian. "Jesus' Baptism in the Jordan." *Theological Studies* 56:2 (1995) 209–36.

McNight, Scot. *A New Vision for Israel: The Teachings of Jesus in National Context.* Grand Rapids: William B. Eerdmans Publishing Co., 1999.

Meeks, Wayne A., ed. *The HarperCollins Study Bible.* New York: HarperCollins, 1993.

Meier, John. *A Marginal Jew.* Vol. 1: *Rethinking the Historical Jesus.* New York: Doubleday, 1991. Vol. 2: *Mentor, Message, and Miracles.* New York: Doubleday, 1994.

Metzger, Bruce M., and Michael D. Coogan, eds. *The Oxford Companion to the Bible.* New York: Oxford University Press, 1993.

Moltmann, Jürgen. *The Crucified God: The Cross of Christ as the Foundation and Criticism of Christian Theology.* Trans. R. A. Wilson and John Bowden. New York: Harper & Row, 1974.

Murphy, Frederick J. *Fallen Is Babylon: The Revelation to John.* Harrisburg: Trinity Press International, 1998.

————. *The Religious World of Jesus: An Introduction to Second Temple Palestinian Judaism.* Nashville: Abingdon Press, 1991.

Murphy-O'Connor, Jerome. *Becoming Human Together: The Pastoral Anthropology of St. Paul.* Wilmington: Michael Glazier, Inc. 1982.

Myers, Ched. *Binding the Strong Man: A Political Reading of Mark's Story of Jesus.* Maryknoll: Orbis Books, 1988.

————. *Who Will Roll Away the Stone? Discipleship Queries for First-World Christians.* Maryknoll: Orbis Books, 1994.

Nineham, D. E. *Saint Mark.* Westminster Pelican Commentaries. Philadelphia: Westminster Press, 1977. First published 1963.

Nolan, Albert. *Jesus Before Christianity.* Maryknoll: Orbis Books, 1978. Revised 1992.

O'Collins, Gerald. *Christology: A Biblical, Historical, and Systematic Study of Jesus.* New York: Oxford University Press, 1995.

_____. *Experiencing Jesus.* New York: Paulist Press, 1994.

Oden, Thomas C., ed. *Mark.* Ancient Christian Commentary on Scripture. Vol. 2. Downers Grove, Ill.: InterVarsity Press, 1998.

Origen. *On First Principles.* Trans. G. W. Butterworth. Gloucester: Peter Smith, 1973.

Osborne, Kenan B. *The Resurrection of Jesus: New Considerations for Its Theological Interpretation.* New York: Paulist Press, 1997.

Perkins, Pheme. *Jesus as Teacher.* Cambridge: Cambridge University Press, 1990.

Perry, John Michael. *Exploring the Identity and Mission of Jesus.* Kansas City: Sheed & Ward, 1996.

_____. *Exploring the Messianic Secret in Mark's Gospel.* Kansas City: Sheed & Ward, 1997.

_____. *Exploring the Resurrection of Jesus.* Kansas City: Sheed & Ward, 1993.

Price, S. R. F. "Rituals and Power." *Paul and Empire: Religion and Power in Roman Imperial Society.* Harrisburg: Trinity Press International, 1997.

Reiser, Marius. *Jesus and Judgment: The Eschatological Proclamation in Its Jewish Context.* Trans. Linda M. Maloney. Minneapolis: Augsburg Fortress Press, 1997.

Reiser, William. *Forever Faithful: The Unfolding of God's Promise to Creation.* Collegeville: The Liturgical Press, 1993.

_____. *Talking About Jesus Today: An Introduction to the Story Behind Our Faith.* New York: Paulist Press, 1993.

_____. "The Sinlessness of Jesus." *The Living Light* 33:2 (1996) 66–73.

Rhoads, David, and Donald Michie. *Mark as Story: An Introduction to the Narrative of a Gospel.* Philadelphia: Fortress Press, 1982.

Riches, John. *The World of Jesus: First-Century Judaism in Crisis.* Cambridge: Cambridge University Press, 1990.

Sanders, E. P. *The Historical Figure of Jesus.* New York: Penguin Books, 1994.

Schildgen, Brenda Deen. *Power and Prejudice: The Reception of the Gospel of Mark.* Detroit: Wayne State University Press, 1999.

Schillebeeckx, Edward. *Jesus: An Experiment in Christology.* Trans. Hubert Hoskins. New York: Seabury Press, 1979.

_____. *Christ: The Experience of Jesus as Lord.* Trans. John Bowden. New York: Seabury Press, 1980.

Schnackenburg, Rudolf. *Jesus in the Gospels: A Biblical Christology.* Trans. O. C. Dean, Jr. Louisville: Westminster/John Knox Press, 1996.

Schweizer, Eduard. *Jesus.* Trans. David E. Green. Richmond: John Knox Press, 1971.

Senior, Donald. *Jesus: A Gospel Portrait.* New York: Paulist Press, 1992. Revised edition.

_____. *The Passion of Jesus in the Gospel of Mark.* Wilmington: Michael Glazier, Inc., 1984.

Shrogen, Gary S. "Redemption (NT)." *The Anchor Bible Dictionary.* Vol. 5. New York: Doubleday, 1992.

Sloyan, Gerard S. *The Crucifixion of Jesus: History, Myth, Faith.* Minneapolis: Augsburg Fortress Press, 1995.

Sobrino, Jon. *Christology at the Crossroads: A Latin American Approach.* Trans. John Drury. Maryknoll: Orbis Books, 1978.

_____. *Jesus the Liberator: A Historical-Theological View.* Trans. Paul Burns and Francis McDonagh. Maryknoll: Orbis Books, 1994.

_____. *The Principle of Mercy: Taking the Crucified People from the Cross.* Maryknoll: Orbis Books, 1994.

Soggin, J. A. "Sabbath." *The Oxford Companion to the Bible.* New York: Oxford University Press, 1993.

Song, C. S. *Jesus, The Crucified People.* New York: Crossroad Publishing Co., 1990.

Soulen, R. Kendall. *The God of Israel and Christian Theology.* Minneapolis: Augsburg Fortress Press, 1996.

Stegemann, Ekkehard W., and Wolfgang. *The Jesus Movement: A Social History of Its First Century.* Trans. O. C. Dean, Jr. Minneapolis: Augsburg Fortress Press, 1999.

Sturm, Douglas. *Solidarity and Suffering: Toward a Politics of Relationality.* Albany: State University of New York Press, 1998.

Tolbert, Mary Ann. *Sowing the Gospel: Mark's World in Literary-Historical Perspective.* Minneapolis: Augsburg Fortress Press, 1989.

Unterman, Jeremiah. "Redemption (OT)." *The Anchor Bible Dictionary.* Vol. 5. New York: Doubleday, 1992.

Viviano, Benedict T. "The Gospel According to Matthew." *The New Jerome Biblical Commentary.* Englewood Cliffs, N.J.: Prentice Hall, 1990.

Waetjen, Herman C. *A Reordering of Power: A Socio-Political Reading of Mark's Gospel.* Minneapolis: Augsburg Fortress Press, 1989.

Wright, N. T. *Jesus and the Victory of God.* Minneapolis: Augsburg Fortress Press, 1996.

_____. *What Saint Paul Really Said.* Grand Rapids: William B. Eerdmans Publishing Co., 1997.

Zanker, Paul. "The Power of Images." *Paul and Empire: Religion and Power in Roman Imperial Society.* Ed. Richard A. Horsley. Harrisburg: Trinity Press International, 1997.

Scriptural Index

Index of Names

Index of Subjects